CÉZANNE
A Taste of Provence

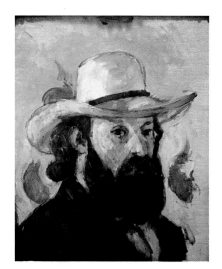

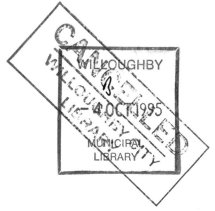

English edition first published in 1995

1 3 5 7 9 10 8 6 4 2

© 1995, Editions du Chêne - Hachette Livre

Original title, 'Cézanne - Le Goût de la Provence'
Illustrated by Jean-Bernard Naudin
Written by Gilles Plazy and Jacqueline Saulnier
Published by Les Editions du Chêne-Hachette Livre 1995

First published in the United Kingdom in 1995
by Ebury Press
Random House, 20 Vauxhall Bridge Road, London SW1V 2SA

Random House Australia (Pty) Limited
20 Alfred Street, Milson's Point, Sydney,
New South Wales 2061, Australia

Random House New Zealand Limited
18 Poland Road, Glenfield, Auckland 10, New Zealand

Random House South Africa (Pty) Limited
PO Box 337, Bergvlei, South Africa

Random House UK Limited Reg. No. 954009

A CIP Catalogue record for this book is available from the British Library
ISBN 0 09 180849 9

Printed and bound in Italy by Canale, Turin

Note to the reader:
Measurements in this book are given in metric and Imperial. When measuring ingredients,
follow one system. The measure 'wine glass' and 'liqueur glass' have been used and these represent
average-sized glasses of 200ml/7 fl oz and 80ml/3 fl oz respectively.

Translation: Henrietta Handford, text and Cathy Muscat, recipes

CÉZANNE
A Taste of Provence

Jean-Bernard Naudin

Text
Gilles Plazy

Recipes
Jacqueline Saulnier

Styling
Lydia Fasoli
Louis Benzoni

Preface
Alain Ducasse

Foreword
Philippe Cézanne

EBURY PRESS LONDON

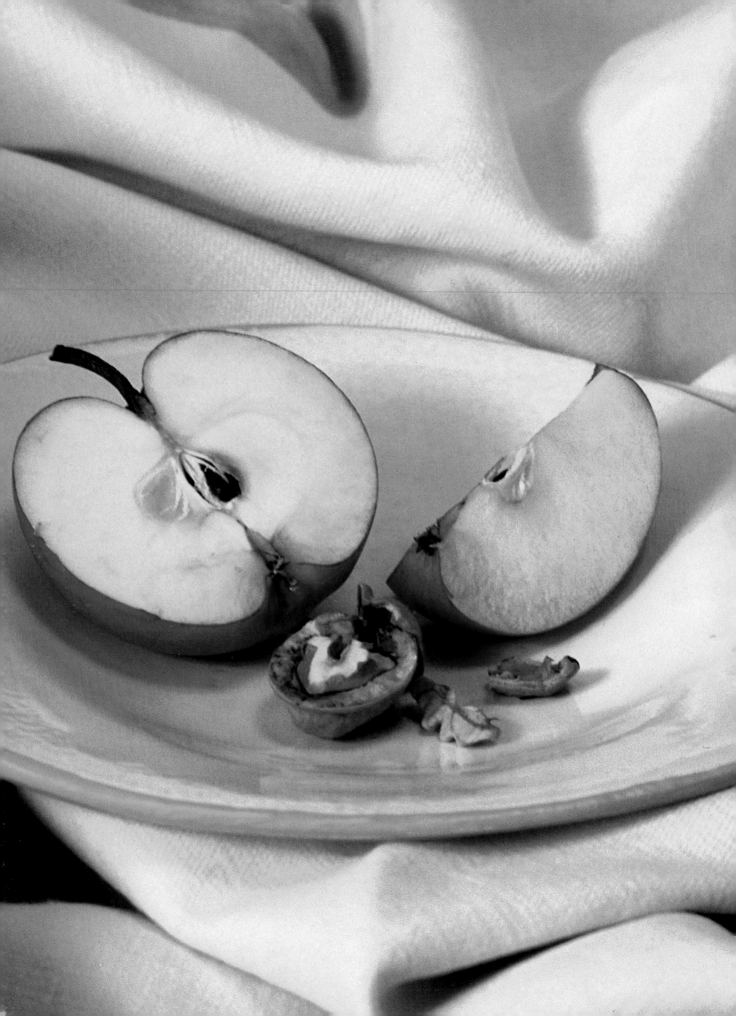

Preface

When Cézanne was once asked to name his favourite dish, his simple reply was 'potatoes in olive oil'. On another occasion, he rose to the defence of a gentleman guest who was being ridiculed by his friends, protesting that ' he is a true connoisseur of olives.' Cézanne never made the trip to Paris without his own personal supply of olive oil. It was his one luxury during hard times. A glimmer of sunshine which reminded him of his beloved Provence. Olive oil is at the heart of my own cooking. Like a ray of mountain sun lighting up a landscape, olive oil brings other flavours to life and regales the palate with different taste sensations.

Cézanne loved the Provençal countryside and exhausted his eyesight in his incessant scrutiny of the landscape. He once said 'Our art should transmit the taste of eternal nature' as if he himself could somehow feel the flavours of nature. When I am creating a recipe using a local product, I do my best to remain faithful to the natural tastes, perhaps in homage to Cézanne and all those like him who respect and rejoice in nature.

Cézanne was on a permanent quest. 'The impossible need to express the whole of nature in a single canvas wore him down,' wrote Zola, his one time close companion.

Cézanne was not a socialite, nor a theoretician, nor a great conversationalist. He was simply a hard worker. The fruit of his labours was a whole new style of painting, achieved without provocation or revolution. His perfectly balanced landscapes of Aix, bathed in light, revealed a new art form and a hidden Provence.

Cézanne lived through all his senses. Sensitive to the nuances of texture and colour, he appreciated the pleasures of food. He was often tempted away from his painting by the enticing aromas of Mme Brémond's cooking. It was not unusual for him to offer the fruit he was painting to passing visitors.

Why the connection between cuisine and art? When considered in the context of the senses art and cuisine are closely linked - they are both an expression of the senses designed to be shared, experienced and appreciated by others. Through my own cooking I try and convey something of the atmosphere of Provence: the olive groves, the fruit and vegetables ripened and often harshly treated by the sun, the fish cooled by the Mistral, the local accent which stretches words, the people who take the time to live. Cézanne always maintained that there are many things in nature which haven't yet been seen. I would have liked, through my own cooking, to have shown him some of these things myself.

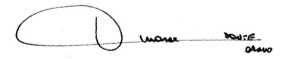

ALAIN DUCASSE

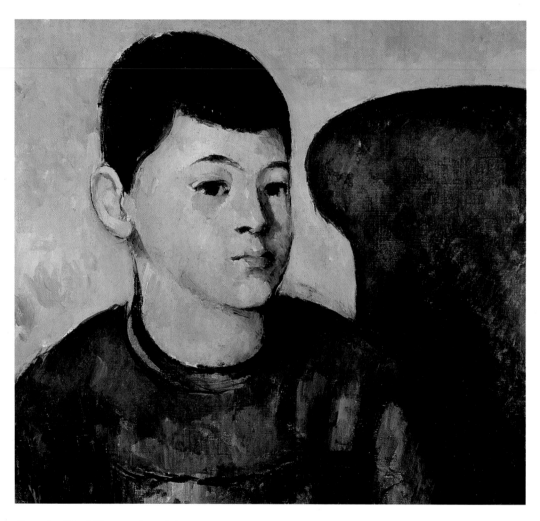

Portrait of Paul Cézanne, the artist's son.

Musée de l'Orangerie, Paris, collection Jean Walter and Paul Guillaume.

Foreword

When Jean-Bernard Naudin first told me that he wished to continue the wonderful series on 'artists and cuisine' by paying homage to my ancestor, Paul Cézanne, my first reaction was one of disbelief. I thought that it would be an impossible task, given the difference between Cézanne's simple lifestyle and frugal eating habits and the more flamboyant life-styles of Claude Monet and Jean Renoir, subjects of the earlier books. Upon reflection, I realised I was mistaken.

Paul Cézanne was a true Provençal, with a predilection for the tastes and smells of his native region: olive oil, herbes de Provence, garlic, tomatoes and Mediterranean fish. He drank great quantities of tea and coffee but could never refuse a small glass of wine cultivated in the vineyards around Aix. His still life paintings in themselves give us a very good indication of the day-to-day life he led.

Although he had the reputation of being somewhat surly and ill-mannered, this shield of aggression concealed a painfully shy man. Cézanne was loyal to his friends and welcomed them into his home alongside many young artists, including Renoir, who he once nursed through an illness like 'a mother hen'. Thanks to his faithful cook and housekeeper, he was able to devote all his time to artistic creation.

I would like to express my appreciation and thanks to the authors of this book for producing such an accurate and evocative portrayal of Paul Cézanne in the context of his beloved Provence.

PHILIPPE CÉZANNE

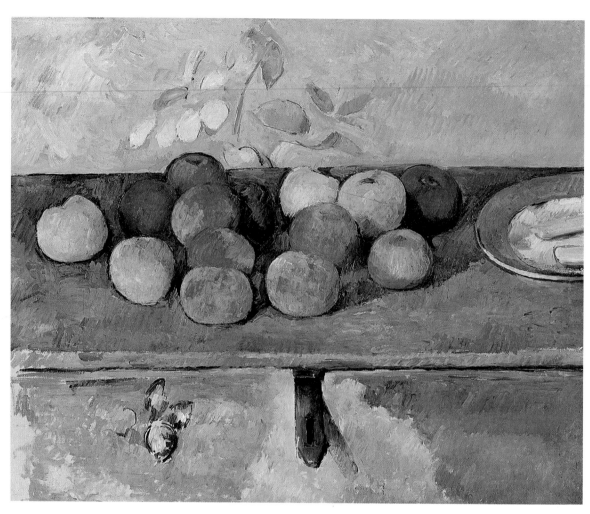

Apples and biscuits.

Musée de l'Orangerie, Paris.

Contents

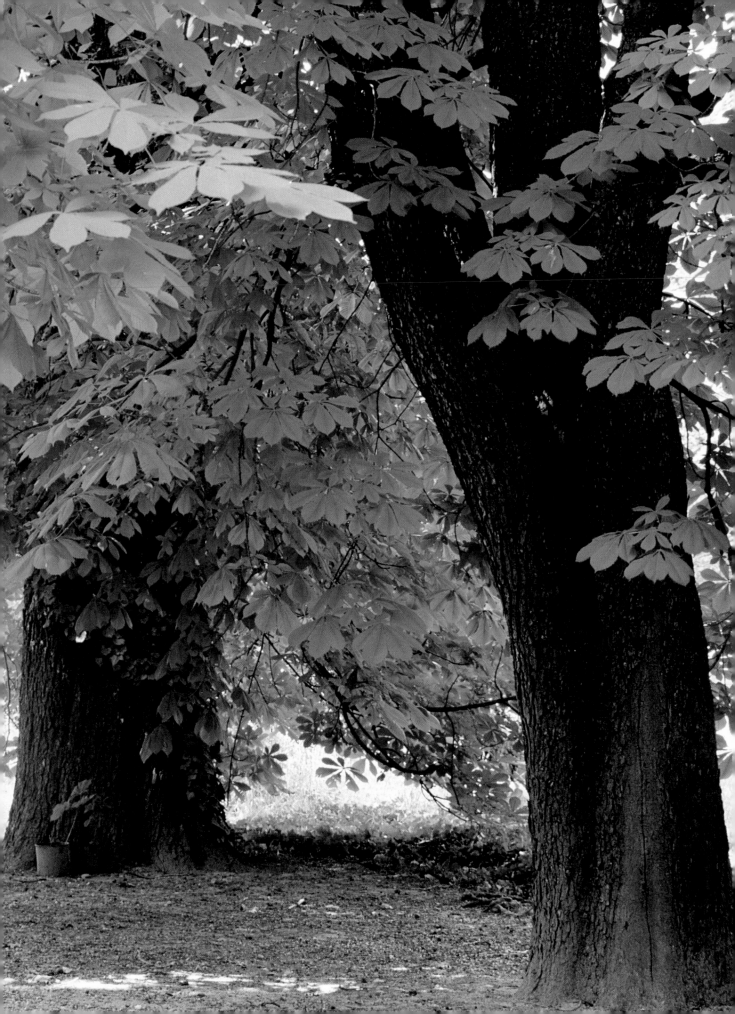

Jas de Bouffan

Think of your future, my son.
You cannot live by talent alone;
money is the key to survival.

Louis-Auguste Cézanne to his son.

Paul Cézanne's Provence in southern France was more than just his birthplace. It represented the destiny of a man who was to become one of the greatest artists of the nineteenth century. He remained loyal to Provence throughout his life, resisting the temptations of Paris. Born in Aix-en-Provence in 1839, Cézanne was the son of a wealthy hatter turned banker. He spent his childhood and adolescence in the centre of the town before the family moved to Jas de Bouffan, their country property a mile or so away. It was a large, square, eighteenth-century house with an imposing façade, high windows and a red-tiled roof, set in fifteen hectares of enclosed grounds with an adjoining farm.

Jas de Bouffan means 'windswept house' in Provençal French. It was perched up high, overlooking Aix and the surrounding plain, with a distant view of the Sainte-Victoire mountain. The grounds included a greenhouse, a wide chestnut tree-lined avenue,

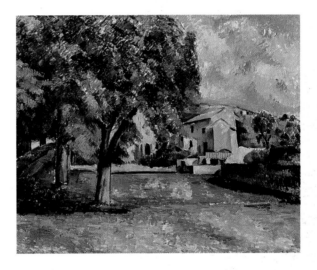

Cézanne's father, Louis-Auguste, bought himself a house in the Aix countryside when he became a successful banker. Cézanne had his first studio there and painted frescoes all over the walls in one of the rooms. He was to paint Jas de Bouffan in every season and from every possible angle.

Maronniers et ferme du Jas de Bouffan,

Pushkin Museum, Moscow.

Left and following pages: Jas de Bouffan as it is today.

11

a meadow and an ornamental pond decorated with stone lions and a dolphin. The land also had vineyards, olive trees and orchards. The property was initially used as a weekend and holiday retreat and for growing the family's own fruit and vegetables. Louis-Auguste Cézanne bought the former residence of Mr de Villars, Governor of Provence, for eighty thousand francs in 1859. He was keen to show off his prosperity, to prove to Aix's aristocrats and landed gentry that he was more than just a mere money lender. This property and its large somewhat run-down park was initially used during the summer months when it got too hot in town. Then the Cézanne family moved there permanently. The house was not in perfect condition and needed a great deal of

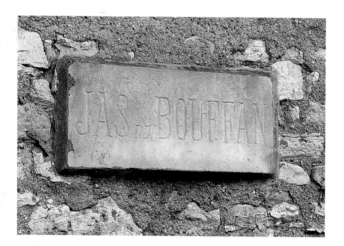

renovation, but it was big enough for them to live in the best rooms and close off the ones most in need of repair.

Louis-Auguste Cézanne was not the kind of man to waste money on luxuries. To him the house was a home for his family and the farm

a source of income, and he saw no need to restore Jas de Bouffan to its former glory. He had only recently made his fortune and was as a consequence naturally cautious. He intended to set his children up for the future, to help his son Paul and provide for his daughters, leaving them with some property and social status. He would never forget his own struggle for success. He was born in humble circumstances in 1798 in the small village of Saint-Zacharie. He had been an employee for a wool merchant when, at twenty-three, he decided to go to Paris and spend four years as an apprentice hatter. Back in Aix, where there was a thriving hat trade, he opened a shop working initially with two associates, then on his own. He increased his capital by lending to suppliers with money problems. By 1848 he was sufficiently successful to take control of the only bank in Aix, which had just gone bankrupt.

In his biography *La vie de Cézanne*, Henri Perruchot describes his hero's father thus: 'Money was all that counted for Louis-Auguste, it was the indisputable sign of social success. He was always clear-headed, intelligent in an inventive way, prudent yet bold, as blunt as he needed to be in business, sharp, meticulous, as hard on himself as he was on others, easily carried away, bossy, with sober taste and as parsimonious as was necessary. Thus he steadily accumulated his fortune.'

Needless to say, he had not planned for his son to be an artist and even saw it as something of a curse, undermining his dream

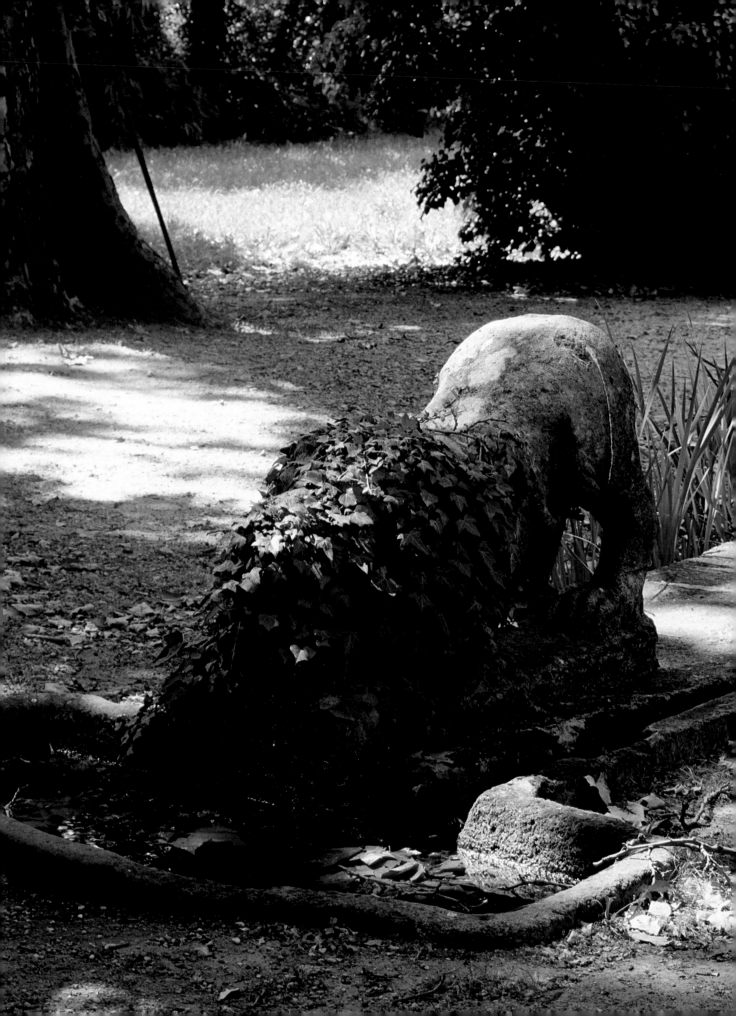

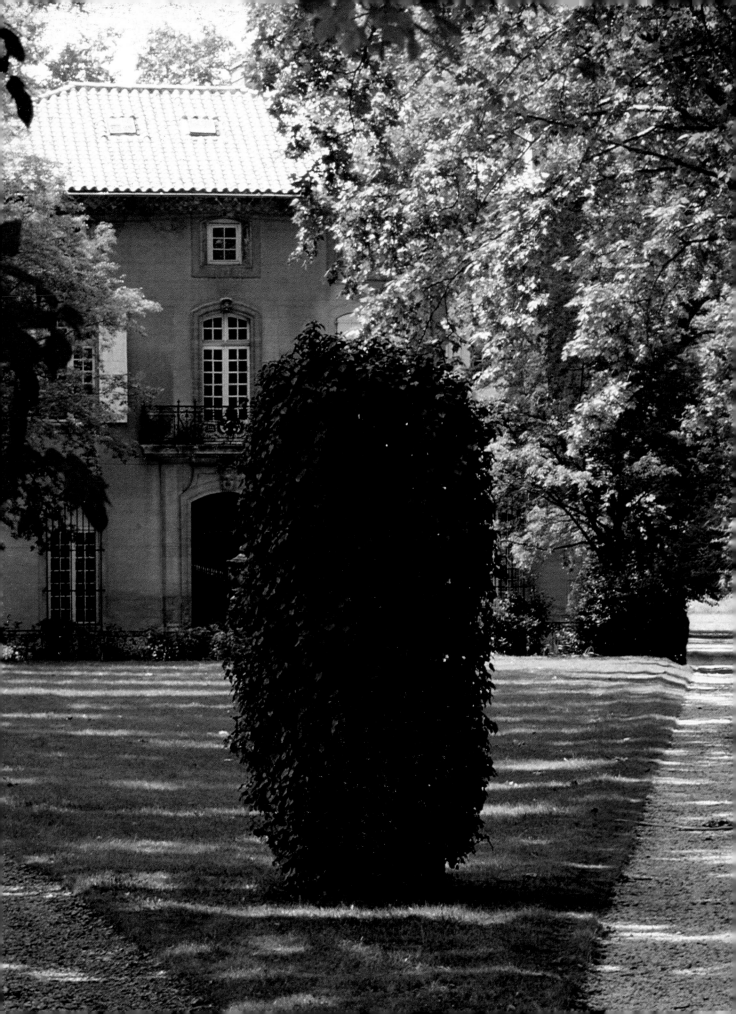

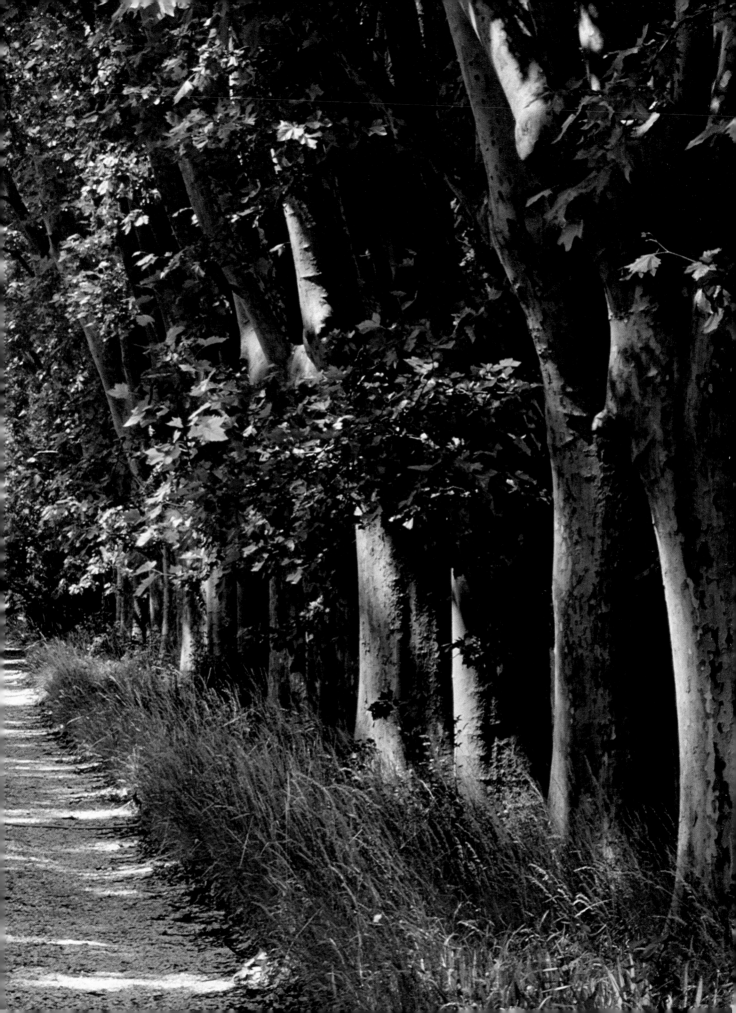

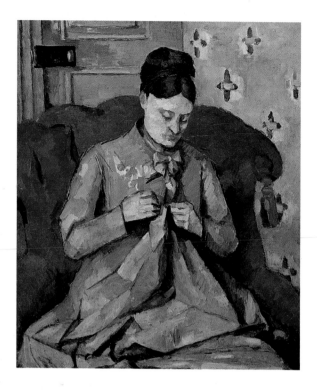

*H*ortense Fiquet finally became Cézanne's wife after 17 years of life together. By then the couple had a fourteen-year-old son named Paul after his father and whose existence had been hidden from his grandfather. Cézanne was a somewhat distant husband but nonetheless left some affectionate portraits of his wife.

Madame Cézanne cousant.
National Museum, Stockholm.

Right:
Fruit preserves and jam in the kitchen at Jas de Bouffan.

of passing on his fortune to found a Cézanne dynasty in Aix.

Cézanne was 20. He was not yet an artist and he only dabbled in painting. He lived at home and was still financially dependent on his family. He had just won his baccalaureate and had begun studying law while also attending art classes. His friend Emile Zola, with whom he had grown up and gone hunting and fishing in the countryside around Aix, had gone to Paris and only returned to Aix during the holidays. They wrote to each other and Zola, already determined to be a great author, hoped that one day Paul would join him in the capital and become a great artist. There is no reference in their correspondence to the acquisition of Jas de Bouffan, which is surprising, as it was a great event in the Cézanne household. Maybe Paul was a touch reticent about Aix and family affairs, unsure of the future and what he was going to do in life or whether his vocation was real. Did he dream of leaving, of asserting his independence, of escaping his parents and sisters?

He soon became attached to Jas de Bouffan and set up his own studio there. Over the next forty years he treated it as home, even after his father's death in 1886, when just he and his mother used the house. His wife Hortense and beloved son Paul remained in Paris while he shared his time between Provence, where he played the role of loving son, and Paris, where he was the family man. All through his life he was like a prodigal son, returning faithfully to Jas de Bouffan. His family weighed heavily on him, as he was to say more than once. He wrote to Pissarro in 1866: '...the most annoying people in the world, my family, the most irritating of all.'

Perhaps he felt misunderstood and insufficiently supported, like most young artists; and he was certainly quite critical of his family. But at least his father never cut him off and his mother provided an affectionate home environment. He had little

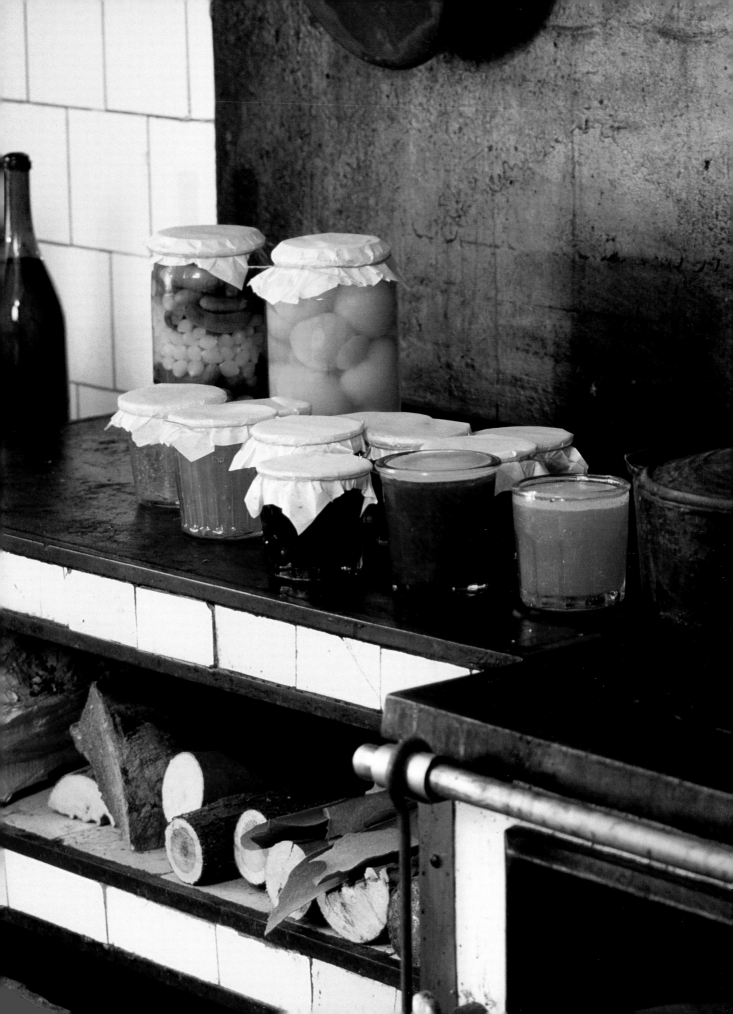

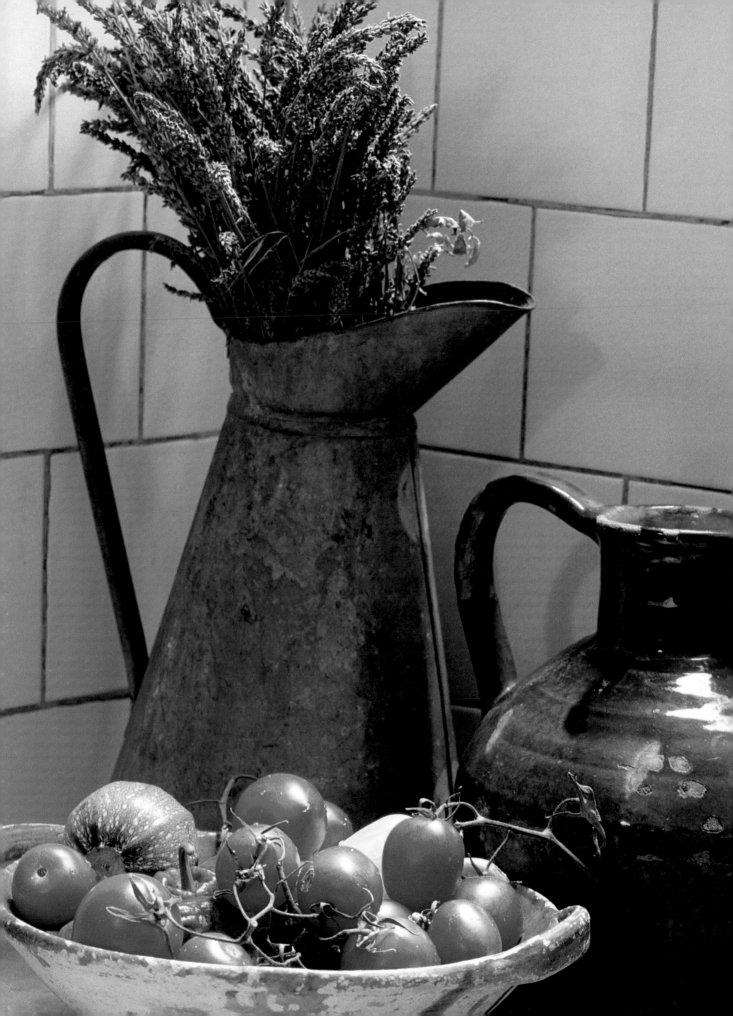

in common with his sisters, especially Marie, who was not very broad-minded, but he was nevertheless very attached to them. A country house and a family had their uses for the young Parisian bohemian who needed some home comforts from time to time. Jas de Bouffan was a family home and he could dedicate himself to his painting there without worries: food and affection were automatically provided. In Paris, the bachelor artist fed himself on soup in cheap restaurants, or on olive oil-soaked bread (as long as there was olive oil, all would be well!). He once remarked in a letter to Zola that he made the sort of meagre soup which Lantier (an impoverished artist character based on Cézanne in Zola's novel *L'Oeuvre*) would have made. So when he went to Jas de Bouffan he appreciated the fact that he was well fed and looked after. Louis-Auguste was not the sort of man to allow excesses in the kitchen, but he did not want people in Aix to say that one did not eat well at Jas. He entertained rarely, but insisted that his guests be well-treated. He

liked simple, good country cooking: stews and cold meats with roasts and legs of lamb for special occasions. His wife was a good cook and ran the kitchen well. Provençal cooking was her forté and Renoir was very impressed by a fennel soup he once had at Jas (he left with the recipe) and a cod brandade she served on a special occasion at their seaside house at nearby Estaque. He wrote to Victor Chocquet about this experience: 'I think I've discovered the ambrosia of the Gods, just taste it and you will surely die a happy man.'

So, Cézanne's family may not have been ideal for a budding artist, but at least they ate well and never wanted for olives! They made traditional anchovy and olive paste, thrush and chicken patés, bouillabaisse and legs of lamb, stews and casseroles, cooked with tomatoes and courgettes, thyme and bay leaves.... Christmas was a time when traditionally thirteen desserts were served all at once: calissons (marzipan sweets), black and white nougat, quince jelly, candied apricots, winter melons, a traditional cake (based on

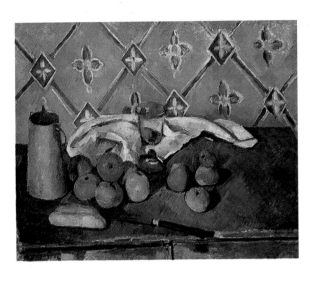

Apples regularly feature in Cézanne's still life painting, he loved their roundness, firmness and colour. Because he painted so slowly, apples were perfect subjects as they didn't change too quickly. He often painted them in a kitchen or dining room setting.

Fruits, serviette et boîte à lait.
Musée de l'Orangerie, Paris.
Collection Jean Walter and Paul Guillaume.

one which the Greeks and Romans offered to their gods), dried fruits - figs, grapes, pears and apples....

Cézanne was a dedicated painter who could work for hours and hours, going for long country walks with his artist's equipment on his back. He had a healthy appetite in the evening, doing justice to what his mother had prepared for him, maybe helping to give him the necessary strength and stamina to follow his chosen path as an artist. At Jas, and at the seaside town of Estaque (which he fondly called 'home to the sea urchins'), he was happy as long as someone was putting his meals on the table. Like his father he had simple tastes in food, and once, when asked in a questionnaire what his favourite food was, replied 'potatoes in oil'.

Cézanne the artist was fulfilled at Jas, but only after a long battle to find his own equilibrium and place in life. John Rewald, writing in his biography Cézanne, confirms that 'Jas de Bouffan was very important to the painter. Nowhere else did he work so often and through so many different periods. The house, the chestnut tree-lined avenue, the stone lions in the pond and the grounds can be seen in many of his paintings.'

Louis-Auguste Cézanne still did not approve of his son's painting. He wanted Paul to follow in his footsteps, work at the Cézanne and Cabassol bank and become a respected

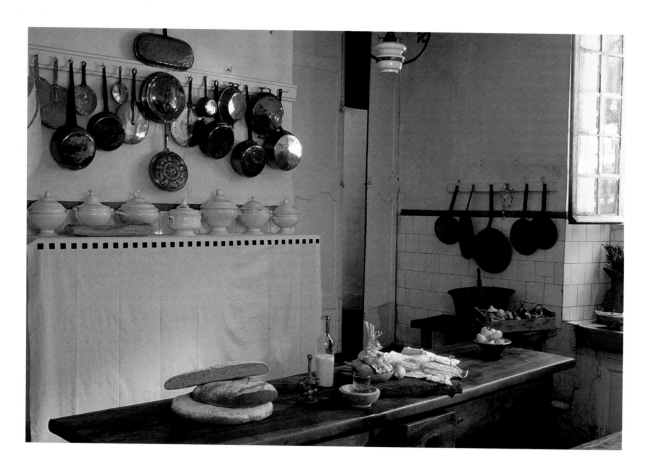

and serious citizen. If his son continued to pursue his studies he would have the means to become powerful and influential. He would not even have to forge his way on his own, because his father would prepare the ground. But he saw his son as a dreamer, a boy who did not know what he wanted, who was more interested in literature than law. Although Cézanne's father was authoritarian and gruff, he nevertheless meant well and simply could not understand why Paul allowed himself to be carried away by his daydreams rather than seeing the sense of his father's point of view. He believed Zola to be responsible for filling his head with ideas and luring him to Paris. In fact it was Cézanne's father who had first interested him in painting by giving him a watercolour paintbox bought at a sale, but he found it difficult to accept that it was he himself who had inadvertently encouraged his son to be artistic. After all, children who filled in colouring books did not necessarily turn out to be artists. Besides, Paul had always seemed more interested in literature and poetry than in painting. He felt there was no need for concern just because his son took art classes, as long as he continued to take his law studies seriously. So he allowed Paul to amuse himself with his paintbrushes, painting on the walls in the laundry room if he wanted to.

Paul was a good son. He drew a portrait of his father sitting on a rickety chair reading the newspaper, a quick sketch in honour of the head of the household. He also painted a portrait of his friend, the artist Achille Empéraire, which was hung in the same room. He often demonstrated a sense of humour in

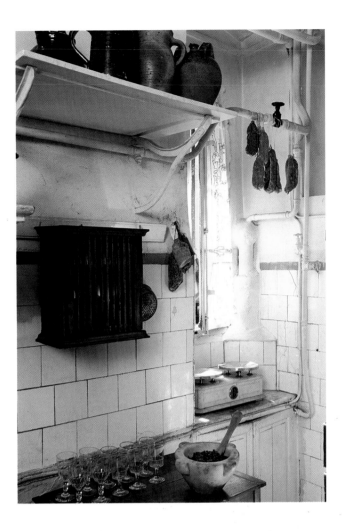

*C*ézanne's mother was reputed to be a fine cook and very knowledgeable about Provençal cuisine. Renoir, who was one of the few Impressionists who became Cézanne's good friend, spoke emotionally about the delicious meals he had at the Cézanne house.

Overleaf:
Preparation of *brandade de morue* in the kitchen at Jas. See recipe page 143.

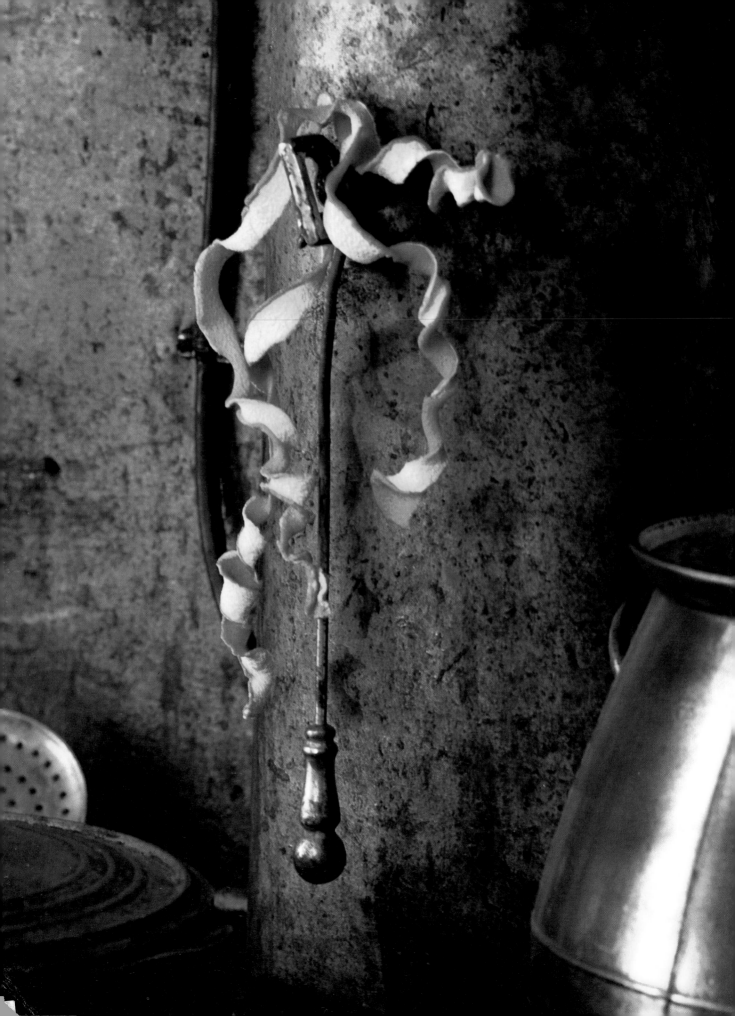

his work. Once, he painted four panels using the four seasons as a theme, in a mock Ingres style, a painter whose neoclassical work he despised. He even signed the painting 'Ingres' and dated it 1811. Later on, when he had mastered the art better, he did a painting depicting a country ball in the style of Nicolas Lancret, a *Christ ressuscitant Lazare* (Christ Raises Lazarus) in the style of Sebastiano del Piombo, and a *Madeleine repentie* (Madeleine Repents) with two men, a woman and a nude bather shown from the back. This seemed a little daring to his father, who said that Rose and Marie, Paul's two sisters, might be shocked by such a spectacle. The artist replied insolently, 'But my sisters have a behind like you and me, don't they ?'

After Cézanne's death, Mr Granel, the new owner of Jas de Bouffan, offered these early paintings which decorated the house to the Luxembourg Museum, the modern art gallery of the day. The museum's curator, Léonce Bénédicte, went to Aix and wrote a report to the Director of National Museums to justify his negative reaction. First of all he describes the house: 'Jas de Bouffan is Cézanne's house and the paintings on offer are part of the decoration. They are all grouped in one room, a large beautiful Louis XIV-style salon which still retains elements from the time when the house was Maréchal de Villars's country residence. A portrait of the latter has pride of place over the door. One end of the room facing the windows has a sort of recess which is decorated by five paintings hung up high. In the middle is a portrait of a man in profile dressed in black

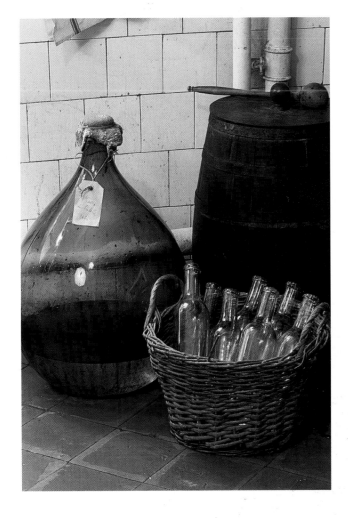

and wearing a cap, painted almost in two tones. It's Cézanne's father. On either side of this are the four panels representing the four seasons. "Spring" is represented by a young woman in a red dress walking through a garden holding a garland of flowers. A decorative vase appears in the background and the backdrop is a dawn sky painted in tones of pink and blue. "Summer" is a seated woman with a bouquet on her knees and a pile of fruits - figs and watermelons - at her feet. "Autumn" is a woman with a basket of fruit on her head and "Winter" is a woman sitting in front of a fire beneath a cloudy, star-studded sky.'

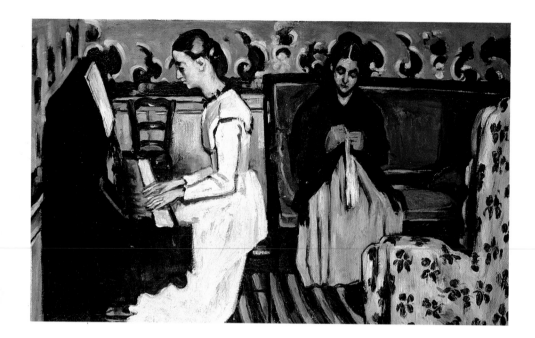

A family scene with Cézanne's sister Marie at the piano. She is playing a piece by Wagner, the great avant-garde composer of the period. Cézanne's mother can be glimpsed in the shadows.

Jeune fille au piano.
L'Ouverture
de Tannhauser.
The Hermitage, Saint Petersburg,

The curator adds, not entirely wrongly, that these paintings are 'awkward and childish'. He is equally critical - wrongly - of the other paintings and concludes: '...Whatever one thinks about the artist's work, it would be strange to honour him by showing these banal and dull images which even he does not seem to have taken seriously.'

To get away from Aix Cézanne would often go to the country with some of his friends, such as Zola and Baille, to climb Sainte-Victoire or swim in the river Arc. Even though Jas was in the country, it was still near enough to Aix not to be completely rural, despite the gardens with the light shimmering through the leaves of the chestnut trees. Cézanne set up a studio in a small room at the top of the house and started to paint seriously. He could see Sainte-Victoire from his studio and worked there in peace and quiet. As Gustave Coquiot, Cézanne's first biographer, was to recall in his

book of 1919: 'He was the only one who could find his way around the jumble of discarded fruits, towels, jam jars, pots, everything related to still life painting. We were forbidden to move anything, to touch anything, to dust... The fruit rotted, flowers died, tubes of paint dried up, yet no-one was allowed to set foot inside his studio. He came down at certain times, the expression in his eyes betraying the struggle of the budding artist fighting against matter.'

Aix was not a lively place in Cézanne's day. It had all the charms of a Provençal town with an agreeable climate; but it was also very cut off from economic development and remained essentially rural and isolated. In 1872, twelve percent of the population lived off the land's revenues, but only forty estates had more than forty hectares of land. The aristocracy, though brought to ruin by the revolution, still despised the lower classes and were suffused with pride. Often sad and morose, they

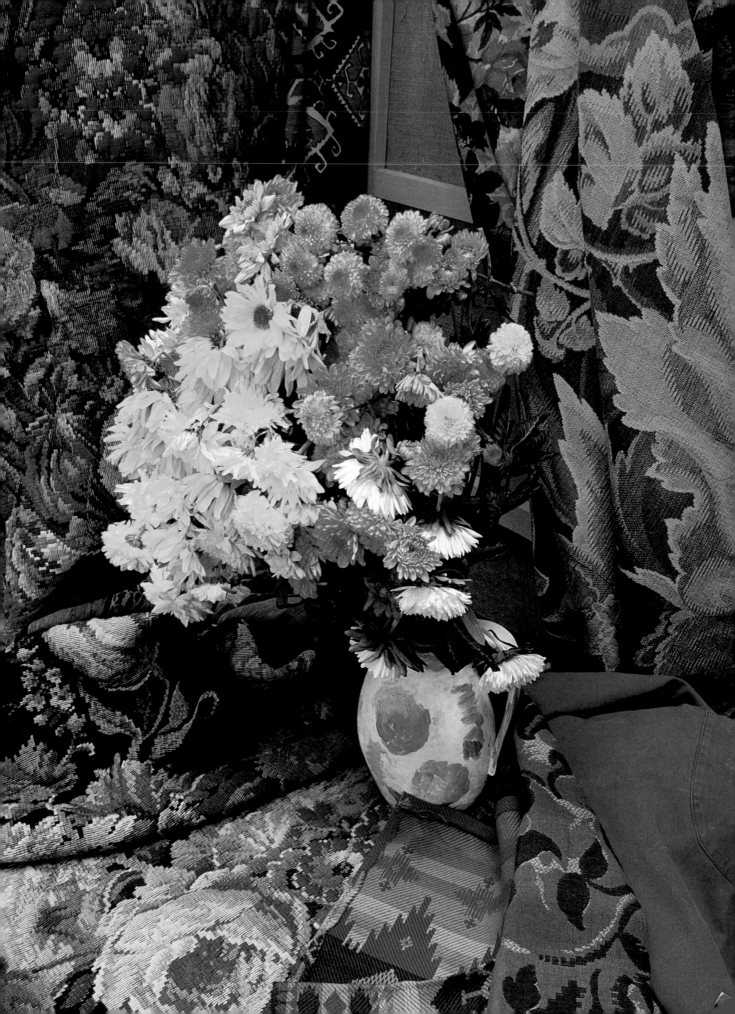

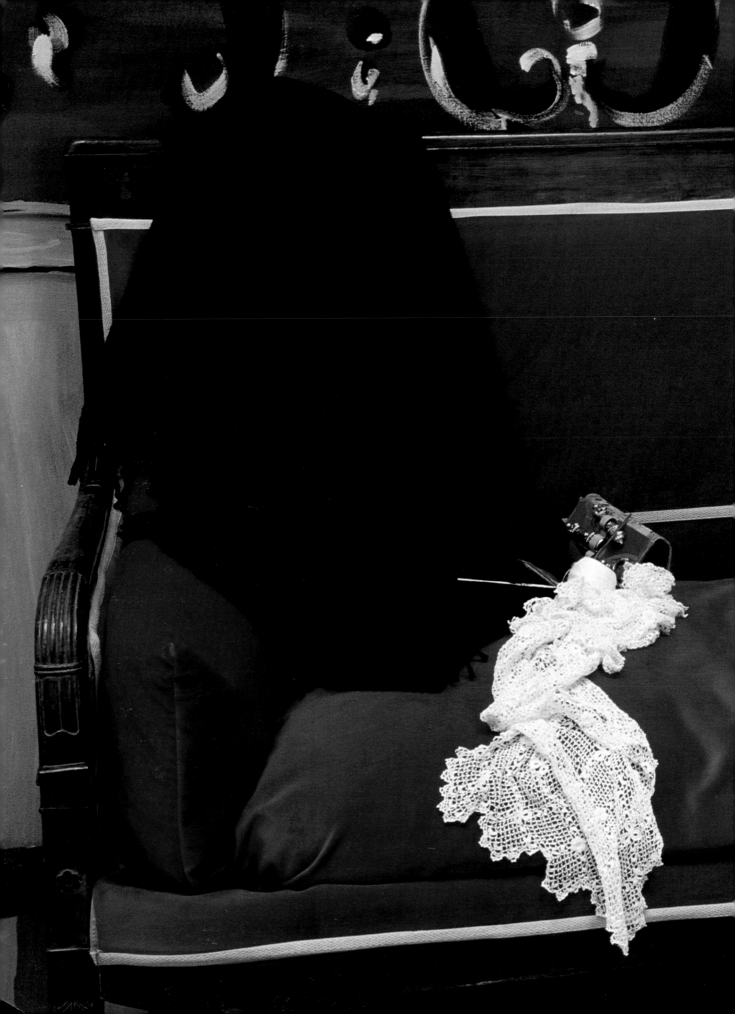

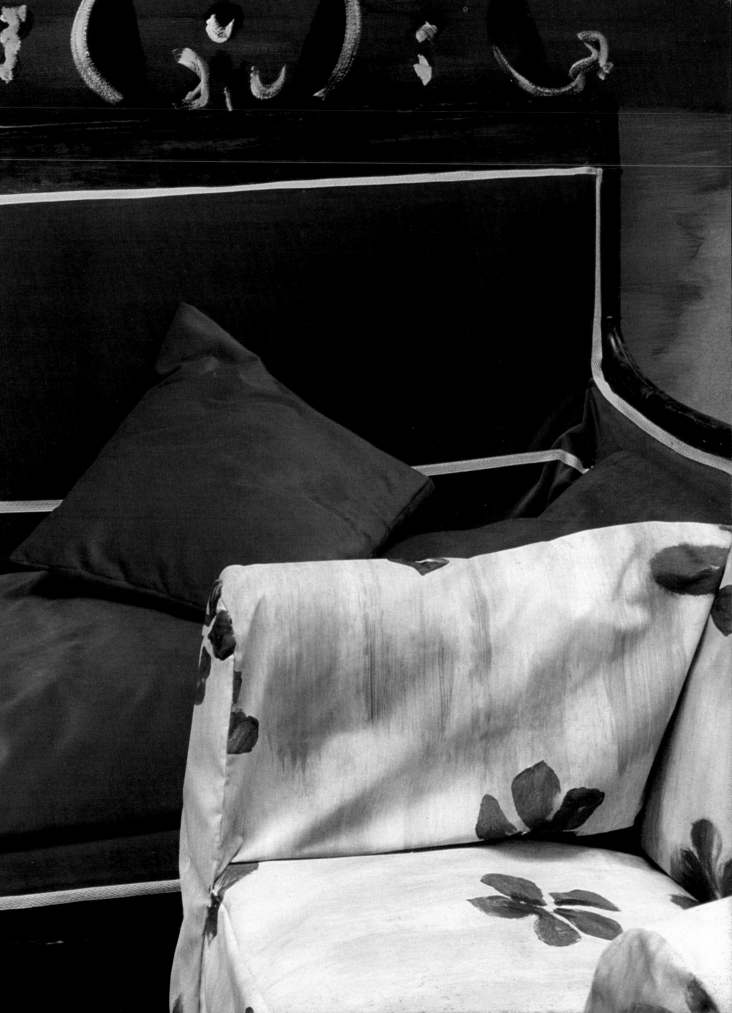

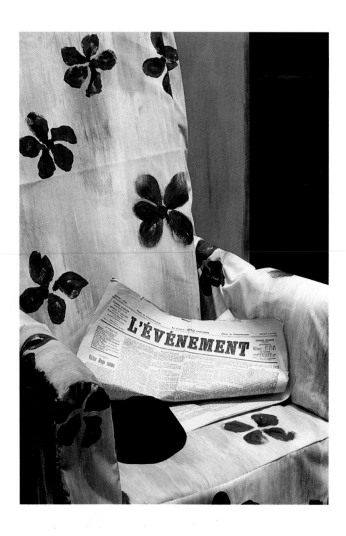

Cézanne amused himself by getting his father to pose reading L'Événement, in which Zola's first articles as an art critic appeared. In these reviews, Zola ridiculed the academic painting on show at the Salon, the annual art show in Paris.

Right:
Louis-Auguste Cézanne, père de l'artiste lisant L'Événement.
National Gallery of Art, Washington, collection Mr and Mrs Paul Mellon.

isolated themselves from the rest of the world, spending the whole winter holed up in their estates surrounded by their antiques and struggling with the upkeep of their houses. Smart receptions were exceptional and only the chosen few were invited: the clergy and the aristocracy. All the old pre-Revolution traditions were maintained. The hub of economic activity was the agricultural market where cattle, corn, oil, almonds, wool and tobacco were sold. A small food industry emerged, and at the turn of the century Aix had a dozen or so pasta factories and flour mills, two syrup and liqueur manufacturers and four carbonated drink factories. Hat making was profitable - seven hat workshops employed over seven hundred people - and also sustained the rabbit-rearing trade as the fur was used to make felt. As for the ancient Roman baths, they were unfrequented and left to go to ruin. The railway line between Paris and the coastal town of Marseilles, which opened in 1837, did not help as it placed Aix off the beaten track and favoured Marseilles with its flourishing port. The Aix-Marseilles section was not opened until 1877, with the Aix-Grenoble line following shortly afterwards.

The town had three kilometres of ramparts and, until as late as 1848, the ten gates were closed at night. They were progressively destroyed in the years up to 1880. Gas lighting was installed around 1850 and then replaced by electricity. In 1876 the Grand Cours was renamed the Cours Mirabeau in memory of a local hero who had played an influential part in the Revolution. A statue of him was placed in front of the newly-renovated town hall. The middle-class Radicals had taken control of the town hall, reflecting the rise of the bourgeoisie, and each class in the town had its area: the south of the cours reserved for nobility, the north for the general public, and the avenue du Mail being reserved for the bourgeoisie.

Aix, however, was not completely lifeless. 'In Aix we take pride in cultivating our minds, it's our desire and tradition to do so', claimed Maurice Gontard. He pointed out that the great Provençal poet, Frederic Mistral, had originally found Aix rather cold, but had finally declared that there was a 'certain charm to the place'. Music had always played an important role in Aix and there were many active musical societies. The theatre was well frequented, there was a university and various local heritage and language societies to keep the past alive, to show that Aix had its own cultural identity.

Cézanne had mixed feelings about Aix, the town where he was born and spent his childhood and adolescence. He disliked the bourgeois hypocrisy of the place, the general lack of interest in the arts and the meanness of spirit. He felt stifled - not an unusual feeling for a young and romantic man. Later, when he was still unrecognised as an artist, he kept his distance, making the most of the fact that Jas was outside Aix. In later years, when his work was more appreciated and he was less rebellious, he took up residence there again, and lived near the cathedral. Even though he spent his entire life moving between Provence and Paris, he was always drawn back to Aix,

the city he never grew to like but which he couldn't live without. In reality he favoured Aix for its surrounding countryside and the landscapes he so loved, which were to dominate his painting. He painted Jas de Bouffan year in, year out. In the winter he painted the front of the house (*Les marroniers au Jas de Bouffan*) (The chestnut trees at Jas de Bouffan), the trees in line, proudly standing straight, bare of leaves - two strips across the canvas: one for the trees, one for the lawn. The houses stand behind, and in the distance is Sainte-Victoire. He paints the same subject in

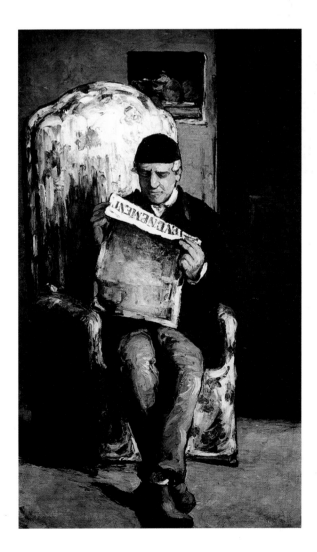

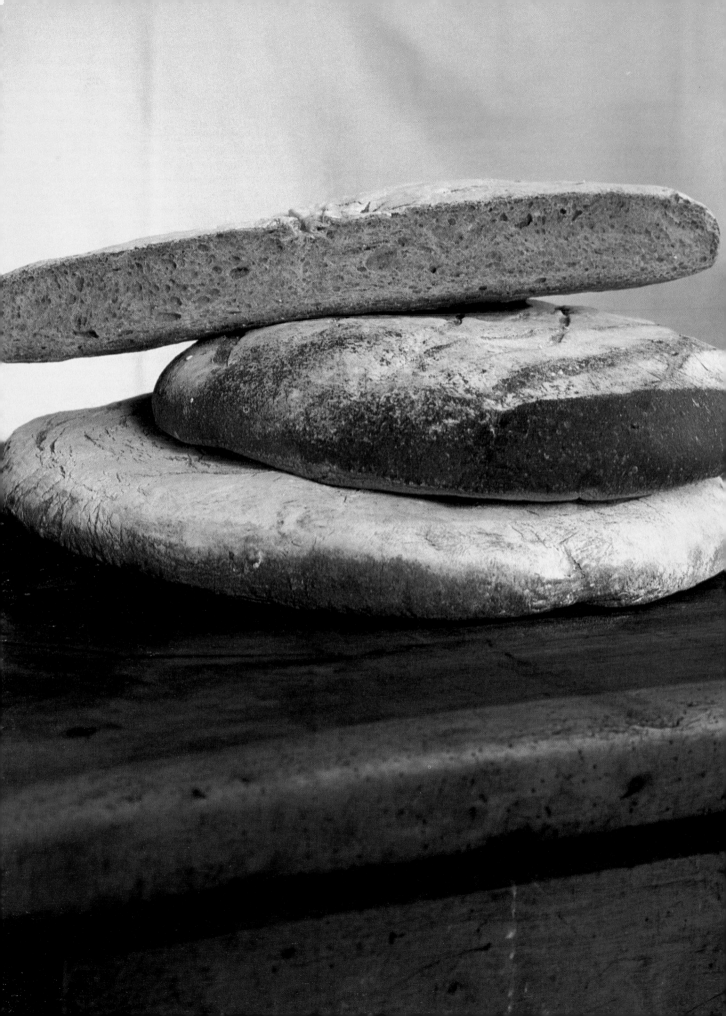

another season (*Marroniers et ferme au Jas de Bouffan*) (The chestnut trees and farm at Jas de Bouffan). The trees are on the left this time and full of leaves, with open countryside stretching out on the right, a few clouds in the sky and, of course, the ever present mountain behind the farm. In his book entitled *Cézanne*, the Italian critic Lionello Venturi notes 'the strength of the spaces, the richness of the foliage, the power of the trees in their struggle against the wind's might, their size, even when stripped of their leaves in winter. Whatever the season, Cézanne found the nature in the house's grounds sufficient to allow him to express the richness of his artistic sensitivity'.

He also painted both houses of the estate together. (*Maison et ferme au Jas de Bouffan*) (The house and farm at Jas de Bouffan). They are slightly askew, in a pale light with their windows open. An air of mystery hangs over the scene. It is a painting which anticipated Chirico's metaphysical style.

When Louis-Auguste died he left his fortune to his children. Cézanne was no longer obliged to wait for his meagre allowance, nor to make it stretch to support his mistress and son, whose existence he had kept a secret. Cézanne's father had finally found out about the grandson who would perpetuate the family name, but relations between father and son on the subject were tense and difficult. In the end it was Marie, Cézanne's sister, who sorted out the affair just before her father's death, by persuading Cézanne to marry Hortense in a family wedding in Aix.

It was almost a marriage of convenience for the couple who were more often apart than together. Hortense and her son lived in Paris and only saw Cézanne for a few months in the year, whilst he remained at Jas de Bouffan living the life of a bachelor son. Nothing was

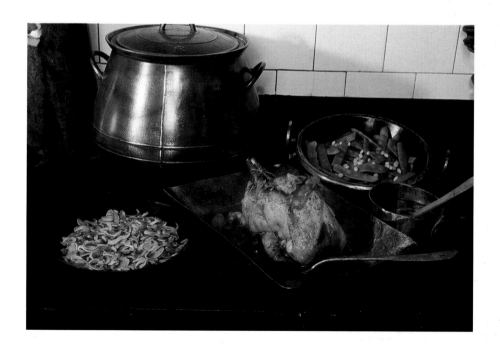

Cézanne liked simple, country cooking best. When he was once asked what his favourite food was, he replied, 'Potatoes in oil'.

Opposite:
Preparation of *pintadeau farci aux champignons*, see recipe page 148.

to change by the marriage, and Hortense was never really made to feel at home at Jas de Bouffan. She disliked being there anyway, feeling unwelcome and bored; and she never succumbed to the charms of Provence. In 1891, Cézanne asked her to move to the rue de la Monnaie in Aix as she was spending too much money in Paris. He was to remain at Jas. However, she did not survive Aix for long and soon moved back to Paris. Cézanne was 'an indifferent husband', according to John Rewald, but a 'passionate and caring father'. No doubt it was his son who brought him to Paris regularly. Nevertheless, Hortense still modelled for her husband - they had met this way, when she used to pose for artists to earn extra money. Cézanne had inherited a large

sum and could now maintain a better standard of living, despite the fact that his wife spent much of it to make him pay for his indifference. The inheritance meant that he could paint in peace at Jas de Bouffan with only his mother near him. His sister Rose had married Maxime Conil and moved to nearby Montbriand, and Marie had taken lodgings in Aix so that she could dedicate herself to charity and religious affairs, thus distancing herself from her difficult relationship with her mother.

Cézanne moved down two floors. His studio was now on the ground floor. His niece, Rose's daughter, was never to forget the room which her uncle permitted her to enter: 'It was a complete mess: fruit, flowers, white tablecloths, skulls on the mantelpiece, and an ivory Christ on an ebony crucifix.' (Jean Arrouye)

It was in this studio that he painted the portrait of Henri Gasquet, a childhood friend who had become a baker and with whom he had remained close. This was a surprising attachment for the man who had often fallen out with old friends, who had distanced himself from a self-important and haughty Zola when the writer caricatured him in the novel L'Oeuvre. Gasquet's son Joachim was a

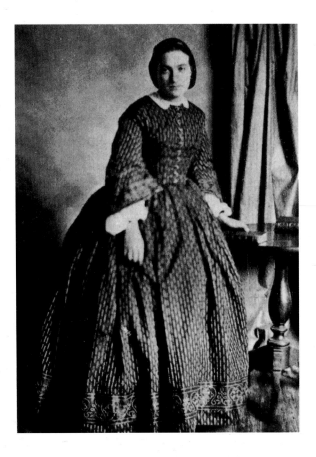

Marie was the sister closest to Cézanne. She was very religious, unmarried and looked after her brother's affairs.

Marie Cézanne, circa 1861.

Right:
Blanc-manger provençal, see recipe page 178.

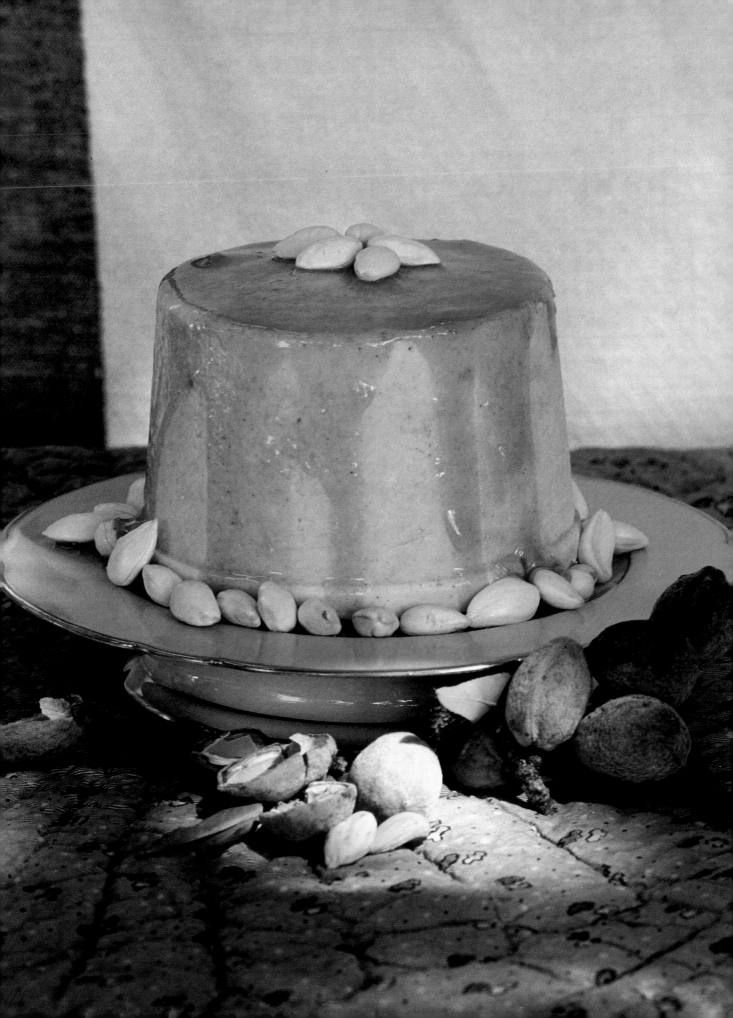

young writer interested in Provençal traditions and culture. He greatly admired Cézanne and attended one of the sessions with his father: 'The studio was empty', he reported, 'except for a small coloured table, a chair for my father, the artist's easel and a stove. Cézanne painted standing up.'

Such personal recollections are few, probably because not many people were allowed into the studio at Jas. Cézanne showed the Gasquets three still life paintings that day, and made the following statement regarding the fruit which he had painted: 'They like to have their portrait painted, it's as if they're asking forgiveness for fading. Their thoughts are exhaled with their scent. They come to you with all their smells, telling tales of the fields they left behind, of the rain which nourished them, of dawns which they beheld.'

He liked to paint still life in the silence of his studio, without the distraction of a human model. At least he could take his time with objects, they did not get restless and move about like models, and complain that they had to come back too often. Of course flowers fade, which was a problem for someone who painted as slowly as Cézanne, and sometimes he had to use artificial ones. And fruit changes colour, wrinkles and rots, but apples, oranges and even lemons were living things which he could have at his disposal in his studio. He could not always be outdoors since the rain, wind or the cold often prevented him from spending the hours he needed to paint outside. But his still life paintings were not very popular. One day he gave one to the coachman who regularly took him out to

paint far from Aix, and the man paid so little attention to it that he completely forgot about it. Cézanne was nonetheless very concerned that his paintings should please those who lived in the country, the peasants and local folk rather than those he called 'oil barons from Chicago'. He painted still life 'for children to look at while eating their soup perched on their grandfathers' knees'.

He was more relaxed at Jas after his father's death, probably because he felt less observed, judged or obliged to justify himself. His mother had always been understanding and rather liked her son being an artist. She once remarked that he even had the same christian name, Paul, as the painters Rubens and Veronese. Cézanne had always confided in her and had told her about his son while his father had remained ignorant of his grandson's existence. John Rewald says of her: 'She was a very intelligent woman, very subtle, quick off the mark and had a vivid imagination. She was tall, very dark-haired, strong with a thin face: like mother like son...'

Strangely enough Cézanne never painted a portrait of his mother, at least none that we know of, whereas he did two of his father. There is only a drawing of her asleep in a chair. Nor did he really paint his sisters, although here and there we see someone who might have been inspired by Marie or Rose reading to her doll. Maybe his two sisters are the two young women in a garden in one painting he based on a magazine illustration, but they never actually posed for him. If he did draw them it was done quickly, in a snatched sketch.

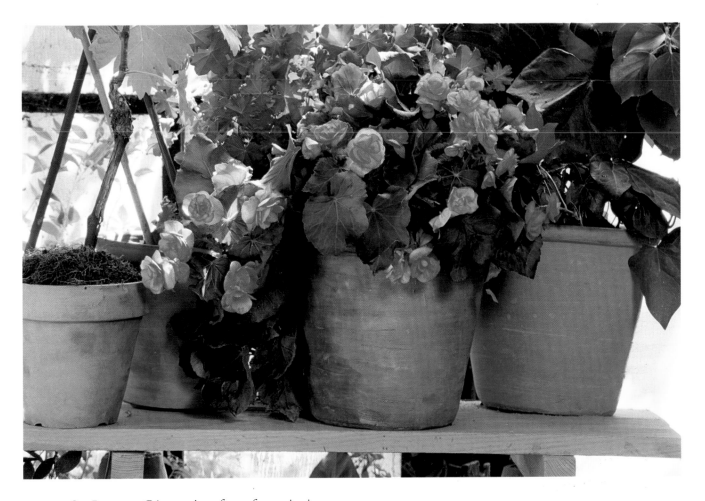

So Jas was Cézanne's refuge for painting. He lived there frugally, looked after by his mother with no need to think about material matters. He worked hard and progressed, moving away from Romanticism and gliding through Impressionism without stopping. He was inventing his own new style of painting, in which he was not content to show only the seductive side of things. He wanted to show the truth of the world, to make his paintings as strong and alive as nature itself. He also worked in Paris throughout those years, but his true source of inspiration was Jas. He was forty-seven when his father died, at which time he had not yet found his definitive style as an artist. He was still experimenting. A new phase of his life and work was beginning, with Jas as anchoring base.

Cézanne spent his life battling with Provence's bright light. He favoured the gentle morning light, softened by clouds and greenery, or playing on the glass of the greenhouse at Jas de Bouffan.

John Rewald wrote: 'Living alone with his mother, Cézanne found the solitude he had been looking for. He worked frequently in the garden which provided an endless spectacle of change over the seasons: in the summer the avenue was shaded by trees, their foliage concealing part of the house; in the winter the bare branches of the trees reflected in the pool and revealed the outline of Sainte-Victoire.'

Cézanne also painted the peasants who worked the land. They refused to pose for him but treated him with warmth. He was more at ease with them than with the pretentious bourgeoisie in Aix. He felt himself become more and more rural and Provençal over the years, drawn to the region by his love of the land which gave him so much inspiration. He had always wanted to

paint portraits, the body, even nudes, but he found it difficult to get a professional model and could imagine the scandal in Aix if he got a young local woman to undress and model for him. It may have been acceptable in Paris, where artists were less concerned about what others thought of them, but in Aix it was unthinkable. He was also embarrassed to be in his studio with a naked woman. He had always been shy and ill at ease with women. So there were no nudes, just figures and portraits. He decided to paint ordinary folk and used local people from Jas as models, not in the intimacy of portraits, but for complex compositions featuring more than one figure. He painted group scenes representing a vision of a community, a homage to the simple folk of Provence, about whom he said to Jules Borél:

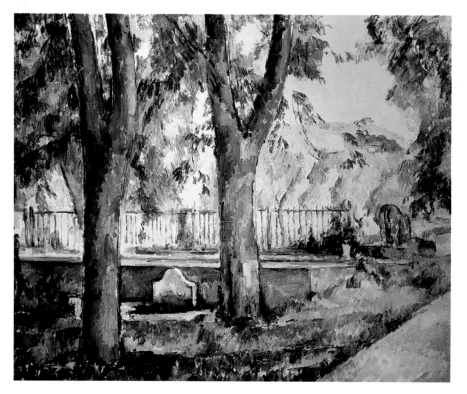

'*H*e [Cézanne] worked frequently in the garden which provided an endless spectacle of change over the seasons: in the summer the avenue was shaded by trees, their foliage concealing part of the house; in the winter the bare branches of the trees reflected in the pool and revealed the outline of Sainte-Victoire.' John Rewald

Bassin et lavoir du Jas de Bouffan.
Metropolitan Museum of Art, New York.

'I particularly like the way these people age according to the laws of nature, without artifice.' He did not imitate Joachim Gasquet in his eulogy of the folklore of Provence, concentrating instead on people rather than traditions. He painted *Les joueurs de cartes* (The card players) repeatedly, striving with each attempt to be more realistic. He did not need the players to model for him. He felt it was enough to observe their movements, to see them as they really were. On Sunday evenings they would get together to play cards, talk and drink and they welcomed Cézanne into their gatherings. They did not regard him as a wealthy landowner, but treated him as one of their own kind. He would sit there in silence and watch, sharing their wine or bringing a bottle himself, making the occasional sketch. This was to become his preferred method. Valabrègue and Vollard the art dealer were witnesses to his powers of observation, his desire to get the exact light, when he painted their portraits. He would watch, absorbing the scene and then begin to paint only after his model had gone. Cézanne observed the card-playing peasants and then, in the solitude of his studio, he painstakingly painted *Les joueurs de cartes*. Joachim Gasquet was another of the privileged few to witness Cézanne's method of working: 'There are a few canvases in the studio depicting sturdy peasants at rest, ruddy faces aged by the sun, with strong shoulders and hands marked by heavy labour. One in particular stands out, dressed in a blue shirt with a red scarf, arms outstretched, he seems to be the very incarnation of the earth as it would be if it

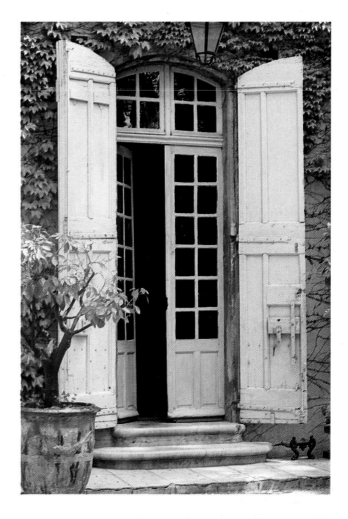

came to life, with his magnificent rough skin burnished by the sun and battered by the wind. There are others painted in a farmhouse room, playing cards and smoking. They all seem to be healthy, well-balanced, fair-minded and peaceful, with no other worry than to love and work the land.'

Lionello Venturi, less poetically, writes about these paintings which stand out among Cézanne's work: 'Peasants in these paintings are seen as individuals, almost portraits, yet there is a universal element to them, and they are as solemn as monuments, solid beings with a moral conscience.'

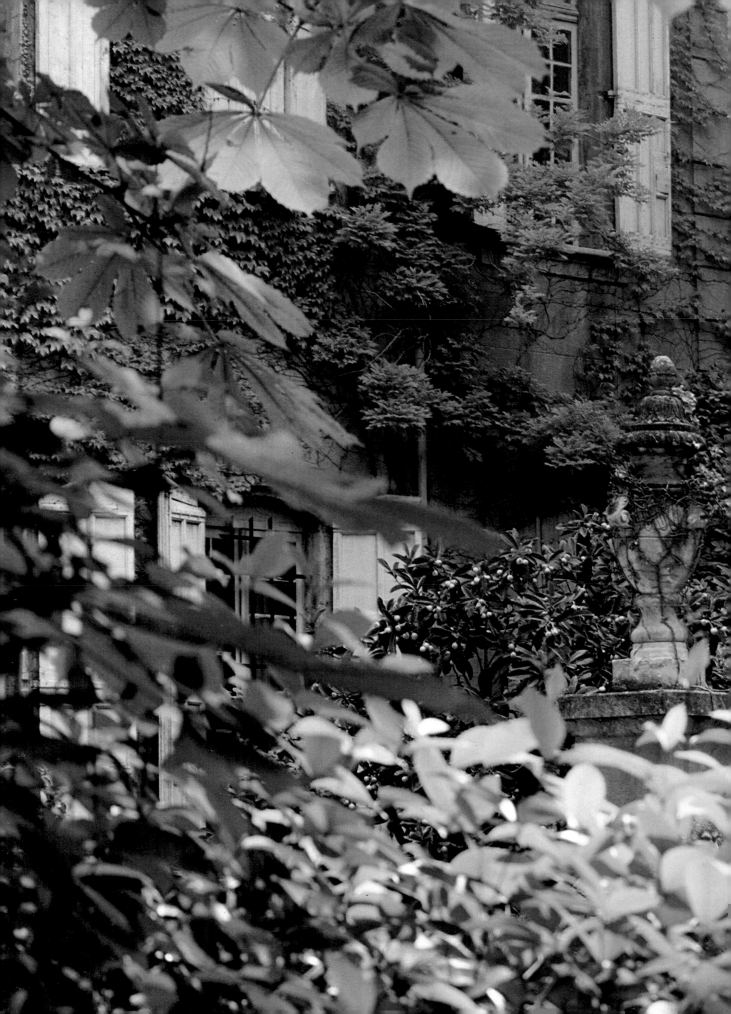

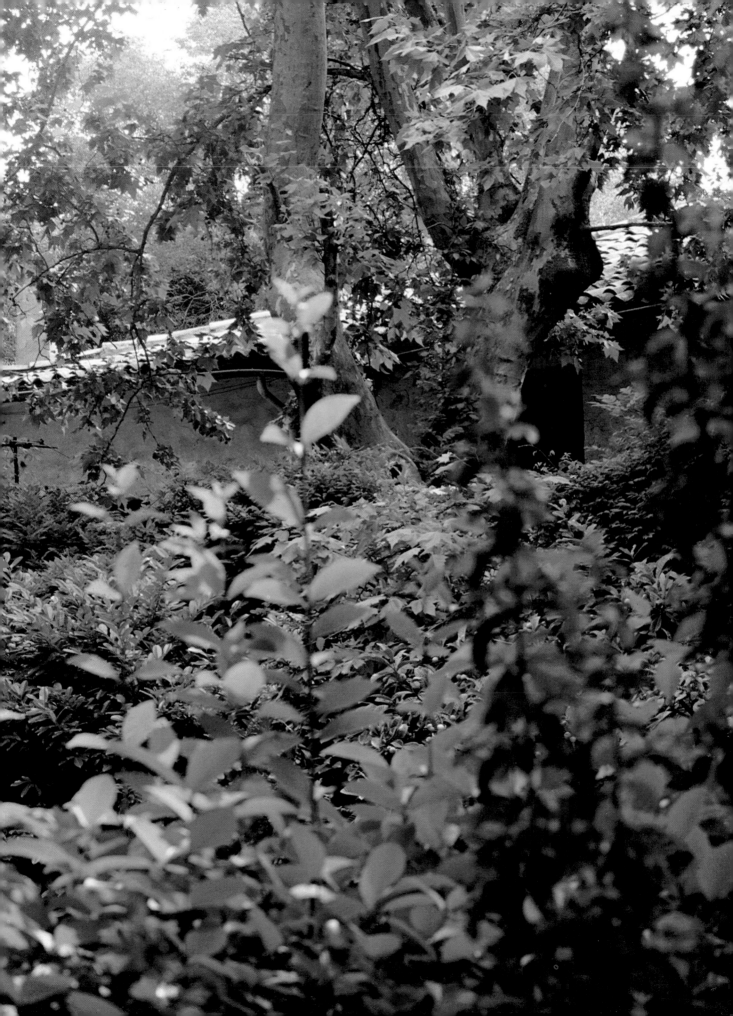

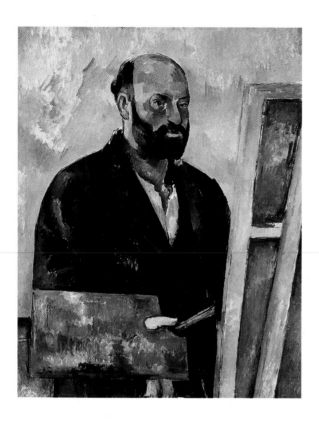

For over forty years Cézanne was faithful to the house and grounds of Jas de Bouffan. From there he could see the Sainte-Victoire mountain, which he had loved from early childhood and which he painted often.

Autoportrait à la palette.
Collection Bührle, Zurich .

Right:
Sainte-Victoire.

When his mother died, Cézanne decided Jas had to be sold. He could have bought his sisters' share but he didn't want to run this huge property all alone. Marie, still single, had run the family's affairs since her father's death, and could have moved to Jas, but did not want to leave town. And Jas without his mother there would be too forlorn, too empty, a house with nothing but memories and ghosts. With great sadness, Cézanne left forty years of life and painting behind him and took a smaller house in Aix. It was better adapted to a man of his advancing years living on his own, with his wife and son visiting rarely. He took a minimum of possessions with him and he burned anything he had to leave behind. Besides, apart from things related to his painting, he didn't have much, such was the place painting occupied in his life. Jas de Bouffan was gone, but he still had his painting. Despite all the self-doubting and many difficulties, painting was his raison d'être. He had given his whole life to art and he still had so much more to give. He left Jas without looking back. His paintings were the most important thing to him and he had to continue, to try and finish them. He had projects and obsessions and felt that this was only the beginning. He wanted to start painting large canvases with people in the countryside, naked bodies in natural settings, water, sky, trees and bathers...

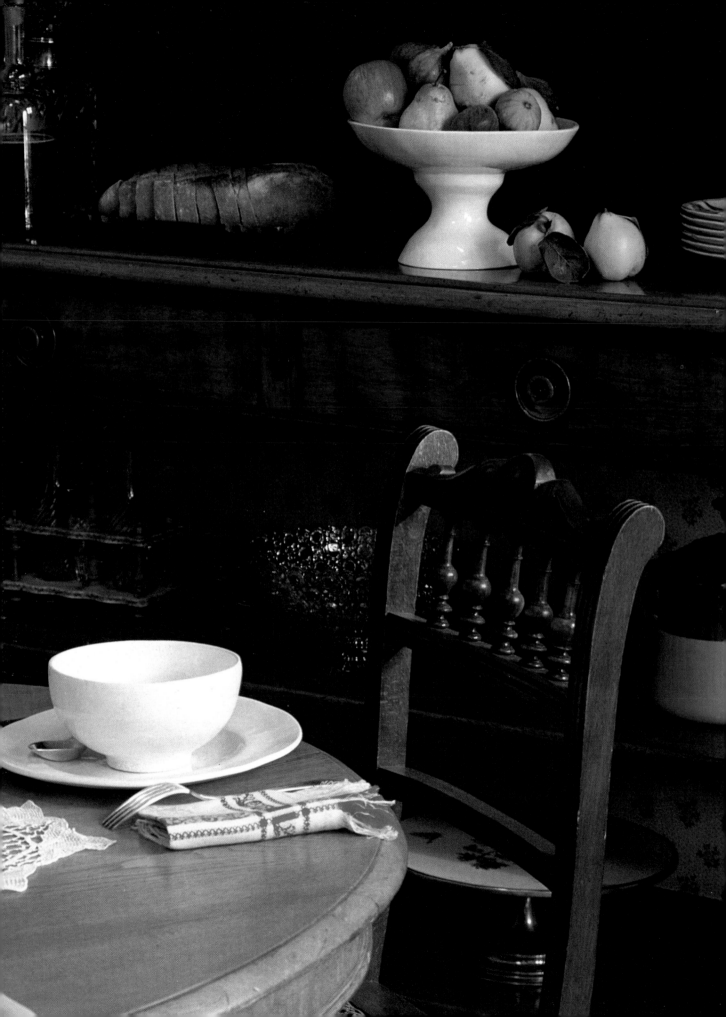

23 Rue Boulegon

'I work, eat and sleep
in peace.'

Cézanne to Coste

By 1899, two years after his mother's death, Cézanne had sold Jas, spent a year in Paris and found a house in Aix at 23 rue Boulegon. It was situated in the very heart of the town, only moments away from his father's bank. He had worked there for a few months after his failed first attempt at living in Paris, when he had managed to persuade his father to let him go and join Zola. He had arrived in Paris the first time accompanied by his father and his sister Marie, who had then left him there to begin his life as a painter. For a while he had lived the life of a bohemian artist, spending his time between his studio and cafés, but had enjoyed it much less than his friends. He had felt discouraged, and began to question his talent. He had been unable to finish the portrait he had started of his companion Zola, and ended up going back to Aix, like the prodigal son. But the subsequent attempt to become a respectable citizen and bank employee failed as well. He had thought he could give up his painting,

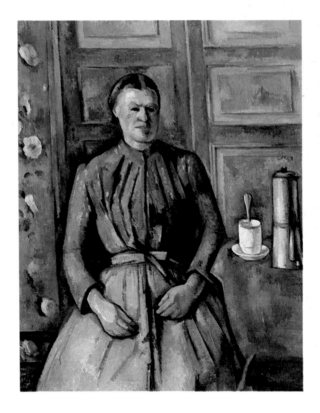

When his mother died Cézanne sold Jas de Bouffan and moved to a house in rue Boulegon in Aix. Mrs Brémond was his cook and housekeeper. It may be she who posed for this portrait.

La femme à la cafetière.
Musée d'Orsay, Paris.

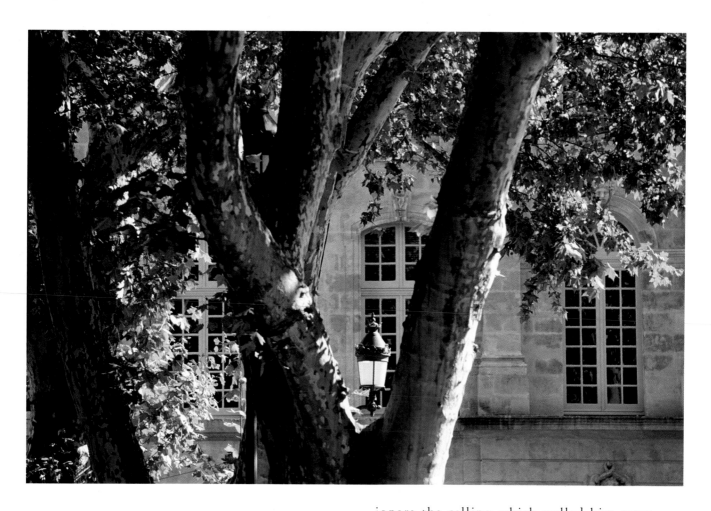

Cézanne created a studio at
rue Boulegon, which he used
when he couldn't paint
outdoors. Later Cézanne
spent the last years of his life
dividing his time between
this house and his new
studio in Lauves, outside
Aix.

Right:
Aix-en-Provence, place des
Ormeaux, circa 1900.

ignore the calling which pulled him away
from the path his father had mapped out for
him. But working in an office and keeping
account books bored him, and he could not
treat the making of money as a serious
ambition in life. He tried very hard to please
his father, but he had to concede that he was
not cut out for a career in banking. His
happiness in life came from roaming the
countryside, breathing fresh air and
contemplating nature. So he had taken up
drawing again and had decided to go back to
Paris. Painting was still part of his life and it
was at this time that he had the studio in the
attic at Jas de Bouffan installed, with the
resigned agreement of his father.

So now, years later, he was back in Aix once
more, living in the very street which brought

back so many mixed memories. The apartment was on the first floor and the studio in the attic arranged just as it was at Jas de Bouffan. He took a housekeeper, who was a calm, thoughtful, slightly plump forty-year-old called Mme Brémond. Marie continued to look after her brother's affairs, keeping the accounts, paying bills and making life easier for him, while he concentrated on his painting. Mme Brémond ran the household, cooking and cleaning for the ageing painter (by now he seemed much older than he was, practically an old man). Cézanne regarded her as more than just his maid. He trusted her and enjoyed her company. It is said that he treated her with great respect and that she treated him likewise. He may even have painted her portrait a couple of times (*La dame au livre, La dame en bleu* - Woman with a book, Woman in blue). However, no one is sure of the date or the model for these two paintings, and even though the dress and hat are the same in both, the figures are different enough for there to be doubt as to whether they depict the same person. Others, keen to put a face to the person who attended to Cézanne in his last years, claim that she was the model for another painting (*La Femme à la cafetière* - Woman with a coffeepot), one of Cézanne's best portraits. However we cannot be sure of this, so Mme Brémond's likeness remains a mystery.

Cézanne's attic studio was not as pleasing as the one he used at Jas de Bouffan. The light was less pure, clear and natural, and he complained about a high red brick chimney which reflected on his work. One Sunday

morning, Léo Larguier was shown the 'attic room under the eaves, a huge room with small windows'. This young man was doing his military service in Aix and was one of Cézanne's admirers - he made the most of his posting to Aix by striking up a friendship with the painter. He was delighted to be admitted into the secret place where the artist was experimenting with a new form of painting, as yet unseen by others. It was here that Cézanne painted still life when he was not out in the open country. He ventured into the countryside every day, weather permitting, going to his favourite places to paint in the thick of nature amidst the trees, just as Pissarro had taught him and as he did during his Impressionist period. He had by now moved away from the Impressionists and no longer sought, as they did, to capture a single moment. Instead, he took his subject further, trying to immortalize the truth within. He decided that he needed another studio much closer to nature, similar to his previous one at Jas de Bouffan, and so he

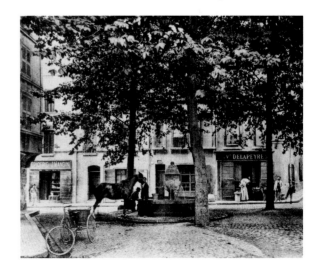

bought some land with his inheritance and had one built. While waiting for the building to be finished, he spent his time between Paris and the studio in rue Boulegon, where one day Léo Larguier, on paying him a visit, was surprised by the overwhelming odour of drying fruit: 'The studio smelt just like a country house in the autumn, when mushrooms and pears are stored and conserved.' Cézanne had just painted a small still life featuring two apples and a preserve jar, the sort typically used for olives in Provence. He took a knife from his pocket, cut an apple in two and offered one half to his guest. There had also been a large bouquet of stiff and faded fake flowers which Cézanne was using for a still life. On the wall there was a small sketch by Delacroix, a picture of a lion alone in the desert…

Here and there canvases were scattered, ready for use or to be discarded. Some of them were taken to Paris in the later years where Cézanne's son presented them to art dealers. Others disappeared, many destroyed by Cézanne himself, when he was taken by one of his fits of anger. He would slash the offending paintings with a penknife and then get Mme Brémond to burn them. Next to the studio was a little room where he kept some watercolours by Delacroix and bouquets of flowers. The dining room was more convivial. It was simple and furnished with things transferred from Jas de Bouffan: a round walnut table, six chairs, a plain dresser. With a 'croix d'honneur' on the wall, and a pipe on the mantelpiece, it could easily have been a retired sea captain's room.

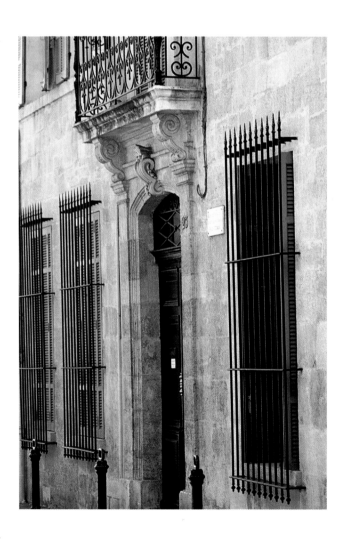

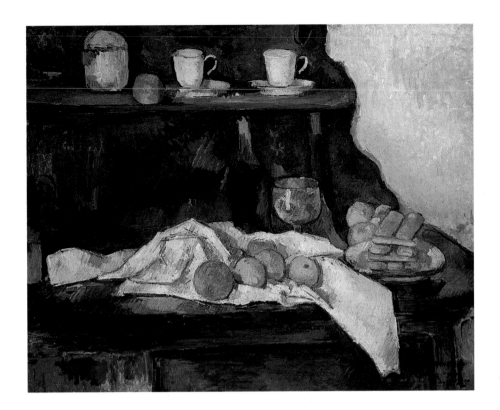

Cézanne painted many still lives in rue Boulegon. The young writer Leo Larguier was often struck by the constant smell of fruit in the studio.

Le Buffet.
Museum of Art, Budapest.

Left:
Entrance to Cézanne's apartment in rue Boulegon.

Cézanne was a ready host to his young friends, often inviting them to lunch. Charles Camoin was another admirer doing his military service in Aix, who arranged to meet him to congratulate him on his work. He was also still friends with the writer Joachim Gasquet. One Sunday they were all invited to lunch along with Léo Larguier. Mme Brémond ushered them in and a relaxed Cézanne recited verse to them. They ate delicious little patés bought from a renowned local patisserie, followed by a chicken fricassé with olives and mushrooms. Cézanne had developed mild diabetes and had to be rather careful about what he ate, especially bread. He nevertheless ate well and generously served his guests with table wine by the litre.

Cézanne loved the local produce and traditional Provençal cooking, and when in Paris would tease his friends by waxing lyrical about the virtues of tomatoes and garlic. He made a point of emphasizing the fact that he came from Provence, unlike many Impressionists who did their best to conceal their accents and origins. His way of complimenting the sculptor Puget for the earthy element he had introduced to the classicism of his sculpture was to say that in him Cezanne could 'smell the garlic'. One day in Aix, Cézanne, now a little less surly than he had been when he was younger, had been walking with some friends who were criticizing a man for having wasted his wife's dowry. Disliking gossip, he said nothing but was nevertheless asked what he thought of the man in question. With a glint in his eye he replied simply: 'He is a true connoisseur of olives.'

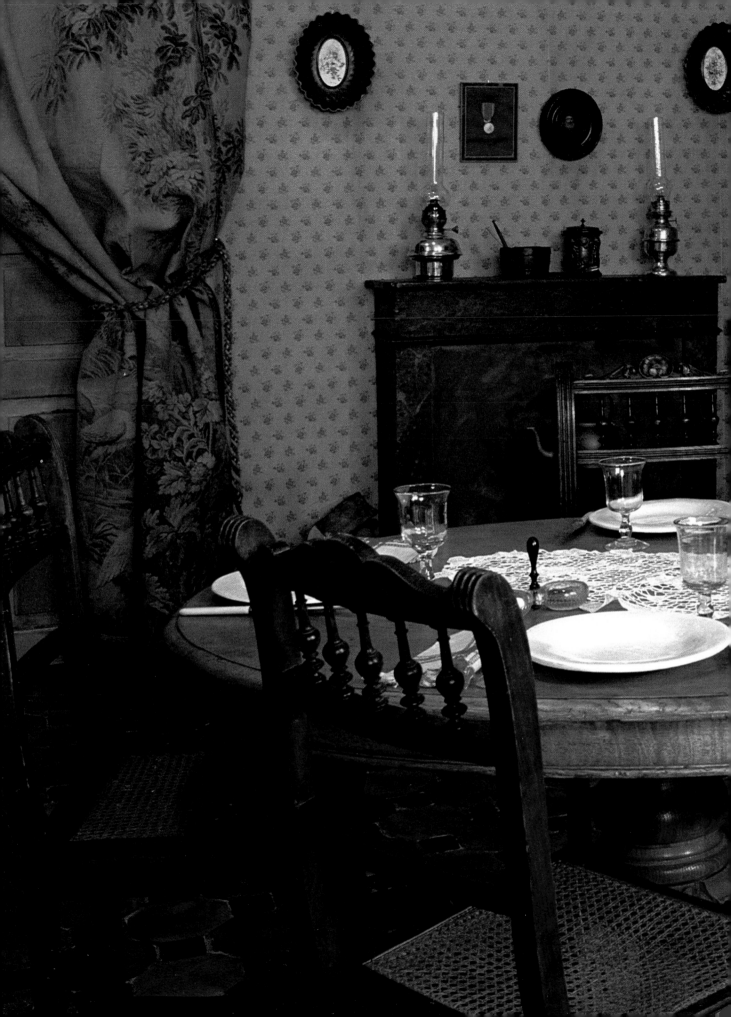

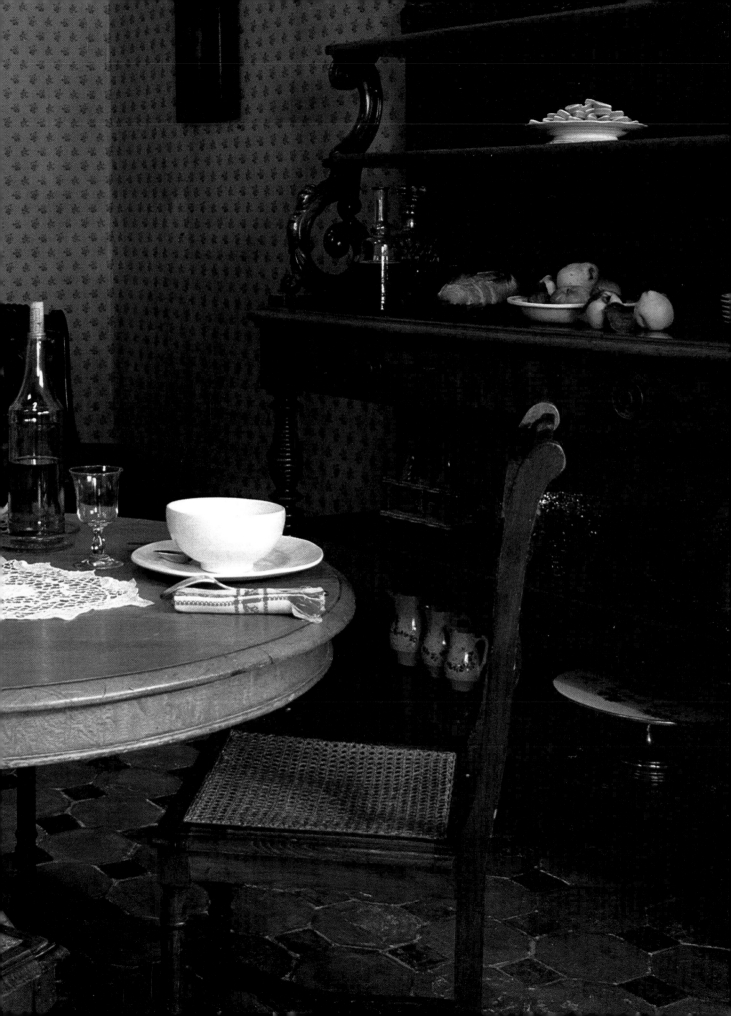

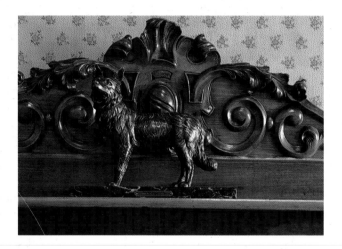

*C*ézanne lived comfortably when he was not painting. His admirers were often surprised when they visited him in his traditional bourgeois home, expecting a more avant-garde style house.

Opposite:
Aïgo boulido, see recipe page 129.

On another Sunday, Cézanne invited Laugier and two other friends - Camoin and Arenche - to lunch. Mme Brémond had roasted a chicken which she carved on the dresser. The scene could have been a still life - a table and tablecloth, a dresser, crockery - a eulogy to food fitting for someone who appreciated it as much as Cézanne. The great artist enjoyed spending time with these young people, who admired and respected him, unlike many of the townspeople. He was talkative when with them, he showed faith in them and encouraged them in their artistic endeavours. He had not lost his youthful ardour when it came to art and became passionately involved when discussing the subject. He was still as obsessive about his work as he always had been. That Sunday he proclaimed that: 'One thousand painters a year should be killed.' 'And who would decide which ones?' Camoin had asked. 'We would, by God!' the great master replied, hitting the table demonstrating the extent of the passion he felt for his art. He had looked at them and said: 'Look, it's all here, you see!' - touching a bottle, a jar, prodding whatever came to hand with his large fingers to prove his point. When Mme Brémond came in to clear the table, taking away the bottle and jar, he watched her and for a few moments it seemed as if he was going to tell her to leave everything where it was, because the articles she was taking away had just revealed some secret of object-relation to him.

Unfortunately there is no record of Mme Brémond's thoughts and opinions on the man she cooked and cared for over so many years. She was partial to using cognac in her cooking and Cézanne occasionally drank some of it to give him a lift while he was working. Mme Brémond had decided that it was not good for his diabetes, and hid the bottles. Therese Gidde, who as a young woman had helped Mme Brémond in the kitchen for a while, found this story very amusing and was to relate it years later to a young student.

It has often been said of Cézanne that he was a misanthrope, that he complained too much, that he was moody and complicated. There is some evidence to back this up. If he felt that people wanted something from him, or that they might disrupt the peace of his studio and break his concentration, then that was enough for him abruptly to break off with that person. Or, more surprisingly, he would be filled with rage and run off if anyone

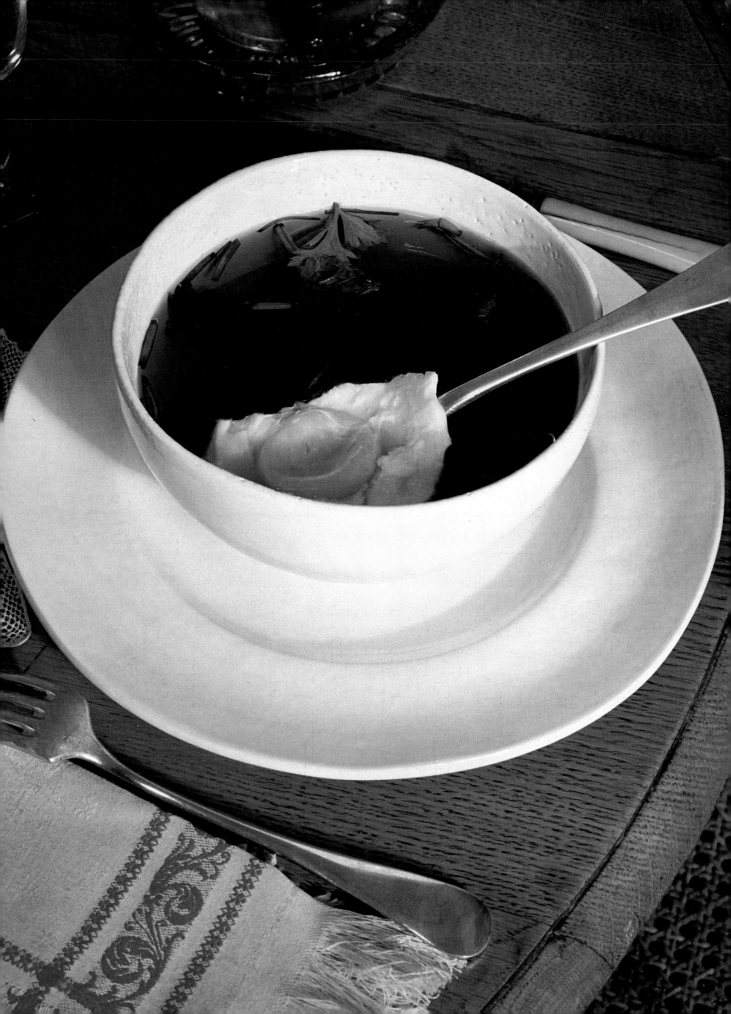

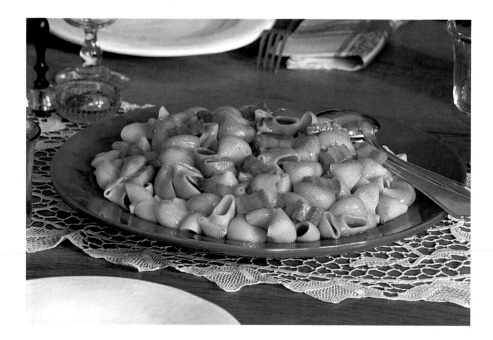

Mrs Brémond was a cordon bleu cook, but Cézanne had diabetes and could not make the most of her cooking. When he had guests, however, he had an excuse to ignore his dietary restrictions.

Macaronade au jus d'agneau, see recipe page 168.

Following pages: *Petits pâtés chauds,* see recipe page 139.

touched him or accidentally brushed against him, as happened with the painter Emile Bernard. But this was an involuntary reaction and he had acted this way ever since he had been violently treated by a friend in his childhood. Even in the early bohemian years in Paris, a waitress had bumped against his chair in a restaurant and he had created a scene about it. Mme Brémond told Émile Bernard, when he asked her what he had done to make Cézanne react in such a way, that she knew it was more than her life was worth to bump into this funny old man.

If he ate out in town, he was very pleasant and attentive to others. But he went out less and less, maybe ill at ease with society people, preferring to be with his old friends. But he was not really the gruff old man that he has been made out to be. The writer Edmond Jaloux, a friend of Joachim Gasquet's, was once invited to dinner at Cézanne's house. He thought he was going to meet a very self-

important man, the artist being a legend in his own lifetime: 'Suddenly the door opened. He came in, his discreet manner and careful step almost too exaggerated. He resembled a well-to-do gentleman farmer. He had a slightly rounded back, healthy ruddy complexion and white hair, a small droopy moustache, small piercing eyes, a slightly red nose. This was Paul Cézanne. He had a nasal voice, spoke slowly but softly and carefully. He talked about art or nature with sensitivity, dignity and depth.'

Léo Larguier, who was one of the lucky few to have a close relationship with Cézanne, said of him: 'It is said of Cézanne that he was a belligerent man. I never noticed that in him, personally speaking. He was shy and somewhat inclined to feel persecuted, but I saw him frequently for over a year and there was never the hint of a problem with him.'

Mary Cassatt, an American who liked to befriend artists, especially Impressionists, confirmed this. She first met Cézanne at Giverny, where he seemed a little daunting, but his kindness and sincerity soon won her over: 'I was somewhat surprised by his manners at first: he scraped his soup bowl and then lifted it and poured the last drops of soup into his spoon. He then picked up a chop and pulled the meat off the bone with his fingers. He ate with his knife, emphasized his speech with it, never once putting it down from the beginning of the meal to the end. However, despite his disregard for table manners, he was more polite with us than any man I have met. He didn't want Louise to serve him before us, according to the normal order of things at a table. He was even very respectful to this stupid maid and when he came into the room he politely removed his beret which he wore to protect his bald head.'

Sometimes Cézanne would go to meet Larguier in front of the barracks and take him to dinner. They would sit at the terrace of the Clement Café, the liveliest place in the cours Mirabeau and a meeting place for officers, students and others. There was music, a piano, a violin and a cello and other admirers flocked around him. He was modest, never hesitating to share his doubts about his work and talk about his aims and whether he was achieving them. Léo Larguier was surprised that the regulars at the café never greeted him, considering who he was and that he had lived in Aix his whole life. But he went there rarely and had long avoided the bourgeoisie. He even eventually distanced himself from Joachim Gasquet, finding him a bit too clingy, too literary and chatty, and

disapproved of the way he crowed in the sort of salons where Cézanne felt ill at ease. Cézanne had always spoken his mind tactlessly on such social occasions, saying exactly what he thought of a fellow artist whom he felt to be without daring, interest and spirituality, or dismissing a museum curator whom he considered ignorant. The renowned moodiness of Cézanne was evident at times like these, if not a little exaggerated.

It has also been said that Cézanne cared little about his appearance and that he was dishevelled. When he was in Paris in the early years he loved to play the simple country boy,

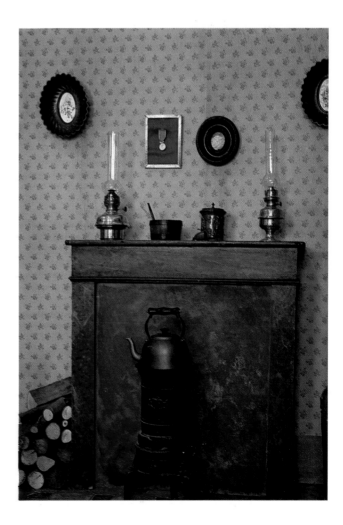

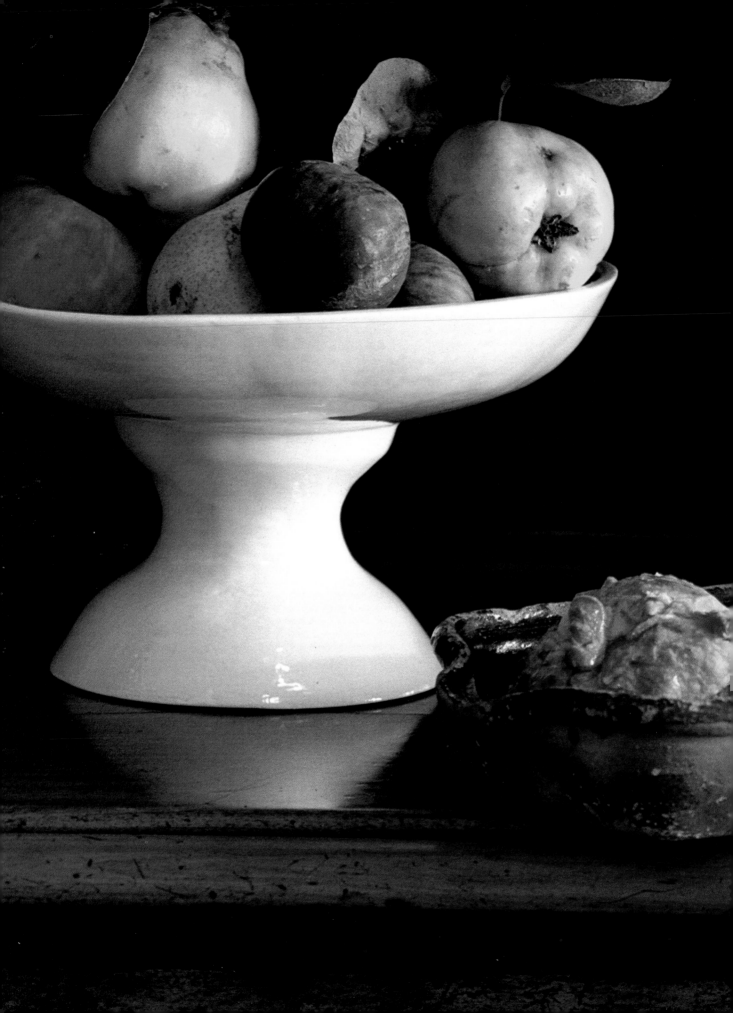

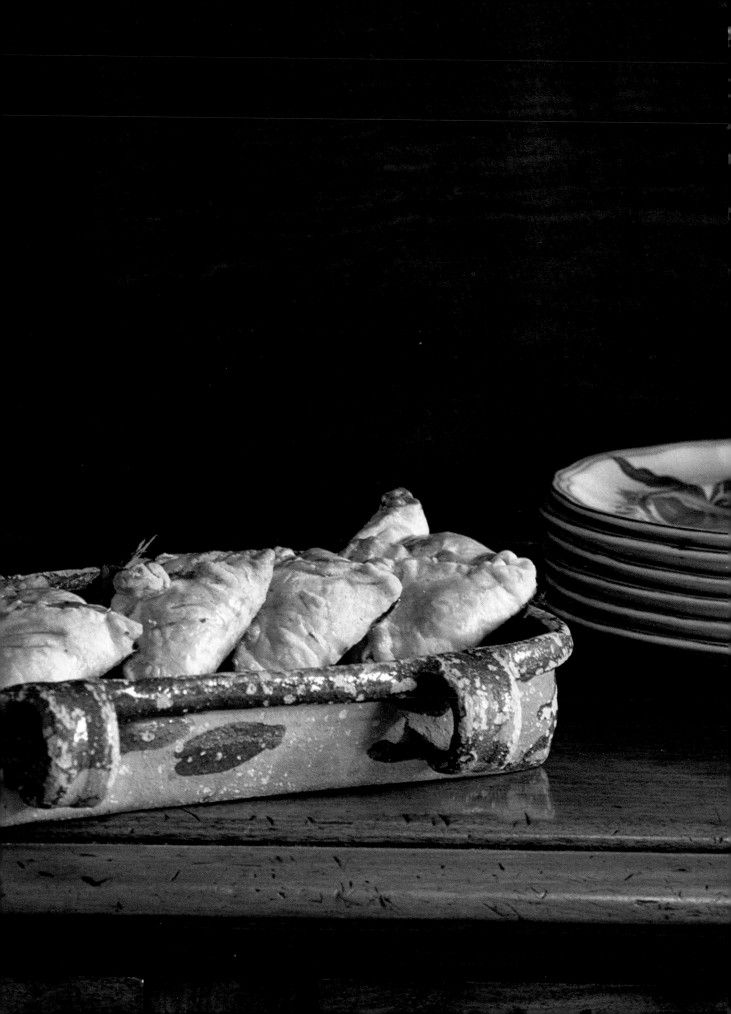

sporting a red flannel belt over his trousers, as was the custom in Provence. But he wanted to avoid looking Parisian or bourgeois, and like many shy people he seemed unaware of ridicule. He never adopted a gentlemanly look like the painter Manet, he did not want to be a Baudelaire-like dandy, and he did not affect an artistic manner of dressing. He was simply unconcerned by his appearance. He was preoccupied by his work and always managed, when juggling with paintbrush, knife and palette, to splash paint on his jacket, waistcoat or trousers. Larguier states that here again Cézanne's reputation has been greatly exaggerated and that he was better dressed than most Aix inhabitants: 'If he wore a

woollen top under his jacket it was not out of place in the cours Mirabeau or the place Saint-Jean and it was ideal to go painting in.'

Gustave Coquiot nonetheless claims that, according to witnesses, Cézanne was 'always dirty, with a ragged tie, clumsy big shoes and a delivery man's greatcoat...'. Trying to separate fiction from fact is not easy, but one can imagine that Cézanne made an effort when he was seeing his friends, bothering less about his appearance when seeing people he cared little for.

Léo Larguier probably knew Cézanne the best, because he had never made him feel that he wanted to use him or that he wanted something out of the friendship. The ageing artist had therefore readily accepted Larguier's invitation to his parents house in the Cevennes, taking Hortense and Paul with him. The visit had been arranged during the shooting season, when 'there was a local woman in the house who knew exactly how to cook game, grilling or frying it to perfection in olive oil and serving it with mushrooms...' According to Larguier, Cézanne 'was like an ageing relative visiting for a few days, and during his stay he seemed for once to forget his painting'. He adds, 'he didn't want to immortalize the trees he saw here on canvas, they were not related to his Provençal olive,

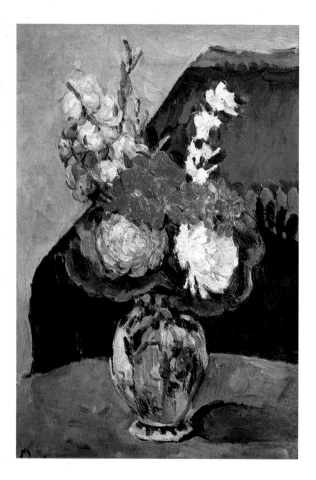

Cézanne didn't often paint bunches of fresh flowers because they usually faded and died before he could finish his painting.

Bouquet au petit Delf.
Musée d'Orsay, Paris.

Right:
Poires et coings au miel,
see recipe page 172.

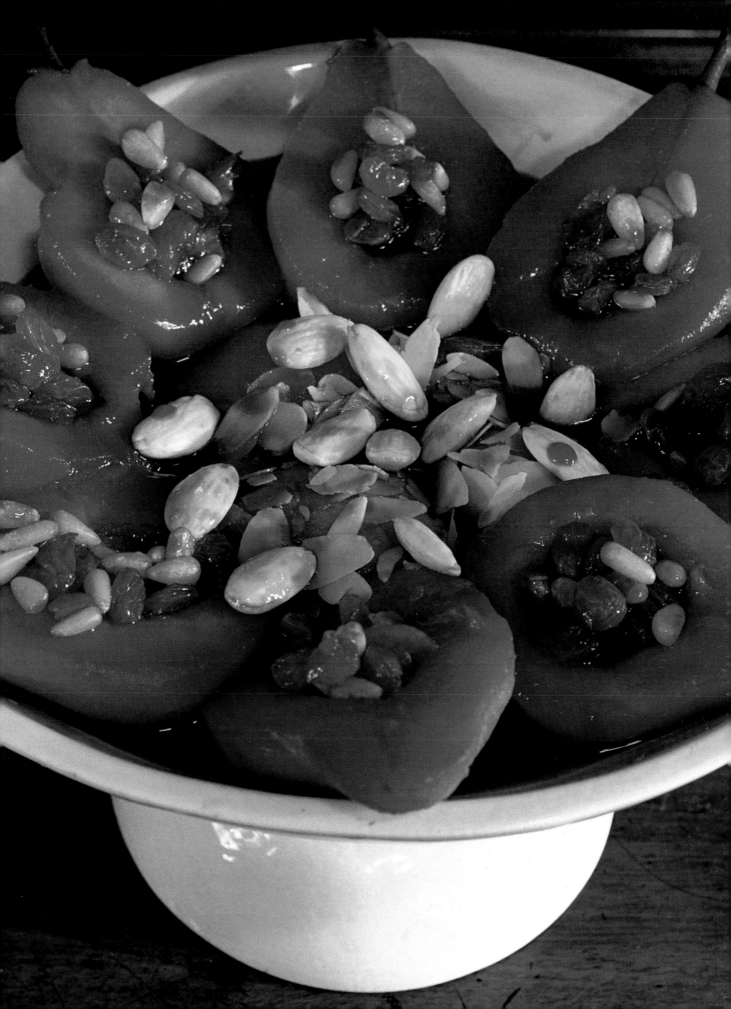

pine and cyprus trees'. While he was there he didn't even react when he heard someone saying something foolish about painting.

So there were many contradictions in Cézanne. The argumentative man had not lost the passion of his youth, a passion he had displayed in the days when he had been an avant-garde artist in Montmartre. But he now attended mass regularly at Saint Saveur's Cathedral, a short walk from rue de Boulegon. He would sit under Nicolas de Froment's triptych of Moses and the burning Bush in a top hat, white shirt, clean tie and jacket. He would contemplate Moses, the man he had often compared himself with, drawing a parallel between the prophet and himself as the pioneer of a new style of painting which

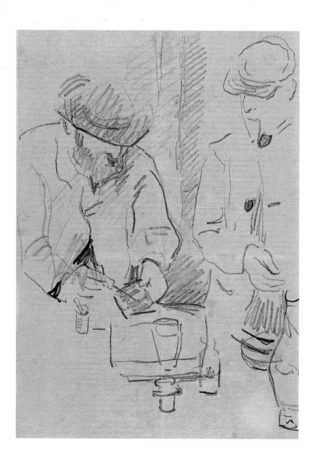

would lead to a 'promised land'. He is supposed to have said to Larguier that 'religion is moral cleansing for me. I am weak, so I lean on my sister Marie, who leans on her confessor, who in turn leans on Rome....'

This philosophy is perhaps a little narrow, but shows that his doubts did not only concern his painting. If only painting was all there was to life. But the absence of a woman in his life bothered him and it had been a long while since he had approached Hortense, or anyone else for that matter. It is possible that he paid visits to the 'house with the red light shining' where he could be sure of a warm welcome. In 1885 he wrote in a letter to Zola: 'I am totally isolated. There is the brothel in the centre of town and a few other distractions, but little else....' Perhaps this was the price he had to pay for wanting to be on his own so much.

Émile Bernard was a disciple of Gauguin and one of Cézanne's fervent admirers. He had dedicated a short book to him without even having met him. He finally met Cézanne by stopping off in Aix on his way back to Paris from Marseilles. He could have perhaps met him earlier in Paris but Cézanne was a difficult man to track down and he was becoming more and more solitary. So he had taken the tramway from Marseilles to Aix and asked around for Cézanne's address. To give people a hint he showed them an old portrait he had of Cézanne drawn by Pissarro, which illustrated the cover of the book he had dedicated to him. In the end he asked at the town hall and finally got the address he was looking for - 23 rue Boulegon. He had started up the steps to the front door when he found himself facing an affable, ageing man with the 'face of an old general', who was obviously on his way out. He was going out painting and as Bernard was 'one of his kind' he took him along. He too had 'the look of an artist' and Bernard himself confessed that his appearance even incited children to throw stones at him.

Bernard was delighted with Cézanne's invitation, so much so that he decided to take a month's lodgings in Aix with his wife. He was invited to lunch at Cézanne's house the next day and at eleven o'clock sharp he was ringing at his door. It was a household where luncheon was taken early and Mrs Brémond was about to serve. The guest remarked that Cézanne's eyes were 'red and swollen', his face 'puffy' and his nose 'slightly red'. He seemed, says Bernard, 'very tired for his age, ill from the diabetes, obliged to eat carefully and watch his diet'. Nevertheless, this did not prevent him from helping himself to a glass or two of wine.

This was the first meal they shared together, but not the last, as they became good friends. The passionate interest Bernard had for the artist's work gave great pleasure to Cézanne, who took him painting and had long conversations with him about art, philosophy and people in general. He trusted his new friend and often went to eat with the Bernards in the rue de Theatre. Émile Bernard returned to the rue Boulegon on numerous occasions. He turned up one Sunday with his wife and the artist seemed particularly happy to see them. 'Mrs Brémond,' he politely requested his housekeeper, 'prepare a special

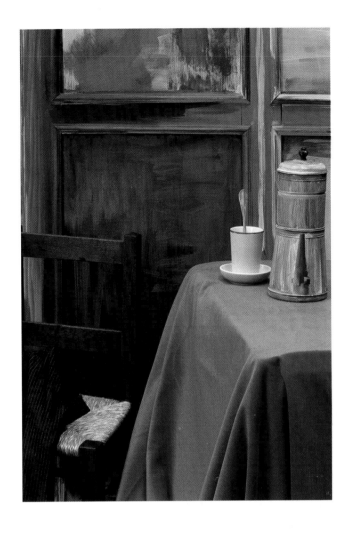

Because Cézanne was very shy and given to mood swings, he was considered to be somewhat unsociable. He could, however, be an affectionate and faithful friend, but he rarely painted portraits of those he was close to.

Left:
Le Docteur Gachet et Cézanne.
The Louvre, Paris

lunch for us today!' He visibly enjoyed these meals with Bernard when he seemed very relaxed and happy: 'At the table he was good-tempered, joyous to an extent I would not have imagined of him, a heartfelt contentment exuded from him which was almost old-fashioned, such was the extent of his bonhomie and abandonment.'

Later on, during another trip to the south, Bernard went back to Aix and lunched once again at rue Boulegon, still faithful to his new friend and keen to listen to his ideas which he always noted down carefully. This time Hortense and Paul were there from Paris to see Cézanne, who went up to Paris less and less. The meal was again very gay. Cézanne was very talkative and praised his son, who dealt with his father's business in Paris. At one o'clock the daily carriage came to take Cézanne painting outdoors, but he sent it away, preferring to accompany Bernard to Marseilles where he was to take the train back to Paris.

Ambroise Vollard was a talented dealer who was very interested in Cézanne's work. It was not yet in great evidence in Paris, shown only by a few collectors or at Tanguy's, an art shop whose owner also sold paintings to help out his favourite artists and to publicize their work. Vollard went to Aix to see the painter Cézannes, both father and son. He helped them immensely by showing and selling Cézanne's work, the latter being appreciated more by the son than by the father. To keep in touch with Cézanne, he sent, at least once, a case of wine to Cézanne in Aixfor whom he had already organized an exhibition, with the help of Cézanne's son, in his gallery in the rue Lafitte (the locals had mocked and laughed at the work in the window). He too says that he was warmly welcomed by the artist whom he had already met without realizing, having talked with him at an exhibition. 'Cézanne was very jolly at the dinner to which I was invited,' he says. 'What struck me above all about him was his extreme politeness with everyone. His favourite phrase seemed to be "Excuse me...!"'

Vollard won and kept the trust of the Cézannes, both father and son. He helped them immensely by showing and selling Cézanne's work, the latter being appreciated more by the son than by the father. To keep in touch with Cézanne, he sent, at least once, a case of wine to Cézanne in Aix.

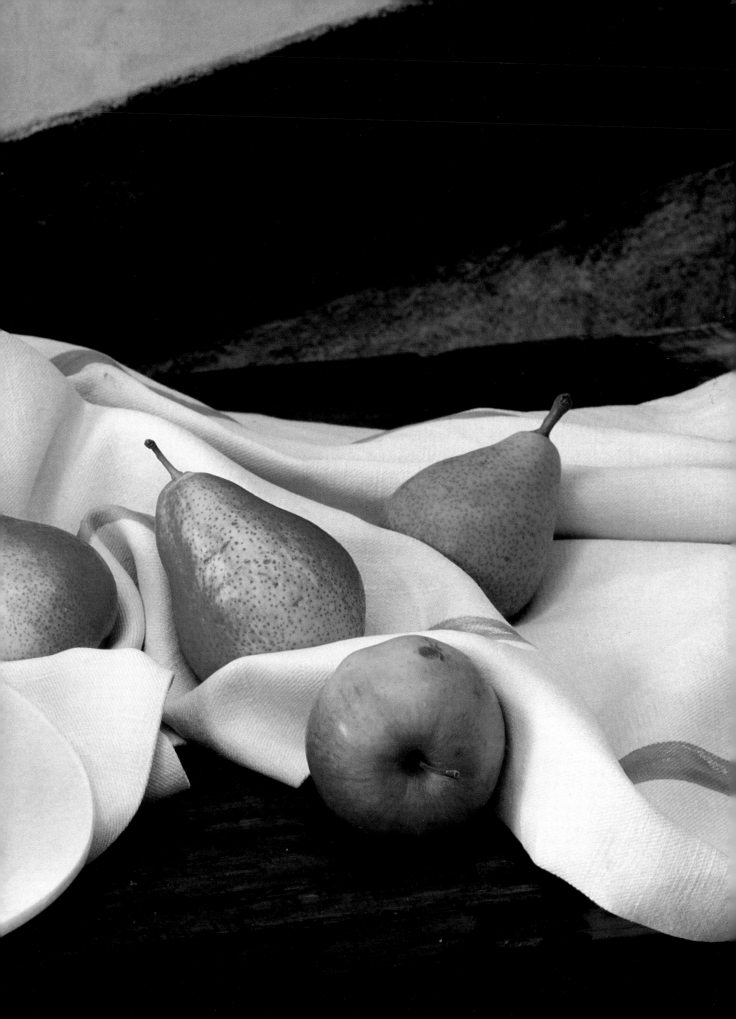

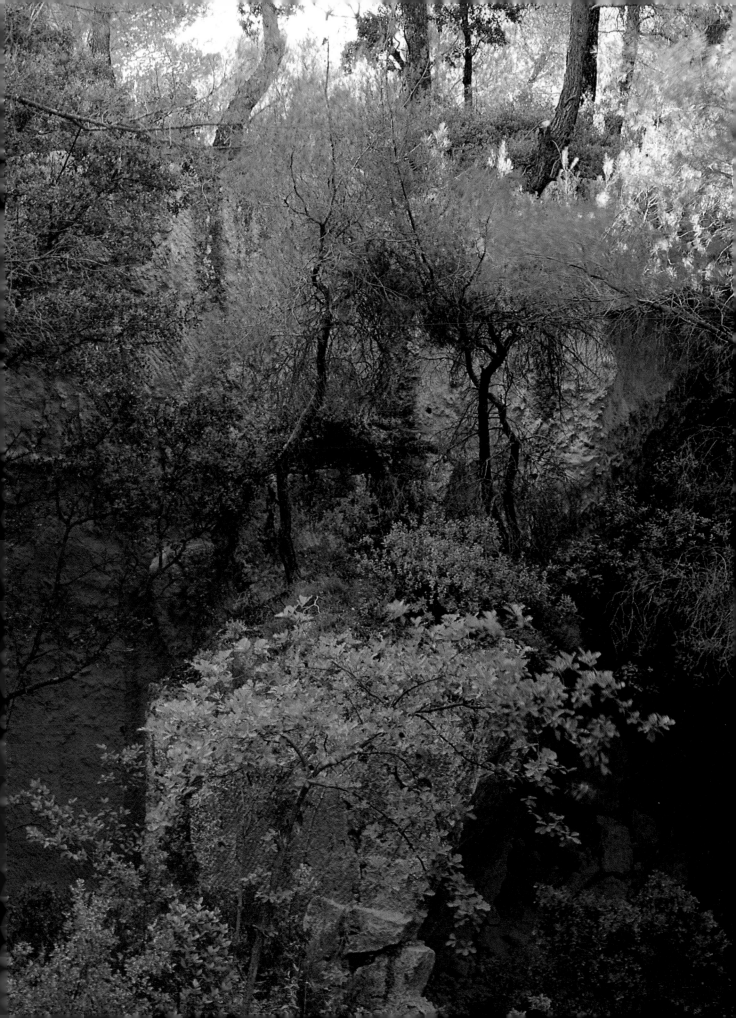

Mount Sainte-Victoire

' We cooked lunch out in the open. ...
Baille lit a wood fire ...
Cézanne tossed the salad in a damp towel.
And after lunch, we took a siesta.'

Paul Alexis

On 8 November 1895 the young writer Emile Solari wrote in his diary: 'Yesterday, Cézanne, Emperaire and I went on an excursion together. As Cézanne walked side by side next to the short and deformed Emperaire, I imagined a dwarf-like Mephisto in the company of an old Faust. They really looked a strange couple. We had been walking for a while and had just crossed a long stretch of wood planted with small trees, when we emerged and saw before us the most unforgettable view of the Sainte-Victoire mountain with the foothills rolling down to Marseilles on the right. The landscape was so vast and yet felt so familiar. Below us we could see the Zola Dam barrier and its greenish water. We had lunch in Saint-Marc under a fig tree, having bought our provisions from a nearby road-worker's canteen. After we had crossed the rocky hills on foot we dined in the evening at Tholonet. We were in high spirits on our return, until Emperaire took a fall. He had had a little too much to drink and hurt himself quite badly. We took him straight back to the house.'

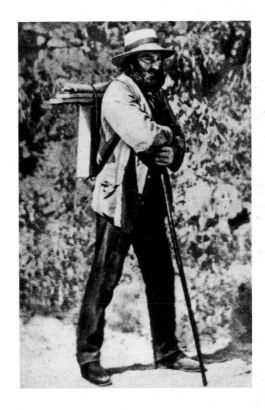

*E*ncouraged by Pissarro, the great Impressionist, Cézanne first started to paint entirely outdoors in the Ile de France region. Once back in Provence, Cézanne allowed other artists to accompany him on his outdoor painting trips.

Cézanne on a painting excursion.

63

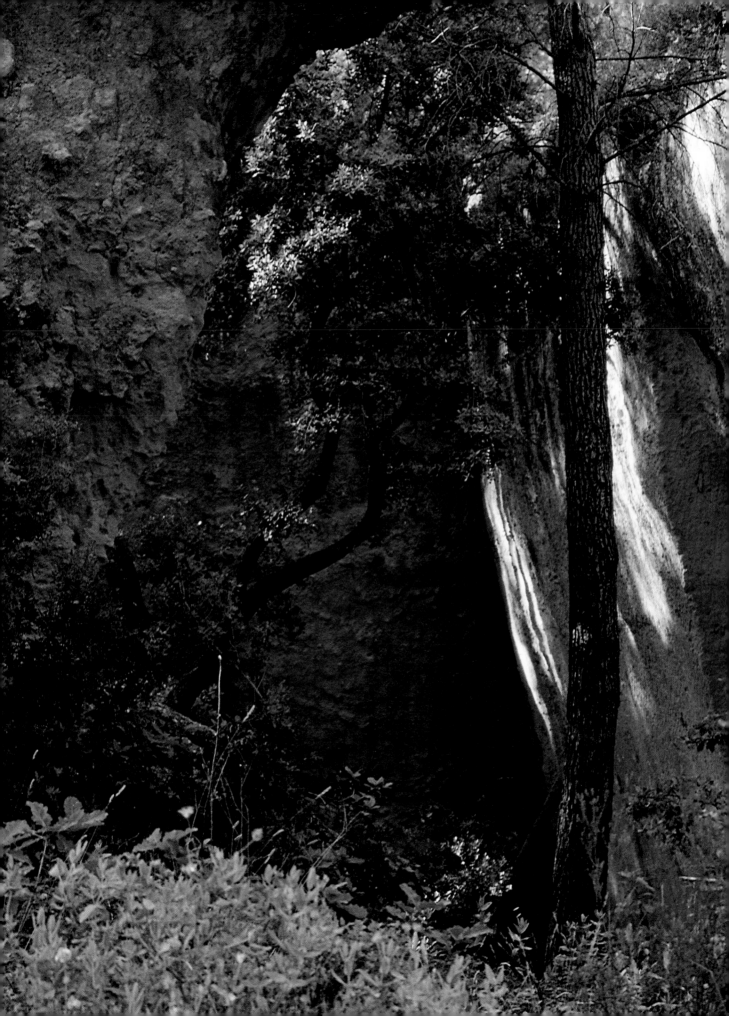

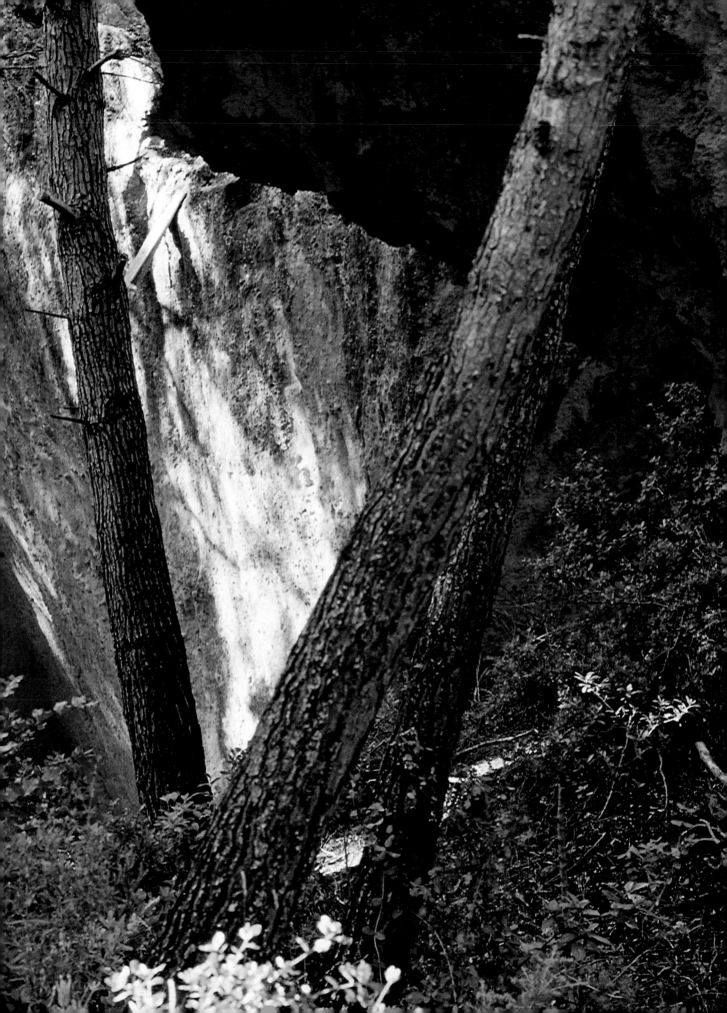

The author of these lines was the son of Cézanne's old friend, the sculptor Philippe Solari, who occasionally painted with him. One day in 1897 Cézanne wrote a letter inviting the elder Solari to join him at eight o'clock the next morning at his cottage at Bibémus on the slopes of Sainte-Victoire. They were to paint a portrait of Achille Emperaire. They painted him on the ground floor and he can be recognised in a later portrait by Cézanne, where he is pictured in his dressing gown sitting in a large armchair. Cézanne held Solari in high regard and valued his friendship. They were then both in their sixties and spent much of

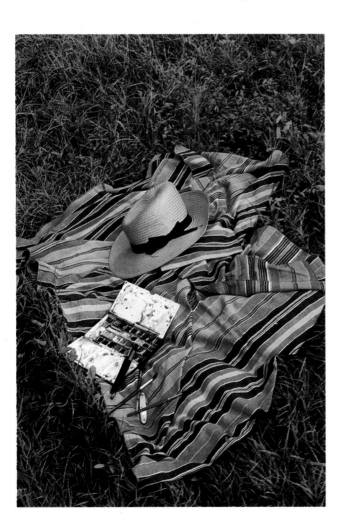

their time together roaming the countryside and reminiscing about their youth.

In the autumn of the same year, they all went on another excursion together. Cézanne and Emperaire accompanied Philippe and Emile Solari, who led them to the slopes of Sainte-Victoire. They spent the night at the village of Vauvenargues in a room 'decorated with large smoked hams suspended from the beams', and set off the next day on the three-hour climb to the top. They had lunch on the summit in the chapel ruins, and on the way down, Cézanne, full of the joys of life, attempted to climb a pine tree to prove to his friends that he had lost none of the agility of youth. He failed, collapsing in fits of laughter.

In his *Documents Litteraires*, Zola recounts how, in 1856, the 'three rascals' got together. The trio consisted of Zola, Cézanne and Baille, who was later to graduate from the Ecole Polytechnique. Whenever there was a holiday they would set off together for 'mad treks across the countryside'. Zola writes that they 'needed plenty of air, plenty of sun and to search for hidden paths at the bottom of ravines...' In the winter they would visit neighbouring villages to eat omelette, and in the summer they would picnic on the banks of the river Arc or down by the dam which Zola's father had built. Autumn was the hunting season, 'a pretext for long rambles', during which they would discuss their favourite poets, Victor Hugo and Alfred de Musset - the 'romantic conviction' of the one and the 'derisive romanticism' of the other.

Paul Alexis, a novelist long since forgotten, describes one particular hunt. He tells how the

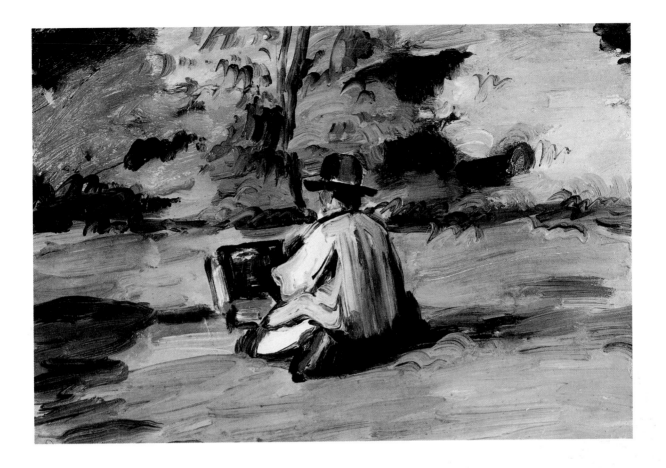

first one up would throw stones against the shutters of the others to wake them. By the time the sun had risen they were already on the trail. Carefully prepared food from the night before was carried in their game bags until it was time to sit and eat. 'We cooked lunch out in the open. Baille lit a wood fire and hung the leg of lamb, seasoned with garlic, from a string above it. Zola turned it as it cooked while Cézanne dressed the salad in a damp towel. After lunch we took a siesta, and then set off once more, our shotguns over our shoulders, ready for the big hunt. We managed to shoot nothing but a few ears of wheat. An hour later we put down our guns, pulled out our books and sat under a tree to read.' Occasionally, when on the Tholonet trail, they would stop

Cézanne spent a great deal of his life outdoors, exploring the countryside around Aix.

Un peintre au travail.
Private collection.

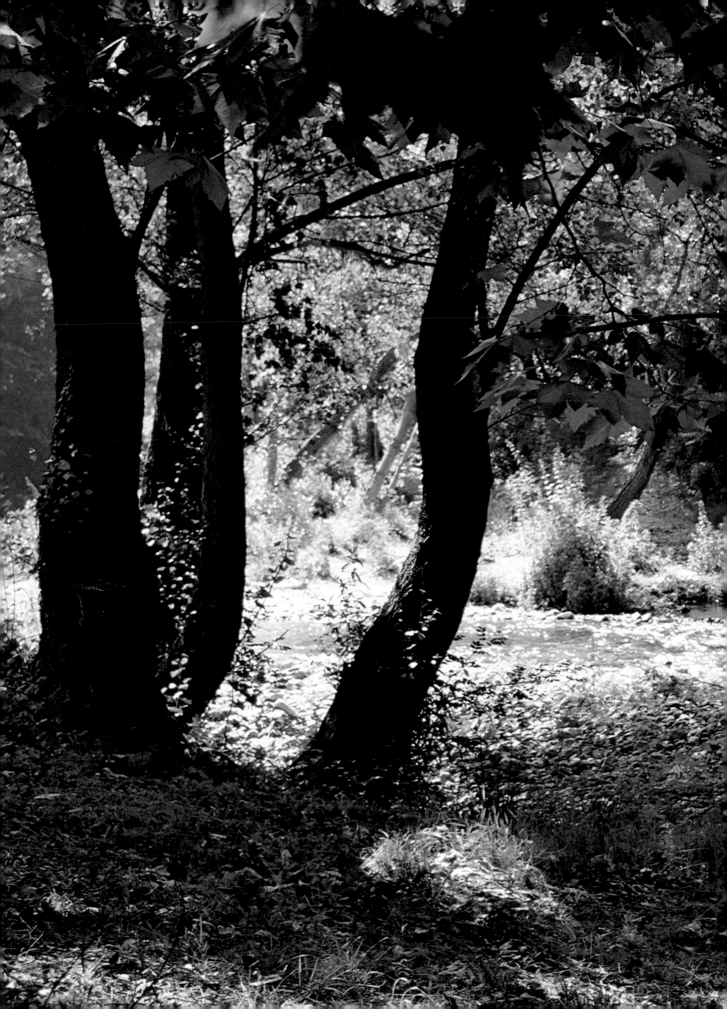

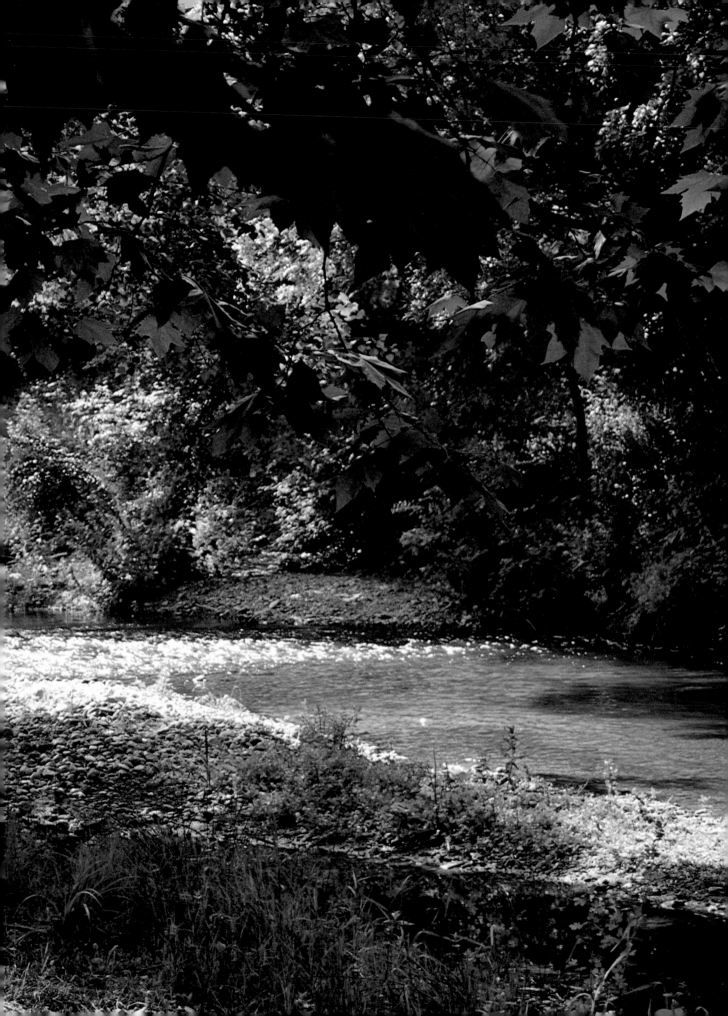

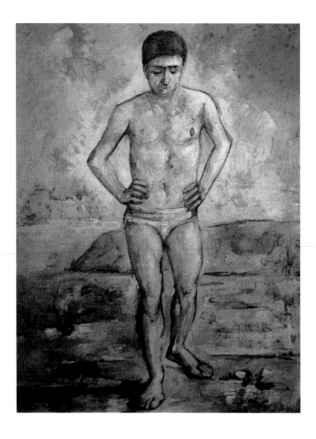

Cézanne's overriding obsession and ambition was to successfully paint a human figure in nature's setting. He seemed to be haunted by a dream of paradise lost which he thought his painting would help him rediscover.

Le grand baigneur.
Metropolitan Museum, New York.

Following pages:
Picnic on the banks of the river Arc.

painting took a hold. His adolescence was dominated by his friendship with Zola. They spent many holidays together exploring the countryside. They loved to wander across the hills and would go down to the river and bathe for hours, trying to catch fish in the waterholes. They would venture eastwards along the road to Tholonet which was then only a small village made up of a few ancient houses. Then they would climb the slopes of the mountain and cross the pine forests until they reached Château-Noir. Climbing higher still, they would go as far as the Bibémus quarry. This strange, chaotic landscape had been shaped by centuries of exploitation and the yellow stone used to build many of the local houses. Large caves had been hewn out of the rock, and trees sprouted from the cracks and crevices. It is a poetic wilderness. The unruly vegetation grew freely from an uneven terrain, yet without obstructing the magnificent view of the river valley beyond, with the dam, the Infernets gorge and Sainte-Baume mountains in the distance. They would also venture southwards to the village of Gardanne or even as far as Estaque on the coast. When they were older they would go hunting, although they spent most of their time discussing their artistic ambitions or their dreams of love. They often slept out under the stars. Later in life, in letters they exchanged during harder times, they would recall these days of happiness and friendship.

Zola used many of their shared experiences for his monumental twenty-volume work *Les Rougon-Macquart*. The protagonist of the tragic novel *L'Oeuvre* is the painter Claude

just after the large house Château-Noir and benefit from the Jesuit hospitality at their Saint Joseph retreat.

Cézanne developed a passion for roaming the countryside around Aix from his early childhood days. He would climb Sainte-Victoire, swim in the river Arc and wander endlessly through the woods and fields. He was possessed by this love of nature and the outdoor life even before his passion for

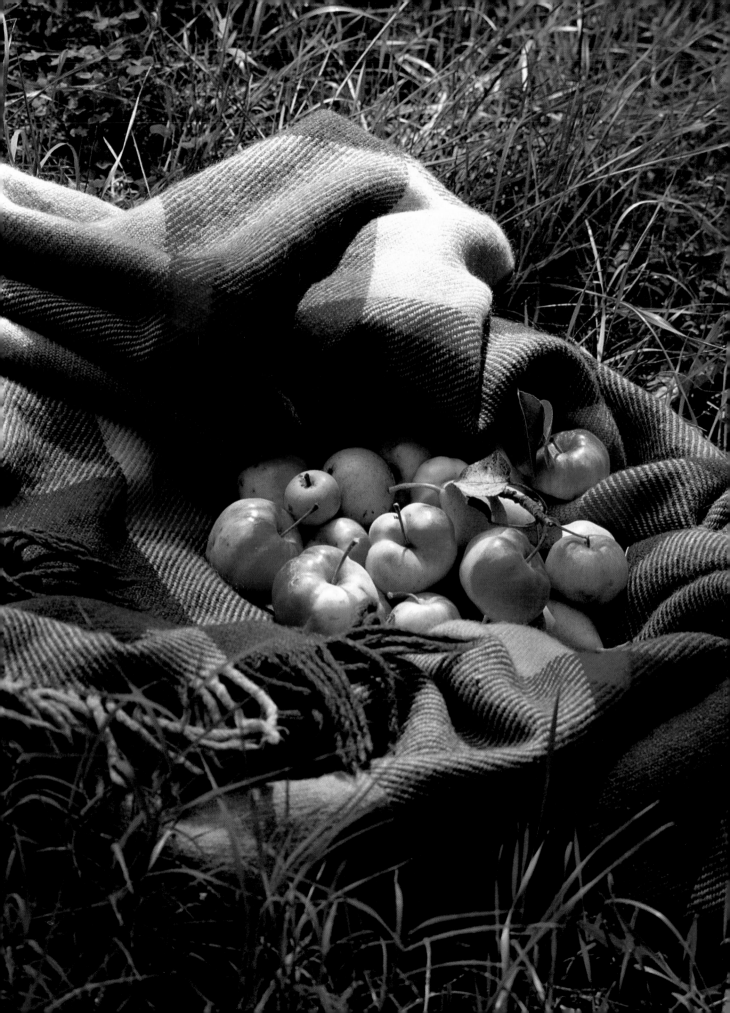

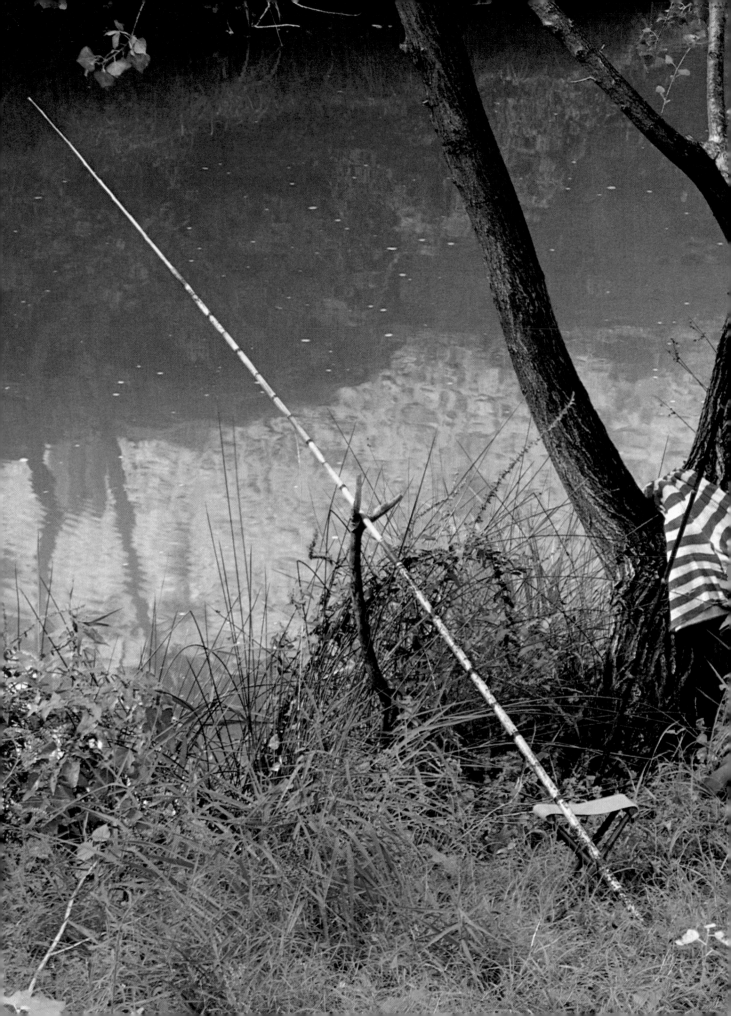

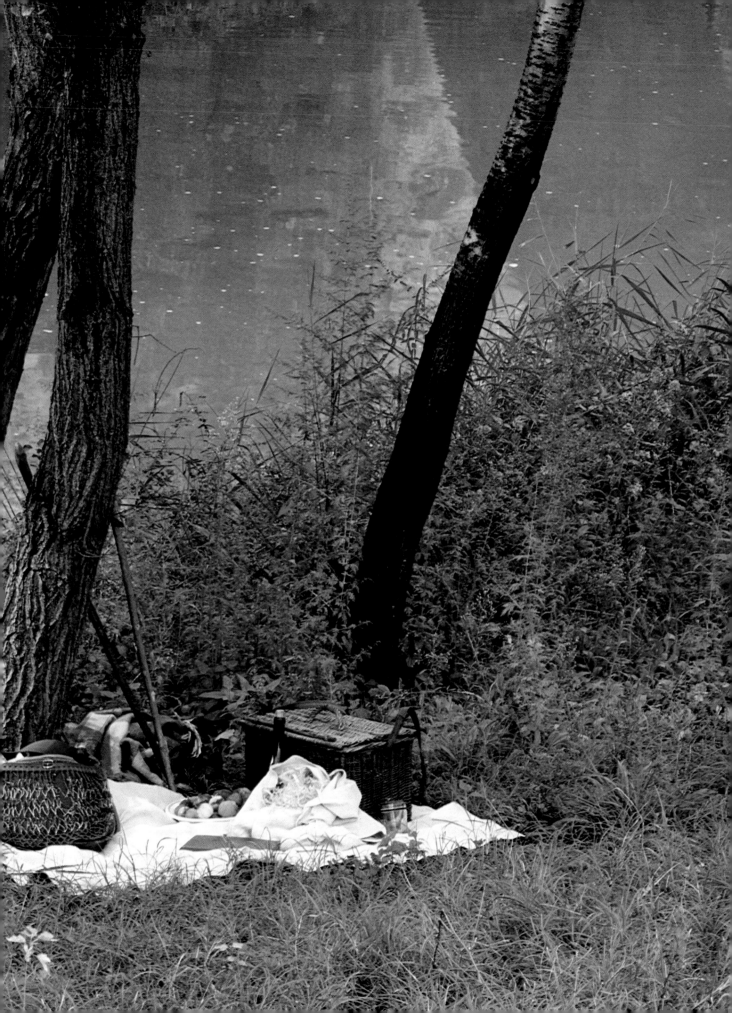

Lantier who, it is said, was partly inspired by Cézanne. He has a fanatical passion for painting but is unable to achieve his artistic goals. In the novel, Aix becomes Plassans, Sandoz is Zola himself and Dubuche is the very portrait of Baille. One day, while in Claude's studio, Sandoz spots a sketch pinned to the wall and is reminded of an excursion they went upon. It was rather a difficult climb during which they stopped to cook some meat cutlets: 'Ah! yes, we each had to cook our own on rosemary branches and I was exasperated with you making fun of me as my branches caught fire and my cutlet burned to a cinder.' Some forty years later Joachim Gasquet accompanied Cézanne on one of his excursions.

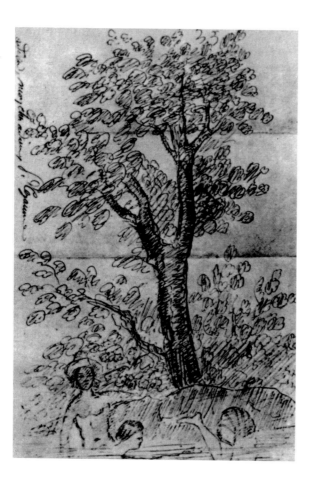

They were above the river Arc, three quarters of an hour away from Aix, on the property of Cézanne's brother-in-law, Maxime Conil. The gamebag hung from a branch. The bottle was chilling in a stream. We sat in front of a small pond in the sunny shade of the pines trees. Our lunch was a frugal one and, like Phedra under the plane trees on the bank of the Ilissus, Cézanne talked while we ate. The landscape undulated in the blue embrace of that hazy afternoon. The white roads, the smiling rooftops, the bunches of trees, the river running between the hills, they all seemed to be participating in our discussion. A dog came by and the old master threw him chunks of bread.'

Cézanne was an outdoor painter, following on from the Barbizon school and allying himself with the Impressionists. He was a great walker and lover of the countryside, who never felt better than when he was in the wilds of nature in his homeland of Provence, to which his painting is inextricably linked. He knew his country, inside out, but he had not spent his life merely observing his surroundings and filling his mind with simple images over the long decades. Cézanne had learned over the years to look beyond the mere appearance of things, to find what lay beyond and beneath the hills and the plains.

Marion was another of his childhood friends who should be mentioned here. As well as being an amateur painter, she was a geologist. They often went to Sainte-Victoire, and it was during the excursions and their long conversations together that she introduced him to geology. We should remember Cézanne's

CHATSWOOD LIBRARY
Tel: 9777 7900
www.willoughby.nsw.gov.au

Customer name:
 Brindle, Lorna Margaret

Items that you have checked out

Title: Cezanne : a taste of Provence
ID: C0603070880
Due: Monday, 30 November 2020
Messages:

Title: The midnigh   se
ID: C0607039616
Due: Monday, 30 November 2020
Messages:

Title: The peacock summer
ID: C0608005880
Due: Monday, 30 November 2020
Messages:

Total items: 3
9/11/2020 11:47 AM
 ecked out: 4

From Mon 2 Nov 2020 regular
    ds will resume. Items borrowed or
        d on or after 2 Nov will be for 21
        ast Reads items return to
        ioans, with no renewal

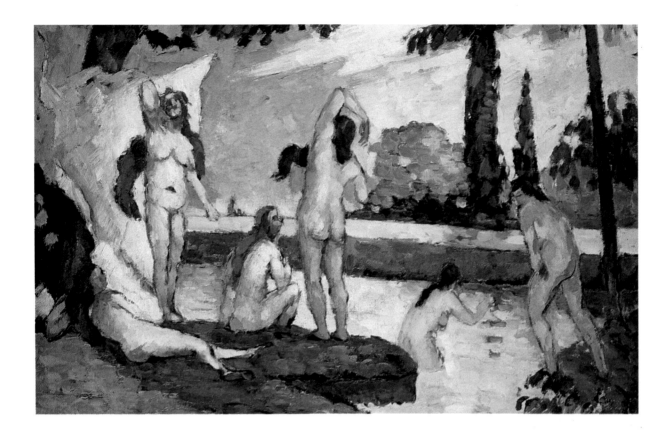

quasi-scientific interest in nature, which clearly separated him from the Impressionists who remained fixed in their simple rejoicing in the beauty of the world. In his preface to an album by Jacqueline and Maurice Guillard, Jean-Louis Ferrier emphasizes, and rightly so, this little known aspect of Cézanne's art. He remarks on the geological variety of the region: '...the bright red formations of Tholonet, dating from the period when the Alps were formed, the thick layers of grey dolomite and the red sedimentary rock of the Infernet gorge, not to mention the Cendre plateau, the Arc river valley and the jurassic rocks of his beloved Sainte-Victoire whose strata form a large fold to the south, an exceptional phenomenon.' Cézanne should not be taken as a documentary painter, nor a scientific popularizer. It is

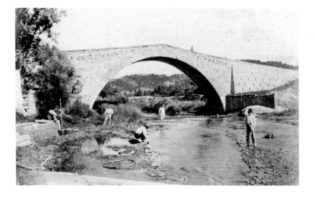

*T*he young Cézanne used to bathe with his friend Zola in the river Arc, just south of Aix. The theme of bathers and bathing runs through the whole of Cézanne's work and features strongly in his larger paintings.

Baigneuses. Metropolitan Museum of Art, New York.

Le pont des Trois Sautets on the river Arc, circa 1875.

Left:
Baigneurs sous l'arbre.
Illustration from a letter to Zola. Bibliothèque Nationale, Paris.

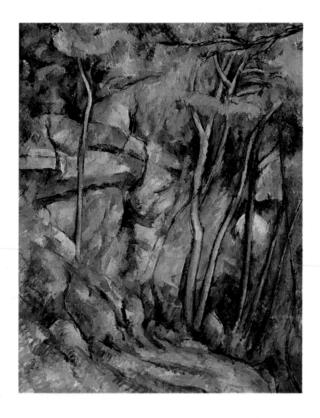

Cézanne liked to walk in the more deserted areas of the countryside, such as the strange grounds of the Château-Noir or the Bibémus quarry. He sought out woods where nature seemed at its most chaotic, dark and hidden from light - and where no-one would come and disturb him.

Dans le parc du Château-Noir.

Musée de l'Orangerie, Paris, collection Jean Walter and Paul Guillaume.

Right:
Aix countryside seen from Bibémus.

work, not only in the petrified vegetation he paints, but even in the almost inorganic appearance of his card players and in the voluptuous, stony bodies of his bathers.

Cézanne painted everything around Aix. He painted the mysterious house at Tholonet, which could easily be thought to be the home of an alchemist, at Bibémus, with its geometrically sculpted yellow stone and at Château-Noir, a property he would have liked to buy, but which the owners refused to sell. He rented a small cottage at Bibémus. It was a wild place, full of scattered rocks and invaded by unruly vegetation, where Cézanne could work undisturbed. Something of a misanthropist, he was content when isolated from his fellow men, but he was not as unsociable as legend would have it. Although Cézanne admitted that he hated to be disturbed while he worked, confiding to Émile Bernard that he disliked being watched, he still often went on his painting expeditions accompanied.

Apart from Marion and Solari, another painter whose company he favoured was the anarchic Joseph Ravalsou. This long-haired, bearded fellow artist was introduced to him by Gasquet. Cézanne paid him the ultimate compliment by telling him he was a true painter, an honour only bestowed upon those of his friends he considered worthy and felt at ease with. He paid the same compliment to Louise Germain in buying one of her canvases then inviting her to accompany him painting, but she protested afterwards that he had ignored her presence, 'It was as if I wasn't there.'

The location was not very sheltered and was poorly suited to watercolour, a technique

important, nevertheless, to consider the educated element of his vision, so centred on the landscape of Provence.

During this age of positivism, with its emphasis on scientific observation of natural phenomena, Cézanne used geology as a privileged means of reading, interpreting and revealing the Provençal countryside as no artist before him had done. This would explain why geology plays such an important role in his

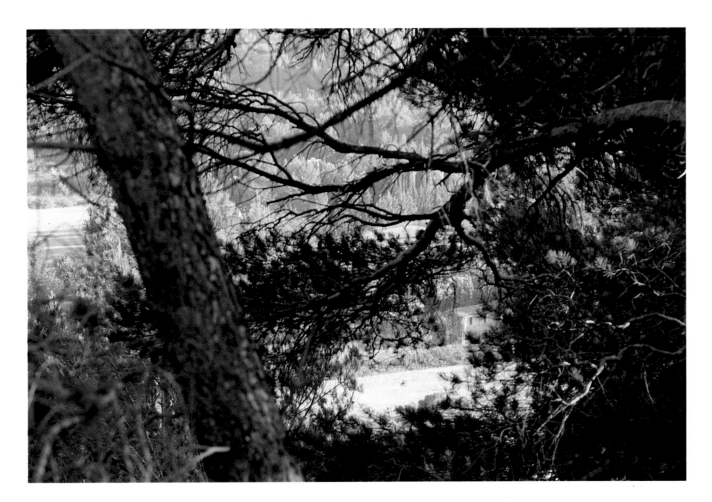

which is particularly difficult in windy weather. 'After the fairly well-kept lawns of Jas de Bouffan, here was a landscape untouched by man with an atmosphere of intimacy, a hidden corner where shrubs spring up from the rock piles wherever they can.' (John Rewald)

The greatest problem for the outdoor painter is the weather. When there was too much rain or wind it became difficult both to make the journey and to paint outside. Then the light had to be just right, neither too bright nor too grey, and the sky just slightly hazy. Cézanne was careful to avoid the hottest and brightest time of day as too much light and heat would flatten the landscape and harden the atmosphere. He would rise early to capture the perfect moment when nature itself awakes. He usually retired early in the evening

but, according to Leo Larguier, 'he was a light sleeper and told me that he got up several times during the night to look at the sky and check whether it was the right time to go out and paint.'

'I began to perceive nature a little late in life,' he confided to Zola in a letter he wrote on 19 December 1878. In this one simple phrase, he expressed what the whole Impressionist experience meant to him. He had begun his painting career studying and taking inspiration from the paintings of others. He copied the style of the great masters, such as Delacroix, Courbet and Manet, trying to recreate dramatic compositions in his own studio or to instil poetry, passion and a sense of the tragedy of life into his own still life paintings. With Pissarro and the other Impressionists he had struck up

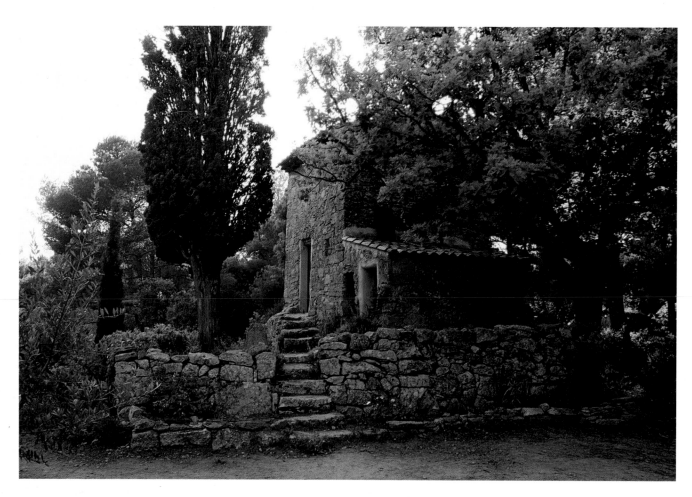

*Cé*zanne rented a shack in Bibémus and kept his painting equipment there to save him from transporting it daily. He also used it as a shelter and a place to heat up the lunches which his housekeeper, Mrs Brémond, prepared for him.

friendships with, such as Renoir and Monet, he had acquired another vision of the countryside and nature. He looked upon nature not just through the eyes of a provincial man attached to his homeland, but as an observer, a voyeur, if this term can be used to describe someone who looks until his eyes are sore. He learned to see things fully and to contemplate without preconceived ideas. He was able to perceive not just the form of objects, but the way the light unites them, the thickness and depth of the space they occupy. In a letter to Victor Choquet, he says, 'There is always the sky. I am most attracted by things which have not been limited by nature and I find the greatest pleasure in contemplating them'. As serious and as austere as he appeared, we should not forget that the the pleasure of contemplating nature and living

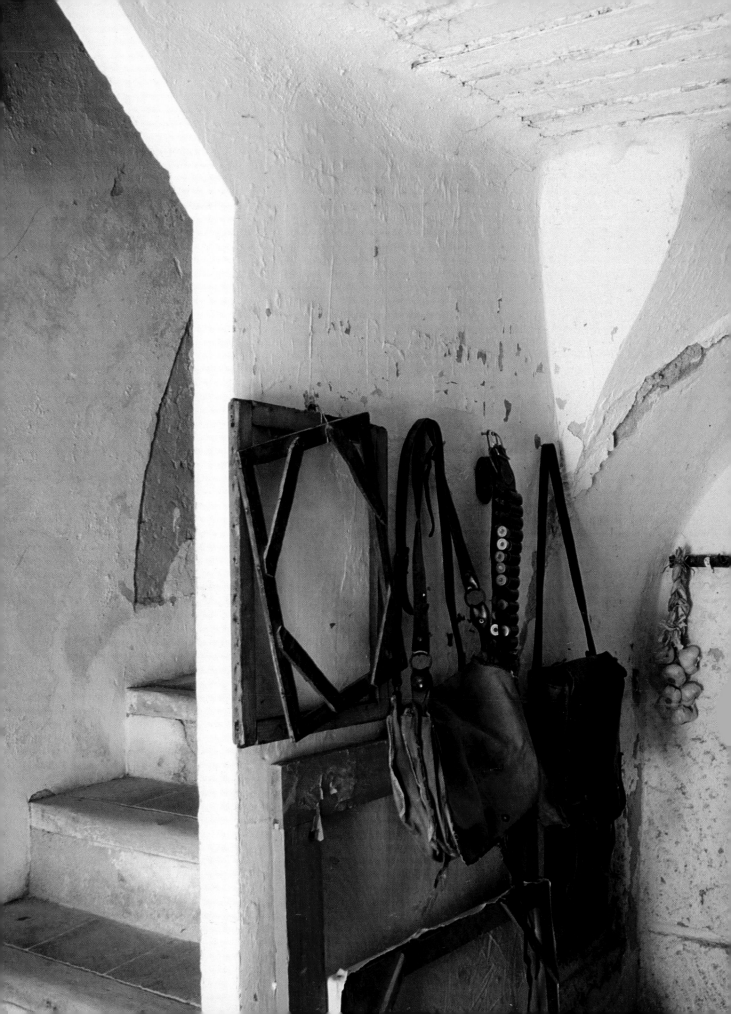

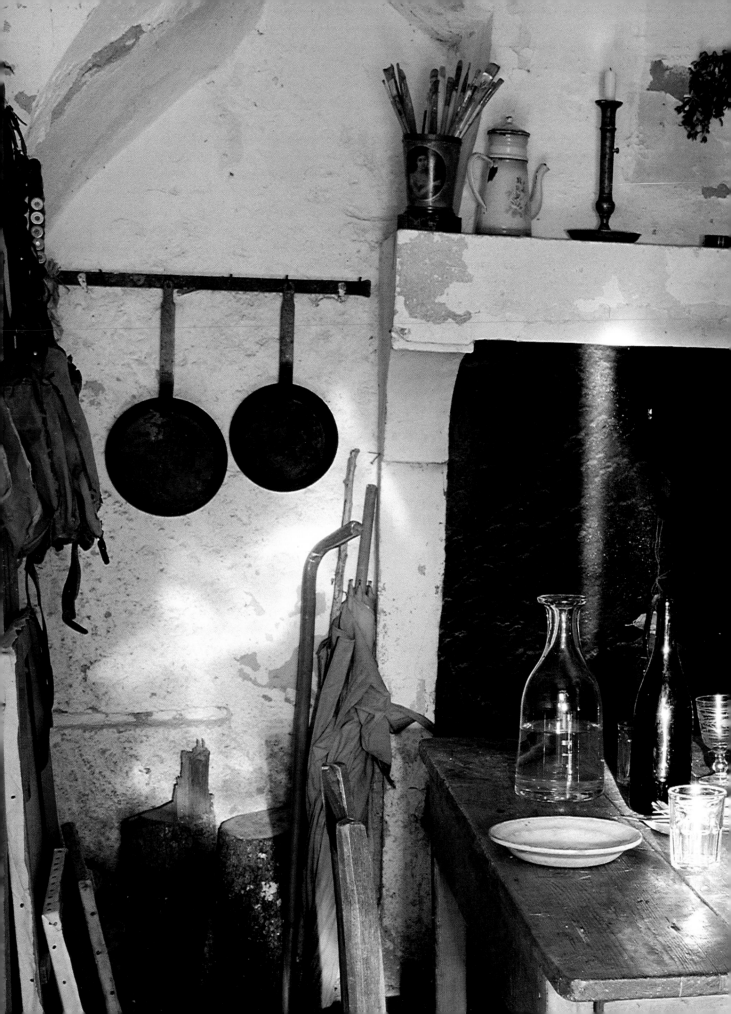

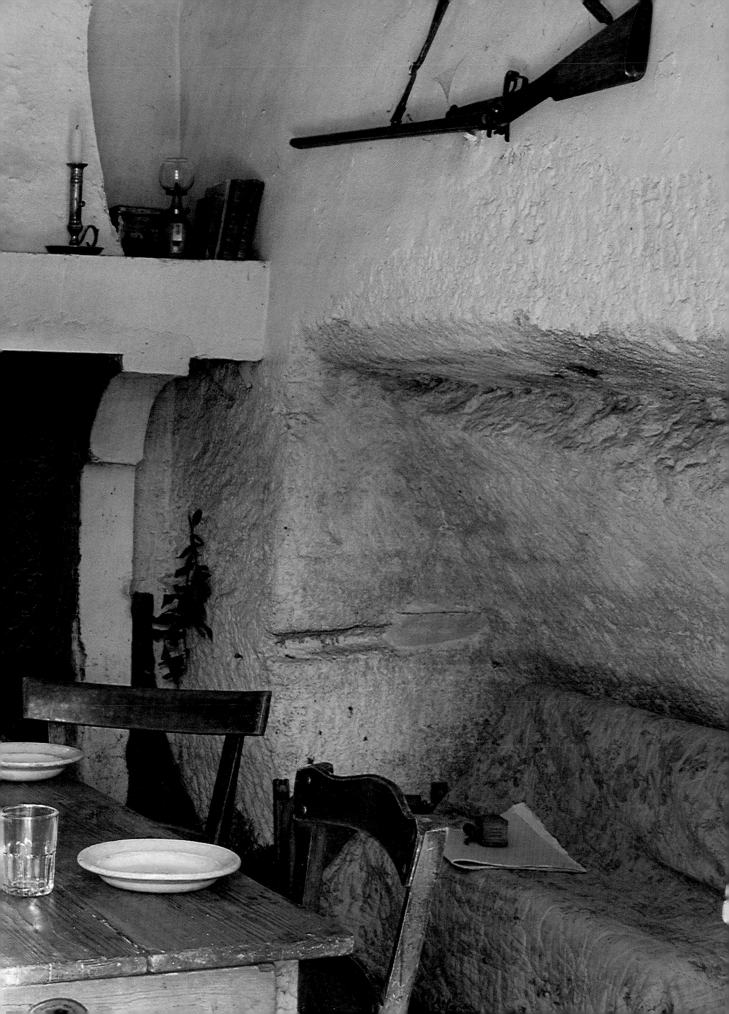

in its heart in his beloved homeland, is the essence of Cézanne's work.

In 1895 the critic Félicien Fagus submitted an intuitive article to *La Revue Blanche*: 'Before nature, he is like a child. You can feel that he is conscious of nothing else and wants to know of nothing else, except the work in hand. He

*C*ézanne was very attached to everything to do with Provence - its countryside, its customs, its buildings and its local produce.

Right:

Brousse au miel et aux amandes, see recipe page 174.

Following pages:

Lapin en paquets, see recipe page 159.

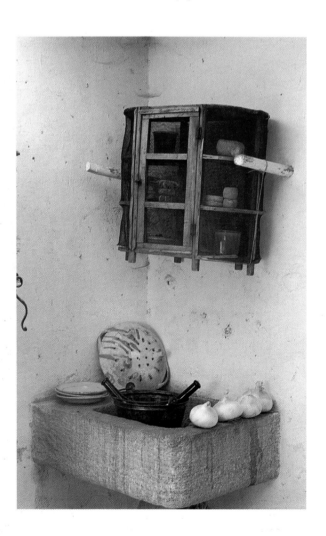

sees and transposes what he perceives with the overexcited sensitivity of his eyes, and the resources he holds in his hands. Thus his work takes on the rough charm of something impulsive and childlike. That naiveté, that innocence, is the supreme effect of the perpetual devotion of science to nature.'

This is a remarkable insight for someone who knew only the paintings, not the painter. Joseph Ravelsou recognized that nature was the key to Cézanne. 'His art gave him great sensual pleasure. He loved nature with a passion, perhaps exclusively, and painted in order to prolong the pleasure.' Cézanne was a man physically attached to his country which he had tirelessly explored. He knew every hidden corner and followed the same paths he had taken as a child, but now as a painter with his easel and canvas under his arm. He rediscovered the places he loved to frequent with his friends, where they had talked, laughed and dreamed together. Stopping at each spot which held a happy memory, he sat down to paint. The link between his life and his land is unbreakable.

He did of course paint in other places, such as the Ile de France, Auvers and Fontainebleau, during his long and numerous visits to the Paris regions. He also painted a little in other towns such as Annecy and Talloires, but nothing could compare with Provence. In 1884, he wrote to Zola that his head was 'filled with that land', and in 1890 in a letter to Solari from Talloires he says, 'when you are born there, you're done for. Nothing else is as appealing'. So finally he painted nothing else but Provence. Although the landscape had already been portrayed by many artists, such as

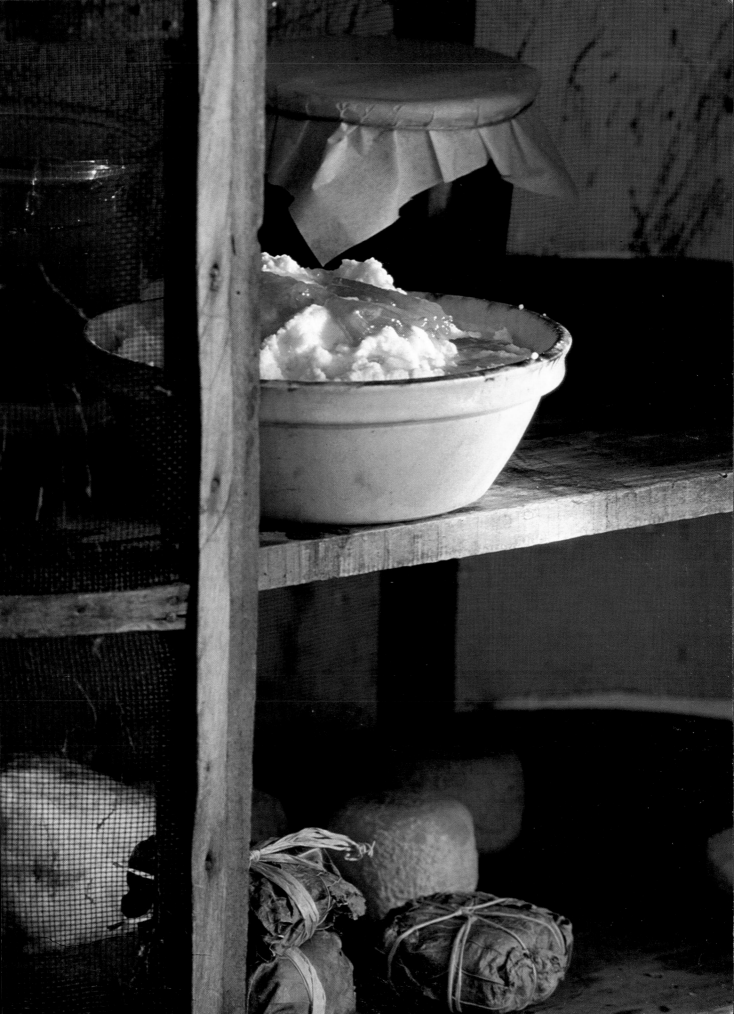

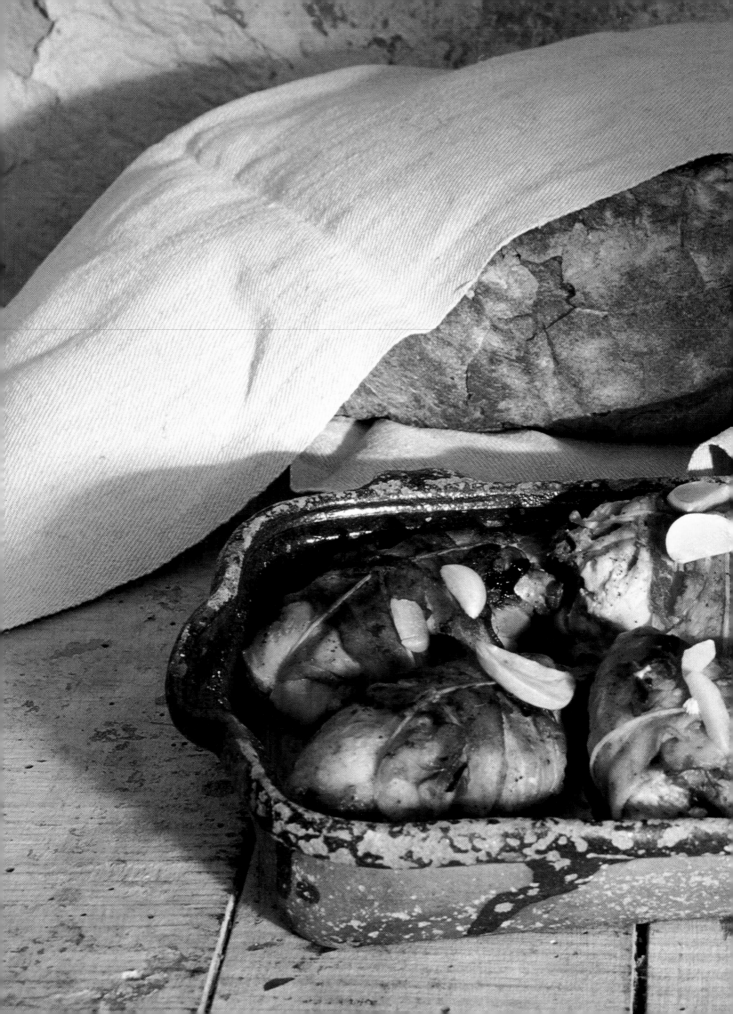

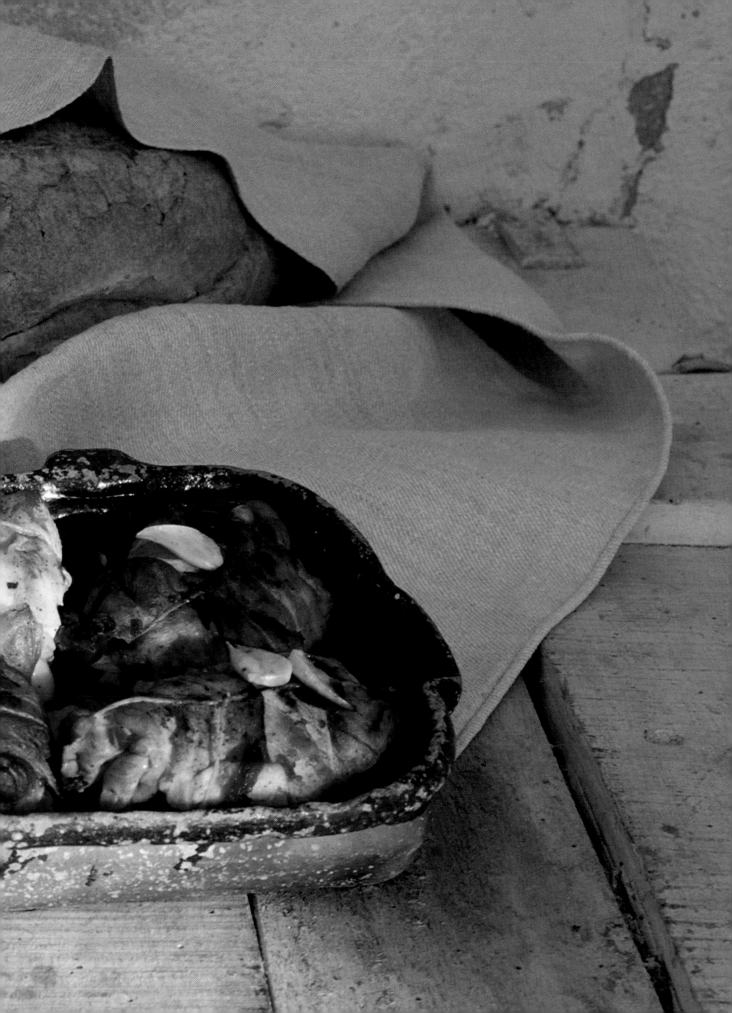

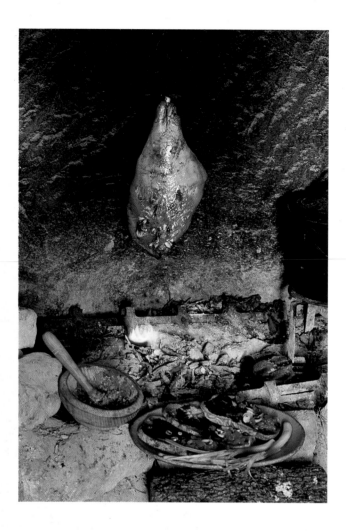

The novelist Paul Alexis recounts a hunting party where more time was spent eating than hunting. Cézanne seasoned the salad while Zola watched over the leg of lamb, which was held over the fire by a string.

Tartines et anchoïade, see recipes pages 141 and 182.

furiously he must work, which he did for the remaining twenty years of his life.

Cézanne, although a Provençal painter, is not a painter of all Provence. He did not thirst to discover all its different areas and aspects, and was not attracted by the towns. He never painted Marseilles, even though it was very close to Aix. He only went there to visit his friend and fellow painter Monticelli whom he greatly respected because he had resisted the seductions and artistic fashions of Paris and painted with his heart and spirit. He ventured no further in his art than Estaque. His mother rented a house in the church square of this little seaside village with its humble port. Cézanne painted the pines and the appearance of the first factory chimneys. From early on, he used this place as a refuge when he needed to get away from his family and his suffocating father. He also used it at one time to house his mistress Hortense and their secret child, Paul. Here Cézanne painted the sea and some landscapes of the surrounding country, pathways and pine trees. He could work in peace and without feeling the weight of Louis-Auguste's presence. When neither his mother nor Hortense were there to look after him, the wife of a local fisherman cooked his meals. And when war broke out in 1870, it was here that he took refuge to escape conscription. Ten years later he was still painting there, putting Impressionism to the test with this landscape whose stark contrasts and sharp outlines reminded him of playing cards. But he began to tire of Estaque and eventually turned his back on the sea and returned to his favoured landscape of Aix.

Grenet, a talented painter from Aix who had often painted Sainte-Victoire, 'there is still no painter who measures up to a true interpretation of the riches of this region'. This was said in a letter to Victor Choquet, when Cézanne was forty-seven years old and had only just begun to feel and to understand what he was capable of, what he must achieve and how

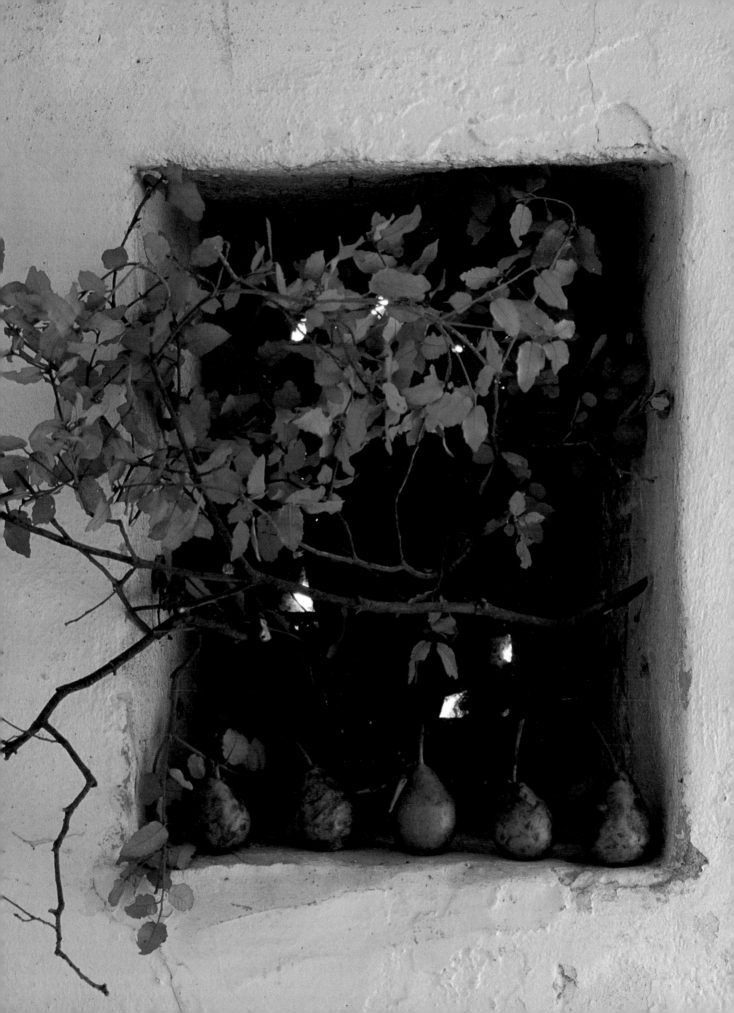

He also lived for a while in the village of Gardanne, just south of Aix, where Hortense had settled with little Paul in the months before their marriage. He moved in with them and they spent these months living together, openly this time. He bought a donkey to carry his materials when he went painting, and the children of the village and his son's little friends took turns in having rides. 'Cézanne sometimes spent several days at a time away on his escapades. He stopped to eat at farmhouses in the company of the local peasants, spending the night where there was a bed and when there was no bed, he quite happily slept under a blanket on top of a haystack.' (Henri Perruchot).

It was while he was at Gardanne that Zola sent him a copy of *L'Oeuvre*. In this novel their youth is evoked and Cézanne appears in the guise of Lantier, a failed painter who is victim of the large inheritance from the Rougeon-Macquart and who becomes suicidal. It is, of course, a work of fiction and Zola, even though he blatantly draws it from his own experience, basing his characters on real people and anecdotes gleaned from real events, nevertheless exercises his freedom as a novelist; and the story he tells is only part of the whole saga of the Rougeon-Macquart family. Cézanne could not help but recognize himself in the portrayal of Claude Lantier, and there are also obvious allusions to Manet and Monet. He felt that many of the memories of their youth spent together in Aix were now tainted, and that their friendship had been badly affected and was beyond repair. For example, the vermicelli which is Lantier's staple food, 'a mixture which he soaked in oil and ate with bread', was exactly what Cézanne ate during the poverty-stricken days in Paris. And the fried gudgeon served with boiled eggs and 'boiled meat left over from yesterday served in a salad with boiled potatoes and pickled herrings' followed by 'a cheese fresh from the

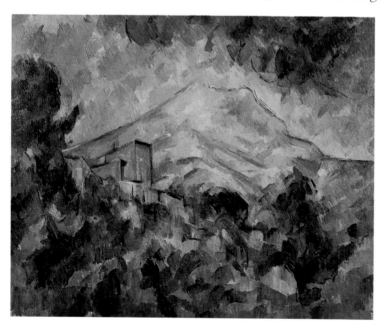

Château-Noir was an attractive property where a strange two-wing house had been built, with Sainte-Victoire visible from the terrace. It was said that an alchemist had moved in and when Cézanne tried to buy it he was told that it was not for sale.

La Montagne Sainte-Victoire et le Château-Noir.
Bridgestone Museum of Art, Tokyo.

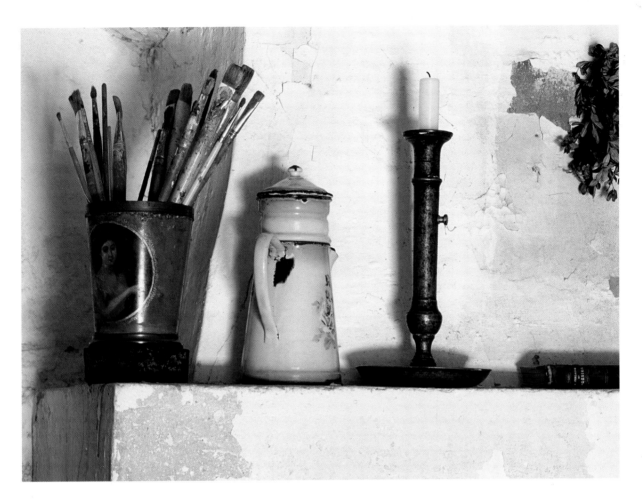

neighbouring dairy farm' and strawberries 'freshly picked' - this was exactly the meal Cézanne had enjoyed with Hortense at Bennecourt when they first became romantically involved. Fifteen years had passed, but Cézanne had not really changed. He was still faithful to Provence, still poor, living from hand to mouth with Hortense, thinking only of that 'accursed painting'. Zola had by now become a famous writer, a bourgeois Parisian, and an impressive and generous host. It is true that Zola entertained lavishly and Cézanne was an honoured guest at his table on more than one occasion, served with such dishes as were described in *L'Oeuvre*: Bouillabaisse, jugged hare, roast poultry, grilled mullet, fillet with cêpes, truffle salad, Chambertin and Moselle wine. But the price of

these meals was too high - too many affectations and empty words - and Cézanne already felt a growing distance between himself and Zola. They no longer belonged to the same world. While Zola was becoming a great and powerful name in Parisian society, Cézanne was still striving for greatness, just like Frenhofer in Balzac's *Le Chef d'Oeuvre Inconnu* (The Unknown Masterpiece).

He did not stay long in Gardanne. After marrying, he had gone back to Jas ahead of Hortense, who stayed a while longer in Gardanne before finally going back to Paris. He had at last settled the family matters which had been weighing on him for so long, he had broken his friendship with Zola in a very cold letter, and now he withdrew to Aix, though in spirit he had never left. He was in his element

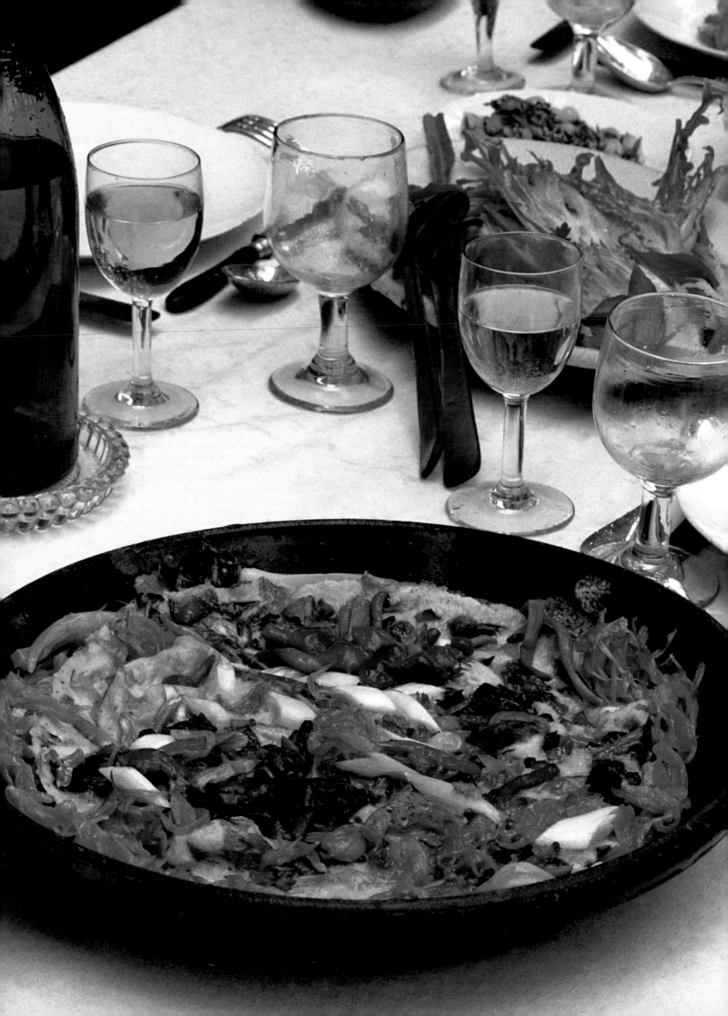

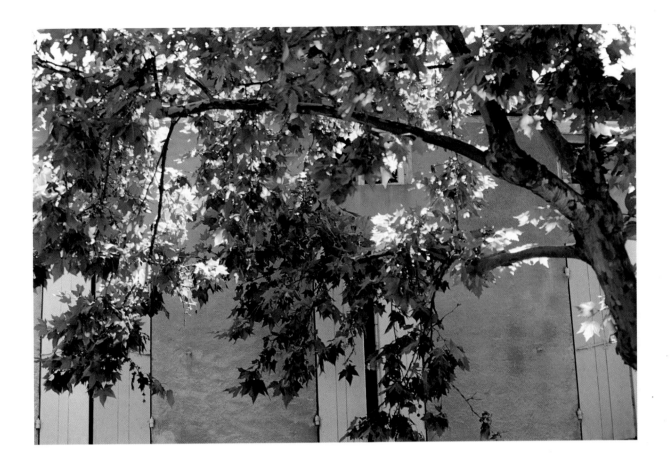

in Aix and he did not need to venture very far to see the world. There was no point travelling across France or indeed the ocean to go in search of new images. Cézanne was not an exotic painter. He was too attached to his Provence because, as he said, 'there are things in nature we haven't yet seen'.

Today, we can trace Cézanne's steps around Aix. Marianne Bourges, curator of his studio at Lauves, has drawn up an exact list of Cézanne's cherished painting haunts and the paths he took in and around Aix to reach them. In the north, towards Lauves, Puyricard, les Pinchinats, the cottage at Jourdan, the Chemin Noir (the black path) and the Etremot plateau. To the west, beyond Jas, towards Roquefavour and Valcros, the pigeon loft at

*A*t Tholonet, a small village east of Aix on the way to Sainte-Victoire, there was a small inn where Cézanne liked to stop on Sundays to sample Rosa Berne's country cooking.

Left:
Omelette aux champignons,
see recipe page 132.

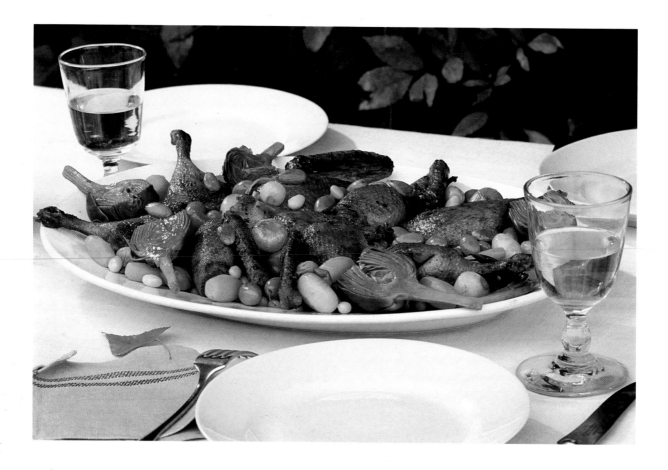

*R*osa Berne's speciality was duck with olives, excellent when accompanied by the local white wine.

Canard aux olives et aux carottes,
see recipe page 153.

Bellevue, Bel-Air and Montbriand (his brother in law's estate). In the south, towards the river Arc, the lock at la Priée, and the Trois Sautets bridge. In the east, towards Tholonet, Château-Noir, the Repentance path, Bibémus, Vauvenargues and Sainte-Victoire.

Cézanne should always be imagined walking through the countryside around Aix, happy in his solitude from dawn to dusk in the thick of nature, painting as no-one before him had done. He was also happy to be accompanied from time to time by some friend or other who would paint with him - Marion, Ravelsou, Solari, Émile Bernard. He particularly enjoyed their company over lunch and they often stopped at the Tholonet inn (which was in fact just a grocer shop) where

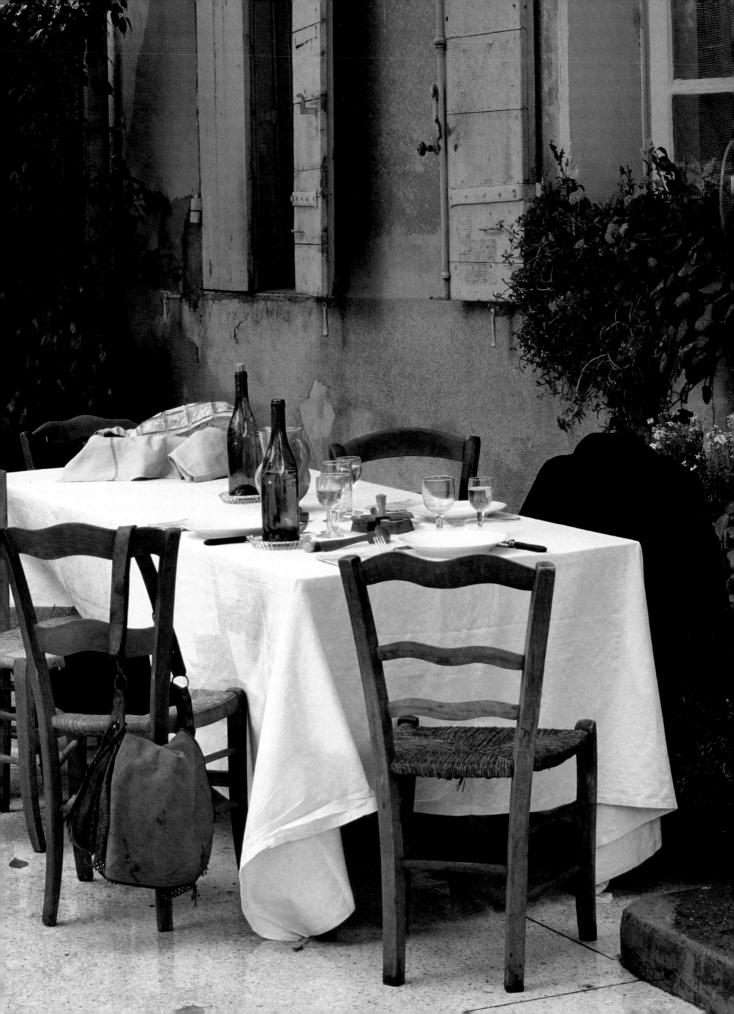

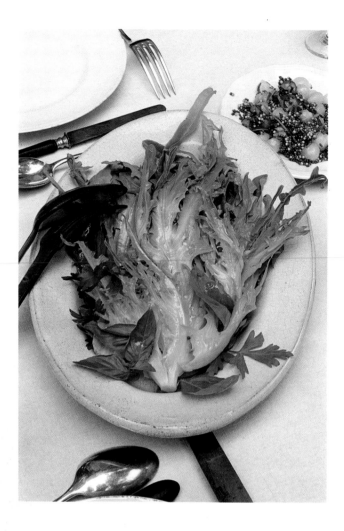

*T*here is another side to Cézanne than the one too readily evoked; he could be a convivial, jovial, witty and humorous man...' Jean Arrouye.

Right:
Gaieto de foie de porc,
see recipe page 137.

the talented cook Rosa Berne would prepare a traditionally rustic meal. She regaled them with truffle or mushroom omelettes, duck in olives, served with white wine produced from the neighbouring vineyards. Being a frequent visitor here, Cézanne soon struck up a friendship with the mayor of Tholonet, Houchart. Jean Arrouye noticed that here

Cézanne seemed to be like a different man, not the austere and withdrawn painter he was reputed to be. 'There is another image of Cézanne which differs from the clichéd portrait: sociable ('Come and visit whenever you please' he wrote to Camoin), hospitable (in 1902 he invited Aurenche to stay with him), conversational ('it does me good to banter, it makes me so happy'), jovial (would such fundamentally literary youths crowd around a grumpy old man?), spirited and with a sense of humour (proven by his quick repartee and his clever correspondence)...'

The Tholonet road led all the way to Sainte-Victoire, but Cézanne rarely went as far as the mountain. His excursions were limited now because of his age, besides which he preferred to look upon rather than climb his mountain. But he was incessantly drawn to it. He would stop at Château-Noir where he painted the strange-looking building and some of the surrounding houses and most importantly the vegetation as described by Jacqueline de Romily: 'Pine trees, nothing but pine trees, growing from rather a steep hillside, leaning over the slopes and tilting in the wind. Sometimes they all slant the same way, forming long concentric lines. Their dry, bright trunks shimmer in the light, while the tree tops are almost golden as if they had passed through the sun.' He stopped at Bibémus, where the chaotic arrangement of the rocks and the trees gave the overriding impression of untamed nature, and recreated the peace and serenity in a sublime painting.

He distanced himself from romantic literature, from theory and even from the more

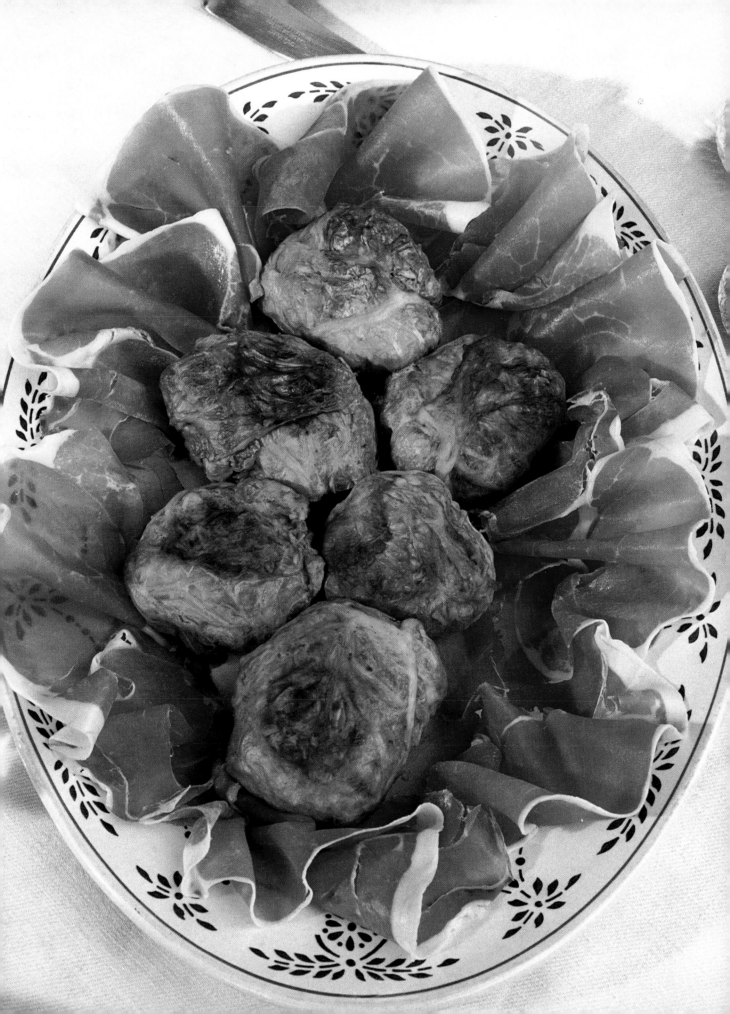

superficial Impressionist game. His painting was uncompromising and expressed that 'sensation' by which he was controlled and which was no more than an intense feeling of happiness and of belonging to the world.

Leo Larguier was one day practising manoeuvres with his soldiers on the road to Sainte-Victoire. When he saw Cézanne's carriage approaching, on his way to a painting session, he was possessed by a strong impulse and gave the order to 'present arms!' as he passed. The old painter, who had received few such honours in his life, was both confused and moved.

Sainte-Victoire is rather like a Provençal Mecca. Though not a very high mountain (600m), it nevertheless dominates the landscape and is considered sacred by the local people, largely because of its history, the legends which surround it and the important role it has played in their lives for centuries. Where does the name originate from? Was it named to mark the victory of Marius over the Teutons and Ambrons in 102 BC? This is possible, though it was rather a late christening as Sainte-Victoire was not named officially until the seventeenth century. It could have been named after a certain Sainte Aventure, a pretty name but one which has never been attested. Or perhaps it could be traced back to Saint Venturie whose name somehow derived from a Celtic divinity? History is unclear on this point, which leaves more room for imaginative speculation. The important thing is that this chalky, triangular, asymetrical mass has remained untamed and unchanged. It still guards the memory of the heritage of Saint Ser, protector of Aix, and the ancient monastery still stands on the summit.

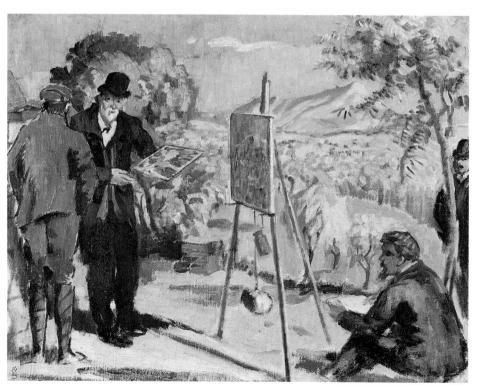

The painter Maurice Denis was a great admirer of Cézanne and visited him in Aix. He went out into the countryside with him and religiously noted down what he said, but unfortunately ended up by boring Cézanne with his over-theorizing.

Maurice Denis,
Visite à Cézanne, à Aix.
Private collection.

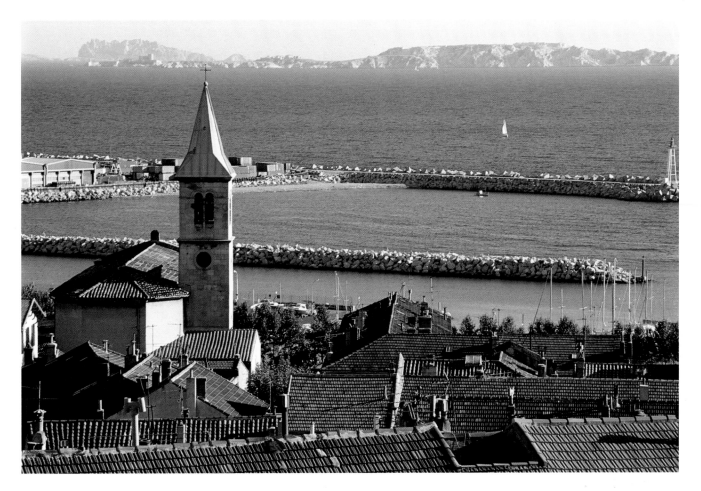

The high cross erected in 1875 still remains, as does the scar of the Garagaï crevice. And it is still the traditional place where the young people of Aix gather to celebrate the feast of St Jean and the summer solstice.

Cézanne was fascinated by this mountain from a very early age. In a painting he made in 1867, called *L'Enlèvement* (The abduction), there is a mountain which resembles it though we cannot be sure. This uncertainty was intentional on Cézanne's part. Soon afterwards he painted *L'Eternel féminin* (The Eternal woman), a strange scene, both ironic and naive. Although the painter appears to be using the woman as a model there is no doubt that the mountain is his main subject. Then in *La tranchée* (The trench) one of his first, and still rather clumsy, Aix landscapes, it is surely

Cézanne often went to Estaque, a small fishing village near Marseilles. His mother rented a house where he stayed for long periods over a number of years. It was the only place where he painted the Mediterranean.

Following pages:
Sainte-Victoire seen from Bibémus.

Sainte-Victoire which stands beyond the newly inaugurated railway. Raymond Jean explains it very well: 'Aix is Sainte-Victoire. Not exclusively of course, but she is the motif par excellence. And each time Cézanne returns to his home town it is upon her that he casts his eye. This mountain in a country full of hills and plains is the protector, guardian and fortress, the horizon, the light and above all the focus of every eye.'

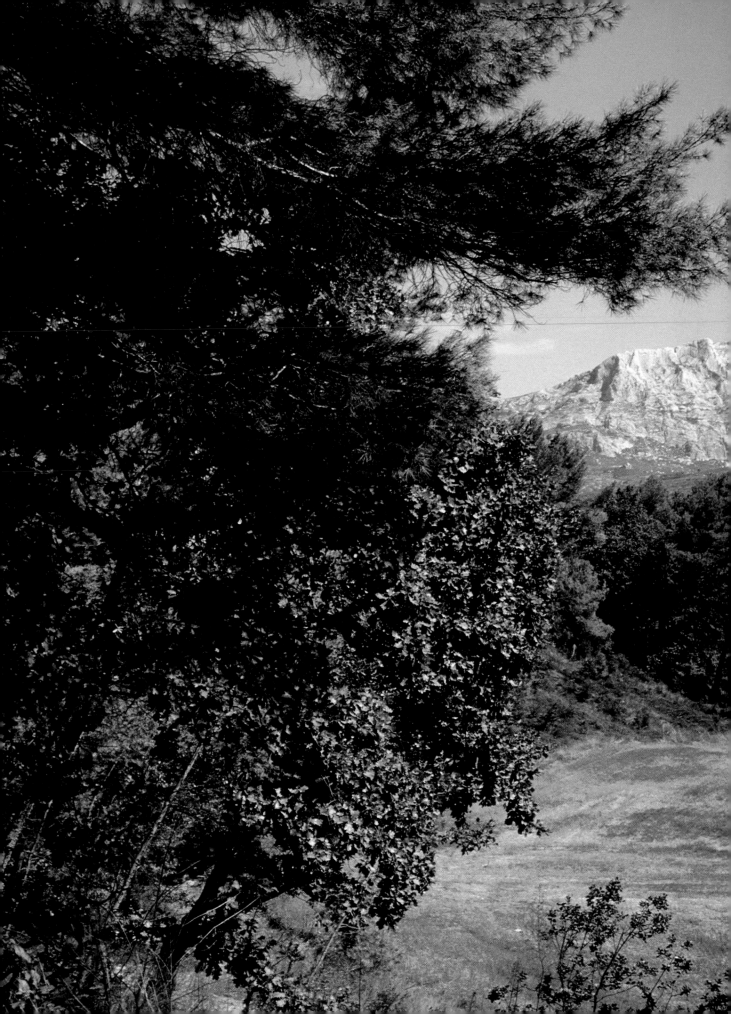

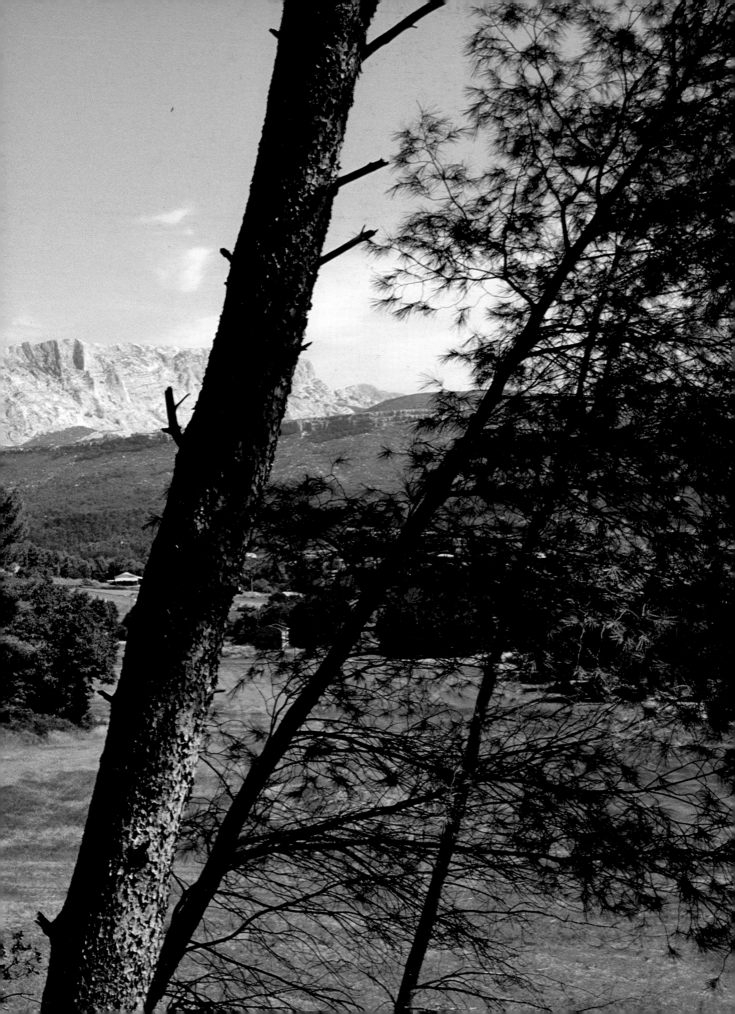

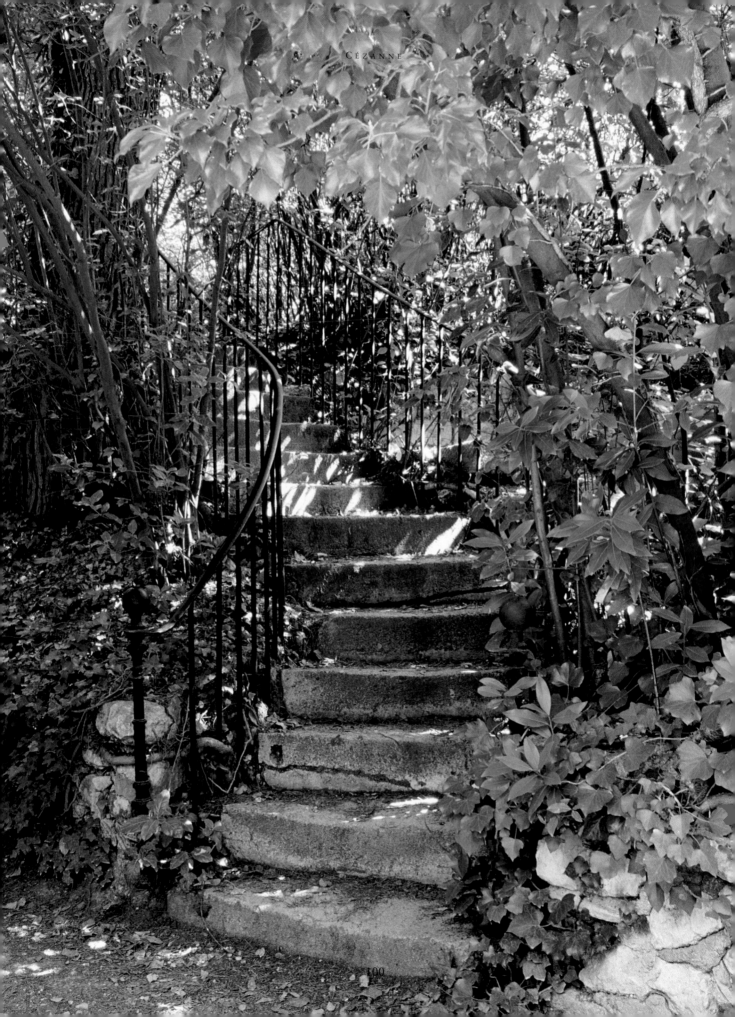

Lauves

' The house is of an orange-hued ochre,
simple and very classical in shape ...
the style is very pure.'

Émile Bernard

The road to Lauves led to the hamlet of
Puy-Ricard. In 1901, Cézanne bought a
piece of land there for five thousand francs. He
pulled down the building which already stood
there to make room for a new studio, where he
could work in closer communion with nature
and with a better light than in Aix. He could
once again be as close to nature as he had been
at Jas, watching the trees and their leaves
change in the light. When he painted outdoors
in the midst of his subject matter he found
what he had been looking for. Jean Arrouye
says of this house at Lauves: 'It leant into the
hillside which protected it from the mistral, it
was a "cagnard" as they say in Provence - a sort
of lean-to - and the whole of Aix was visible
from it at that time: the pink-tiled roofs, the
octagonal spire of Saint Saveur cathedral, the
bent arrow of Saint Jean de Malte which
marked the spot where Cézanne had first learnt
to draw.' The whole region was visible, and if
Cézanne walked a little way up the path he
could see Sainte-Victoire which was one of his

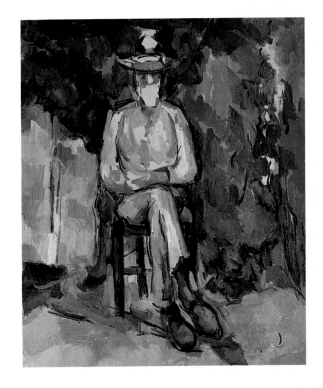

*C*ézanne entered a new
phase of his life with the
Lauves studio, sharing his
time between the two
houses. He would spend the
day in Lauves and the night
in Aix.

Le jardinier.

Bührle Foundation, Zurich.

101

favourite subjects. From Lauves he could see everything which he loved, everything which had an influence on his work. Only Estaque was missing, beyond the horizon. From the studio in Lauves, Cézanne could go in search of any of his favourite motifs: the undergrowth of Bibémus, the Château-Noir woods, or the open countryside from which Sainte-Victoire rose majestically. He kept the house on rue Boulegon and perhaps the only drawback now was the distance between Lauves and Aix.

The architect who dealt with the construction was a man called Mourges, and the brief he was given was quite vague. What was needed was a studio, not a house, and Cézanne specified that he wanted a large room measuring five metres by eight, with plenty of light, something simple and efficient. But the architect had his own ideas, and wanted to show off his talent and taste. Since Cézanne left him to his own devices, rarely visiting the site, the result was, according to Gustave Coquiot, 'a strange villa with a wooden balcony and uneven roof, lots of tiles and varnished wood'. Cézanne was furious when the architect, proud of his design, showed him the end result. He had a fit of rage as only he knew how to, and had all the unnecessary items and adornments destroyed so that the house resembled 'a true Provençal one, surrounded by olive and fig trees'. The façade was ochre, the roof tiles red. It was a traditional local house, true to itself with no superfluous details. On the ground floor a few rooms were used to store things. On the first floor was the studio, fifty square metres and four metres high, with three large windows, including a bay. Sainte-Victoire

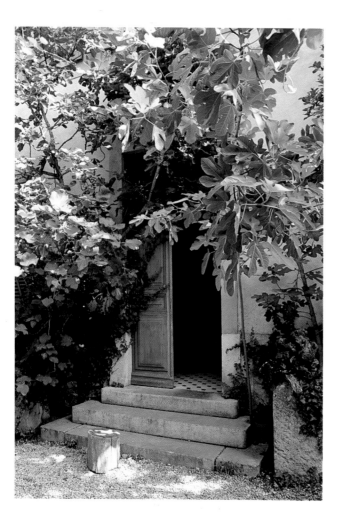

Lauves was Cézanne's workplace in the final years, a place he had designed specifically to meet his needs. The whole of the first floor was taken up by his studio. The studio at Lauves was in the thick of nature. Cézanne only had to step out of his front door to be right in the middle of the countryside. His style became lighter, fresher and younger than ever.

Right:
Les pétunias.
Bührle Foundation, Zurich.

Following pages:
In the garden at the Lauves studio.

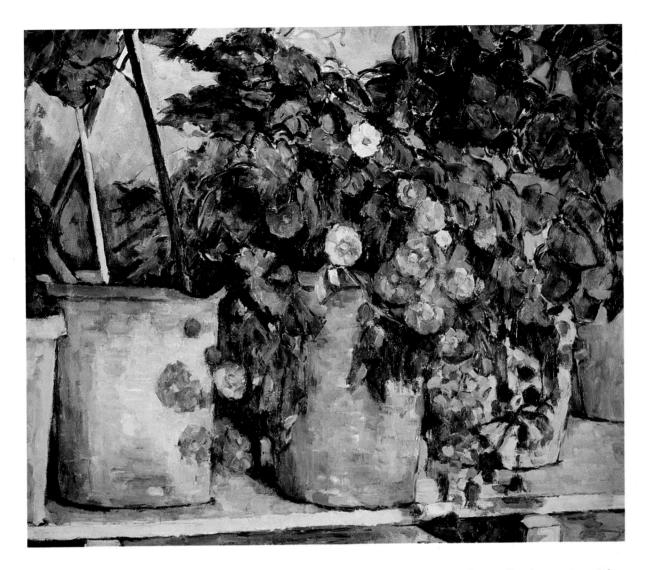

could be seen clearly through them at a glance.

Cézanne moved in, furnishing it simply with just a bed and a table. And of course he had all his painting materials, including a large easel for his huge canvases, in preparation for the enormous paintings which had become quite an obsession. He painted *Les baigneuses* (The bathers) there, celebrating nature and the human form. He also had a small table for his still life paintings, more canvases, paints and paintbrushes, boxes full of lithographs and photographs, some of which he put on the walls, by artists like Rubens, Delacroix, Signorelli, Forain. There were unfinished paintings scattered about, to be completed one day. Nothing was superfluous. The only complaint he had was about the green light which reflected from the trees. Soon he had recreated the disorder that reigned in his studios elsewhere.

He only had to step out of his house to contemplate the fabulous view the land commanded. The hills and plains of Provence lay before him in all their splendour, a constant inspiration for his work. John

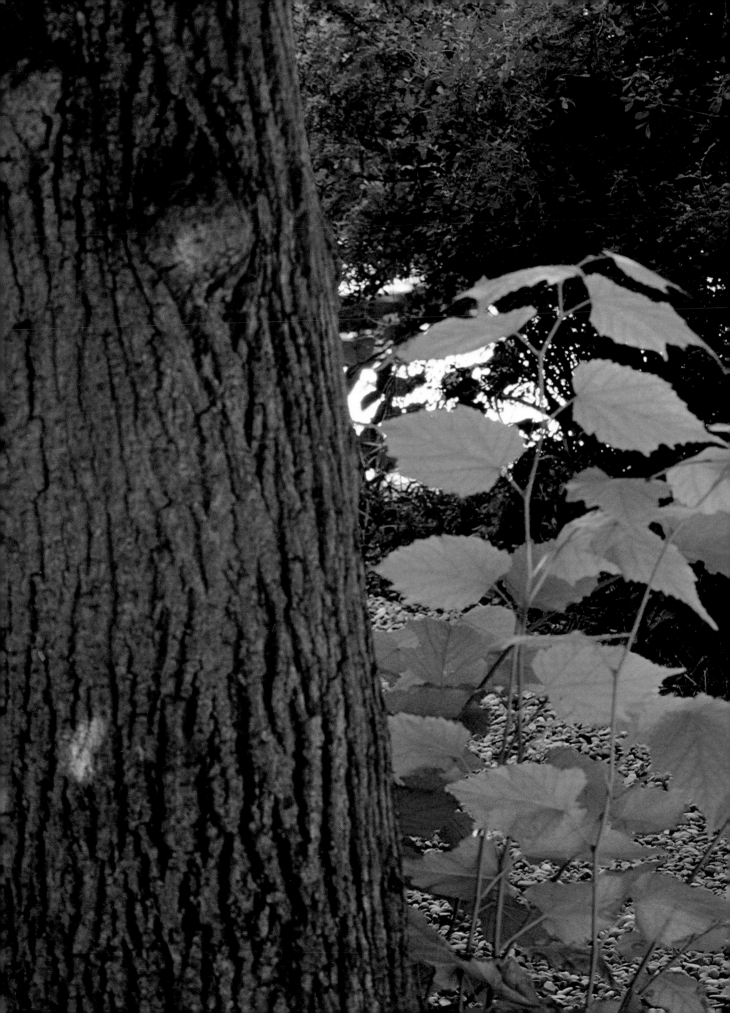

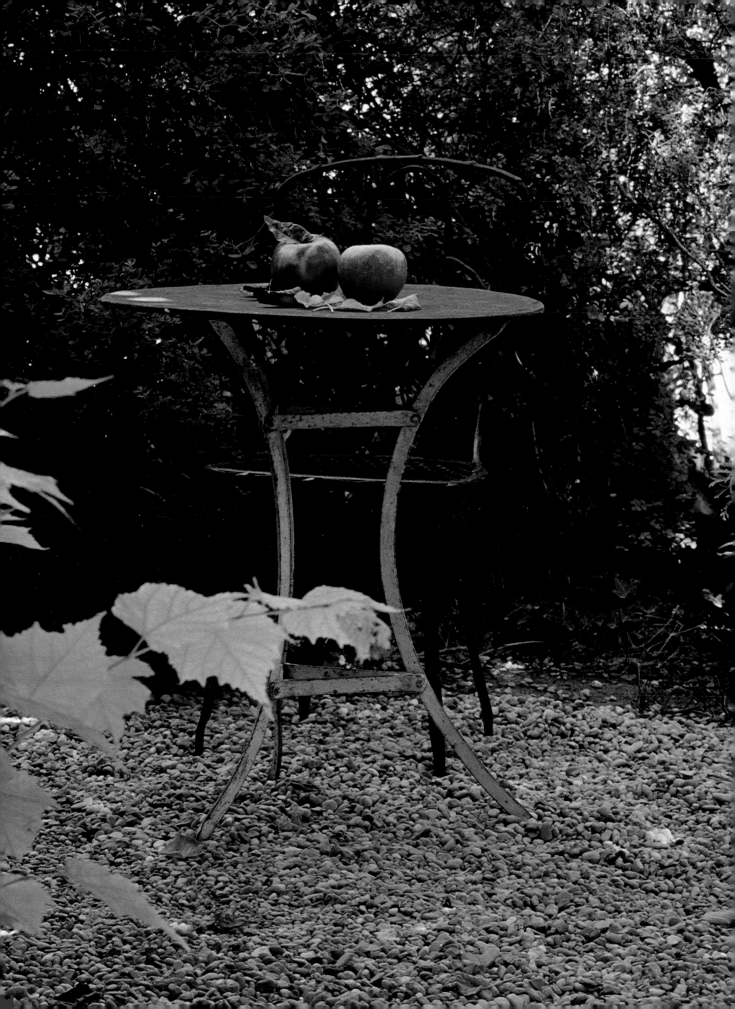

Rewald started a campaign in 1954 to buy the studio (in which the writer Marcel Proust lived after Cézanne) in order to give it to the town of Aix. As a passionate biographer of Cézanne, he had plenty of opportunities to contemplate this view during his many trips to Lauves. This is how he describes it: 'In the midst of this splendid panorama, Sainte-Victoire seems to float in the Provençal light, suspended like a glorious symbol. The near-obsessive fascination which Cézanne had about the mountain seemed to draw him endlessly to this place where he painted most of his last landscapes. There he rendered a final homage to the mountain, painting it on its own against a deep blue sky, majestic in its solitude, not disappearing into the horizon but standing out, superb.'

Cézanne entered a new phase of life in the Lauves studio, sharing his time between his two houses. He had one house for the day and one for the night. Mme Brémond took care of everything in the house in Aix where he slept, with his ever-attentive sister Marie also keeping an eye on the smooth running of the household. Rue Boulegon was his base camp, in mountaineering terms. Cézanne, like a true mountaineer, always strove to climb further and higher, urged on by his sense of adventure and his calling. His art was his life, and he was fulfilled by this great dream which increased in importance for him. Sometimes he would go back to Aix for lunch, especially if he had decided to paint something away from Lauves that afternoon, or Mme Brémond would take his lunch to him in a basket, serving it to him on the ground floor of the house, where he never tired of contemplating the light in the trees outside.

One day Emile Bernard went up there with him. They passed through the wooden gate and Cézanne lifted a large stone to retrieve the key. They went in, contemplating the far end

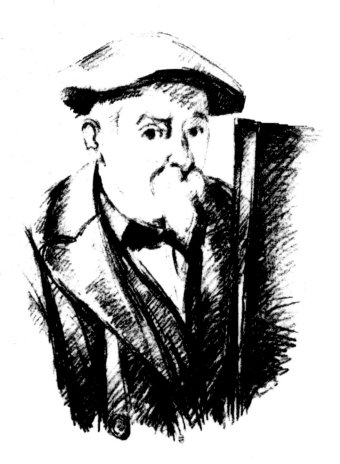

Cézanne worked without respite, never going on holiday and sleeping only when exhaustion overwhelmed him. He looked older than his age, partly due to his diabetes.

Autoportrait au chevalet.
Bibliothèque Nationale, Paris.

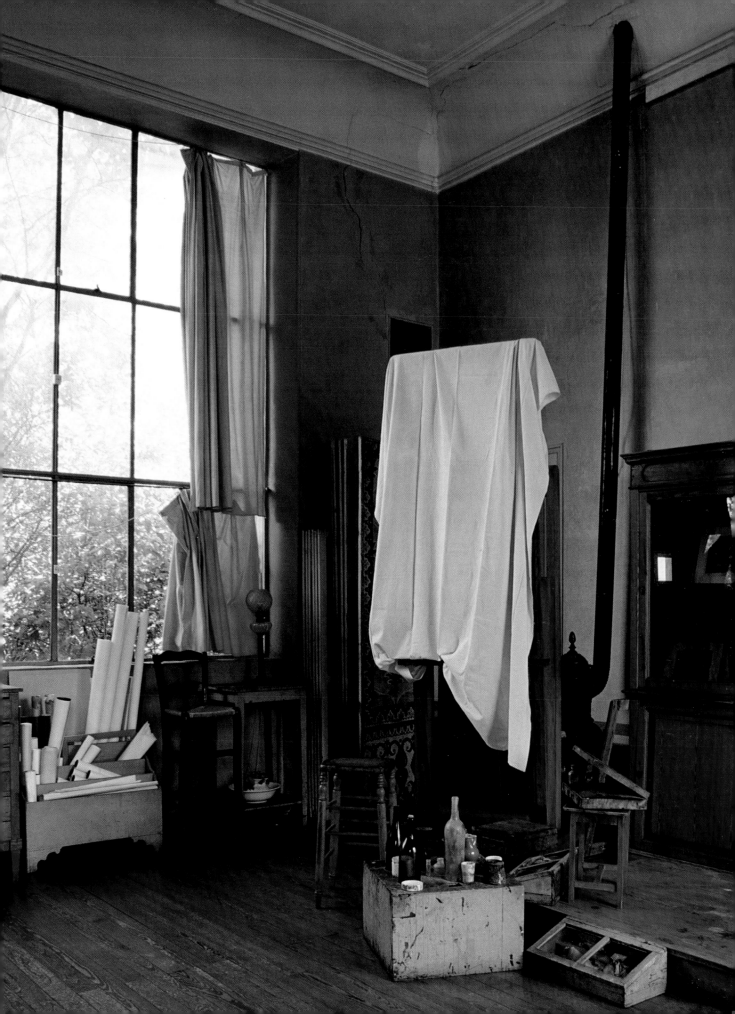

of the garden, and the small stream there. Bernard tried mentally to record the whole thing, sensing that he was witnessing something historical, a feeling that he would be urged to recall every detail. They didn't go up to the studio, not that day, the light was good and Cézanne wanted to paint outside. They went into a room where Bernard noticed a sculpture of Cézanne in red clay by Philippe Solari. The painter had not posed for it, hadn't had the time or the patience… he had to get back to his painting. Solari had done his best, working on the ground floor while Cézanne was in his studio on the first floor. Eventually he had given up, 'leaving this!', Cézanne had exclaimed, picking up the sculpture, going out to the garden and smashing it on a large stone. The shattered pieces remained there throughout Bernard's stay.

Bernard was to go back to Lauves again, which he describes: 'The house is of an orange-hued ochre, simple in shape, very classical. The style is very pure, apart from the chimney which is too narrow. The roof is in two sections, with arabesque cornices as in all traditional old Provençal houses.' Of the studio, he says: 'It is a huge room roughly painted in grey, facing north with the light coming in at the height of the window sill.' Cézanne was working on a still life, 'three death heads on an oriental rug'. He worked on it every morning for a month (during the afternoon he was outdoors). Every day Bernard was stunned by the changes, not understanding why Cézanne seemed to be destroying his painting, unravelling the threads: 'The painting has changed colour and shape every day, even though when I arrived at the studio it could already have been removed from the easel as a finished piece. It would seem that Cézanne uses it as a form of meditation.'

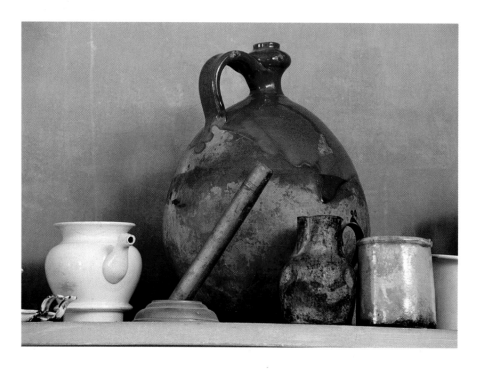

'*It* was a large room which faced north. The light entered the room at a fairly low level'.
The painter Emile Bernard was one of the privileged few allowed into the studio.

Preceding page:
The studio at Lauves.

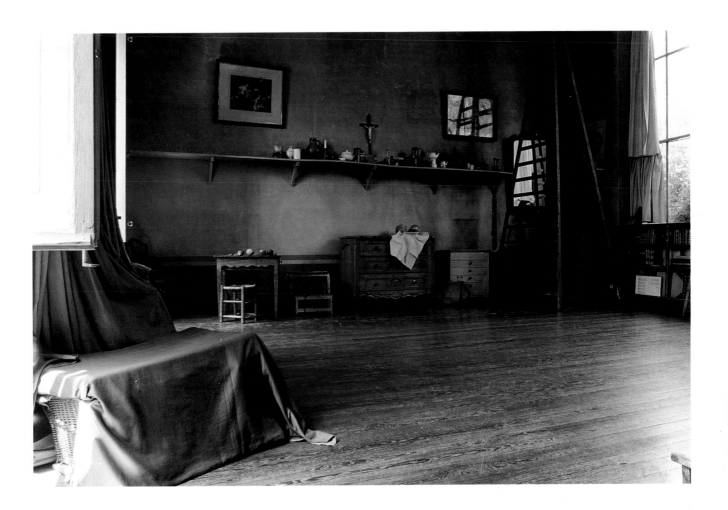

Bernard saw the painting as a sort of testament, which may not have been far from the truth. Even though Cézanne's last great works, *Les baigneuses* or his work on the Sainte-Victoire, were more remarkable, the small still life incorporated elements of religious painting, a meditation on death and vanity. Was it a question of vanity in life - or vanity in his art? Cézanne never showed off about his work and was an example in modesty to future artists. And even at Lauves, at the height of his talent, he worked wracked by self-doubt.

Cézanne had been envious of Monet and his home at Giverny. He watched one of the few painters of his generation whose work he admired and whose friendship he valued set up his studio in the middle of the countryside, creating a garden for his painting. Giverny was Monet's place of work as Jas de Bouffan had been Cézanne's. But it had been time to leave Jas and even while he was there he had not wanted to tame nature and create a garden to paint in, he had not wanted to intervene in nature's work. He had never had a family home where the life of the house was also in harmony with his work. Monet was a contented man and artist, for whom life was easier, or so it seemed to Cézanne. Cézanne had never wanted to be anything but a painter, he had lived for his work. Now he had Lauves, his retreat and place of meditation. There were to be no smart society evenings there, just Cézanne and his paint, striving to

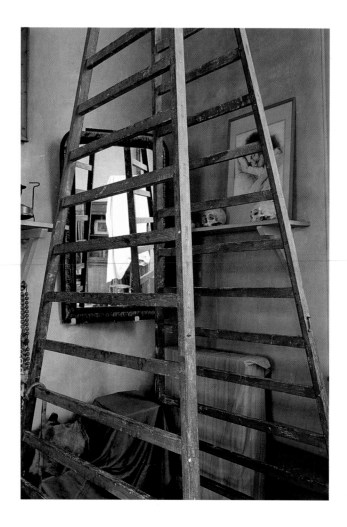

artist before he even met him, something for which Cézanne was grateful. Cézanne also admired Rodin and on leaving an exhibition of his work had bought a photograph of one of his sculptures. He had not been indifferent to Clemenceau either, an imposing political figure who supported Dreyfus, was a friend of Zola's, and who was so interested in the work of the Impressionists that he had written a book on Monet. Mirabeau he admired for his style, the strength of his realism and for his insights into art when he wrote on the subject. So the luncheon at Giverny had been a big event and Cézanne's humility and emotion was remarked upon by the others present. He had even shown pride when Rodin shook his hand. On another occasion when Monet had organized a party to pay homage to the artist, inviting friends such as Renoir and Sisley, Cézanne had fled from it, thinking that they were making fun of him when they had proposed a toast to say how much they all admired him!

All that had been ten years before, in 1894 at Giverny, the artists' paradise. His own 'Giverny' would be more austere, wilder and Provençal of course, being far from Paris and all those self-important people. He would not invite people there, it was for him and his painting alone.

In January 1905, two young painters went to see Cézanne and were allowed to go to Lauves. H.P Rivière and J.F. Schnerb described what they observed: '...in the corners of the room there were canvases, rolled up or stretched in their frames. Rolls were left on chairs and had been squashed. Both the

reach that promised land he had been seeking for so long. He recalled that at Giverny he had met the sculptor Auguste Rodin and the politician Georges Clemenceau; and one day the writer Octave Mirabeau and the critic Gustave Geffroy had also come to lunch. The way Monet had been at ease with such people had surprised Cézanne, who was himself shy, convinced that he was misunderstood and timid when confronted with strangers. Monet, making the most of the fact that Cézanne had taken lodgings at an inn to paint in the region, had arranged for Cézanne to meet Geffroy, the art critic. Geffroy had written an article on Cézanne, singing the praises of the

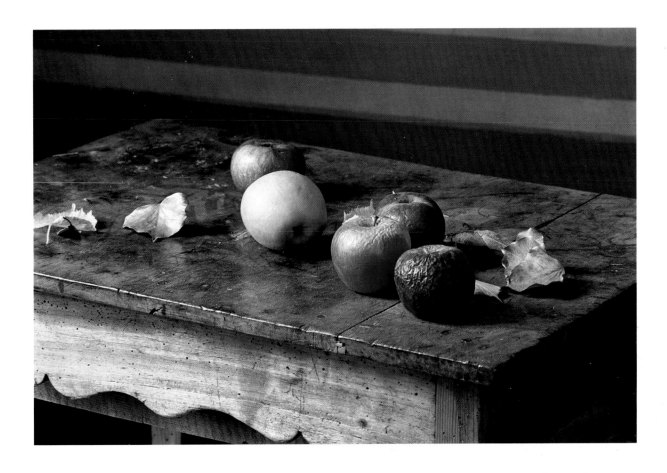

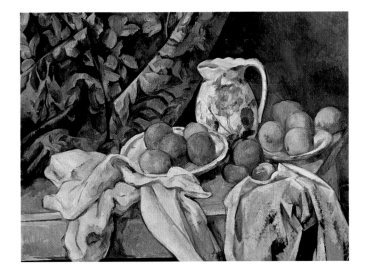

Nature morte au rideau et au pichet à fleurs.
The Hermitage, Saint Petersburg.

*C*ézanne in his later years remained faithful to the still life style he had developed in his youth, painting apples or oranges, draped folds of cloth and a few objects. Here he has chosen plates and an earthenware jar, everyday objects in Provence at the time.

Aix and the Lauves studios were in disorder, a seemingly random disorder. The walls were bare, the light raw. Half-empty tubes of paint, stiffened, dried-up paintbrushes and leftovers of dinners which then became still life subjects, were all over the tables. In one corner there were some parasols, basic ones bought from a local town merchant, and hunting bags for taking food into the countryside when he painted outdoors.'

Cézanne was getting old and tired. It is perhaps old age that gave him his sense of urgency - the sense that his goal was not yet achieved. He was still hesitating over the *Grandes baigneuses* and had not found a way to finish it to his liking. So he tried, through still life painting, to work on something which he would not have to go back to over and again. A finished painting. It is not surprising that he ventured out less and less in his last years and was seldom seen in town. Bernard was a witness to how he drove

himself remorselessly: 'I've seen him so tired by his work that he could barely speak or hear anything. He would go to bed as if in a coma, and the next day he would start again.'

Jean Arrouye said that: 'Still life was Cézanne's way of experimenting and progressing, his master school of thought.' During the Impressionist period this was unusual, and marked Cézanne as someone who followed the ancient tradition of studio art in the Flemish style. It was radically opposed to nature and outdoor painting and considered a heresy by academic art teachers, who placed still life at the bottom of the scale of all types of painting. The still life painter composes his subject himself (as Monet composed his garden...) with a view to his canvas, and he dominates it because the subject is no bigger than the canvas. Cézanne mastered both types of painting: the Impressionist style of being dominated by nature and concerned by realism, and the

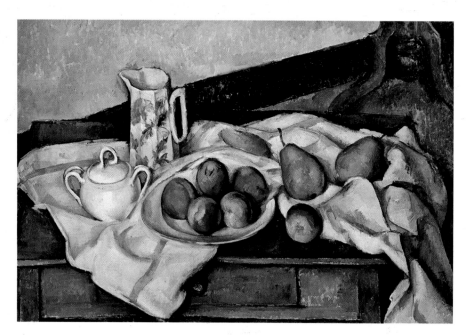

'*S*till life was Cézanne's way of experimenting and progressing; his master school of thought.'
Jean Arrouye.

Nature morte.
The Hermitage, Saint Petersburg.

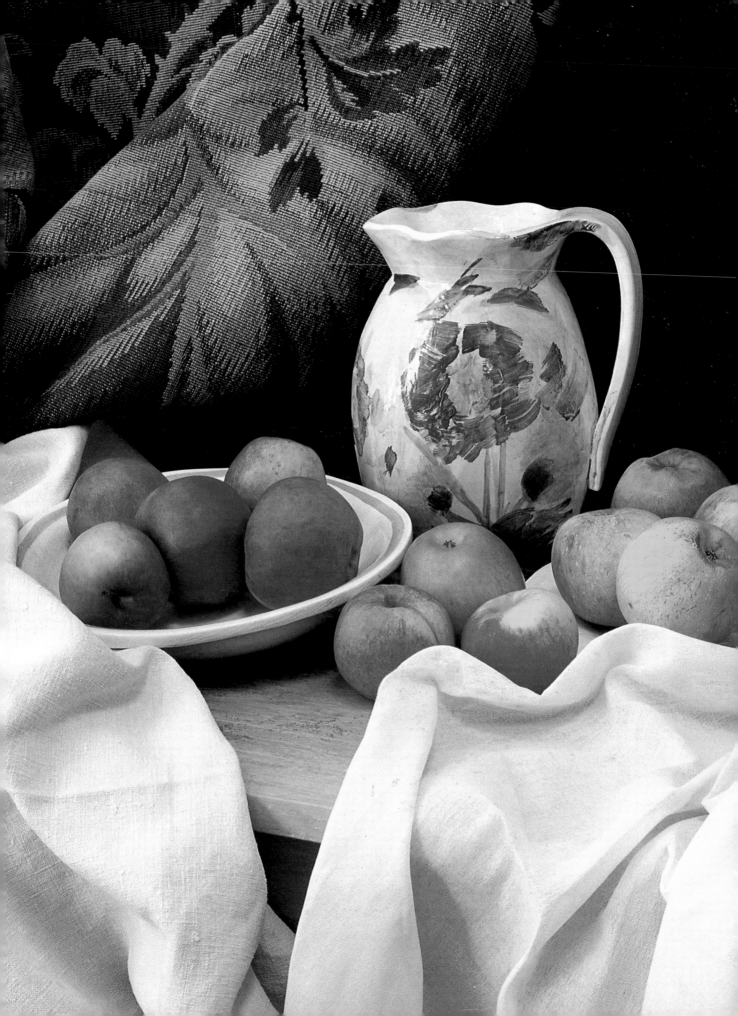

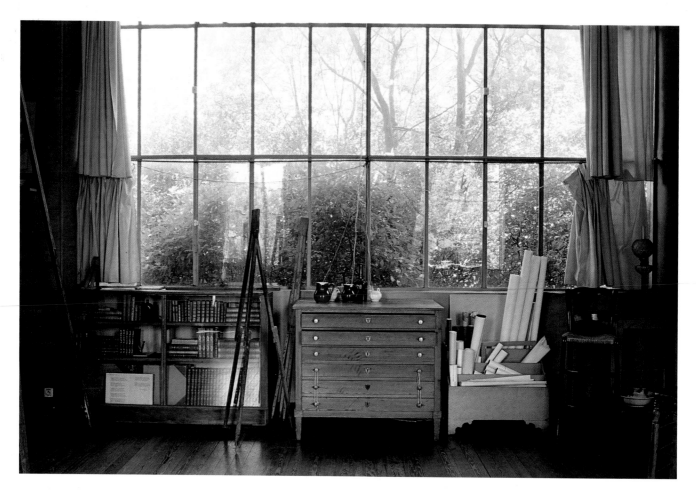

studio style of concentrating uniquely on the subject, forgetting the outside world. For an artist who returned dissatisfied again and again to his paintings and took time finishing his works, still life painting had the advantage of not being subject to the vagaries of the weather (even though the light varied in the studio according to the weather). Still life was never still as far as Cézanne was concerned. He could see the subtly changing reflections on an apple and could create life between inanimate objects, he could see the play of light which breathed life into them. The most humble of fruit was noble to Cézanne, whose aim was to see, really see and transfer what he saw onto the canvas.

Cézanne confided in Bernard, saying: 'Look at God's work! That's what I'm trying to do.'

He did not want to tell a story and he was suspicious of literature when it tried to explain a painting, reducing its role to that of an illustration. This divine work was best contemplated out amidst nature itself, among the trees. But it was not that simple, an apple on a tree was not just an apple but part of the tree. To really see the apple he had to single it out, place it in front of him, and contemplate it without the distraction of the landscape. This was what still life meant, the object alone, and he felt that this relationship was sufficiently complicated without the landscape and the rest intervening. There was a stability in still life work that was absent from landscape painting. Jean-Marie Baron and Pascal Bonafoux quote Cézanne in their book on his still life painting: 'Nature is always the same, but nothing lasts. Our painting must give the impression of eternity, capturing nature on canvas and making the observer shiver when faced with its changeability. What is there to it ? Nothing maybe, or perhaps everything.'

That is what Cézanne's still life work is about. Seeing, but seeing beyond appearances. It is a matter of interrogating nature and looking for the presence of God. Perhaps Cézanne was in search of a promised land, or trying to recapture paradise lost, or perhaps he was like St Francis of Assisi, trying to prove the existence of the Creator in his creations. Painting was not merely contemplation for him, but also action, a celebration in which man was fully implicated, in the here and now. Cézanne's work, unfinished and tormented as it was, was also a eulogy, and the painting's harmony had to be in line with nature's harmony. This is what Cézanne means when he says that his painting is parallel to nature. His studio at Lauves was like a temple to him where the painter could get closer to God through his journey along the hard and difficult path of painting.

It had been forty years since he first painted a still life - a few peaches. During the period when he used to paint quite densely with a palette knife, he had painted some

*B*ecause the boundaries of the town of Aix have spread out into the hills, Lauves is no longer in the heart of the countryside. The studio, however, can still be visited today.

pears with a sugar bowl and a blue cup. He was following Courbet and Delacroix's example, in strongly emphasizing shade and light. He then learned from Manet and composed in shades of grey. Then, on the fringes of Impressionism, he lit his subject and painting more, and lightened the whole composition. Now far away from the heavy, sombre style of his youth, which was merely the surface expression of realism, Cézanne concentrated as much on the light as on the subject of his paintings. It is this aspect which unifies these works which go against the rules of perspective and composition, so that his

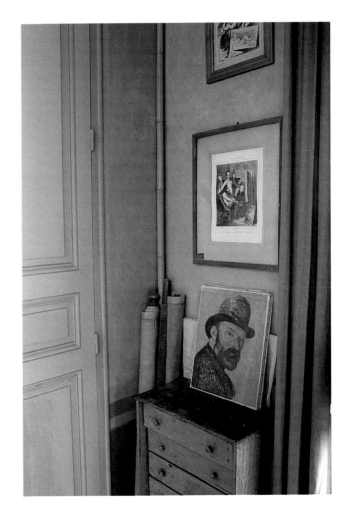

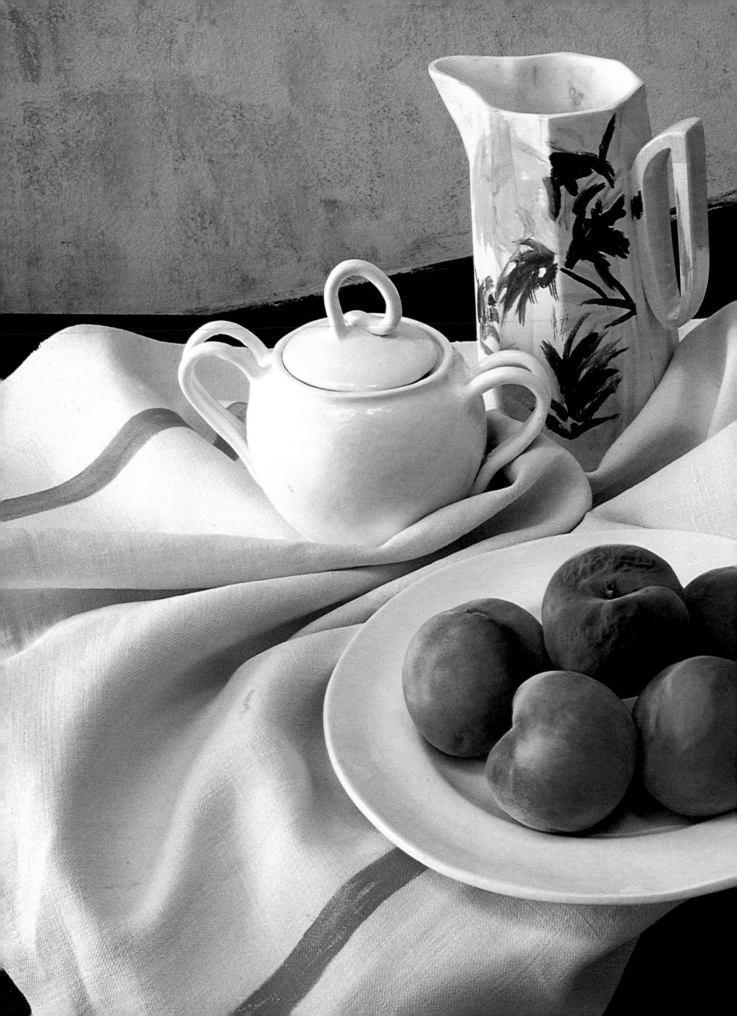

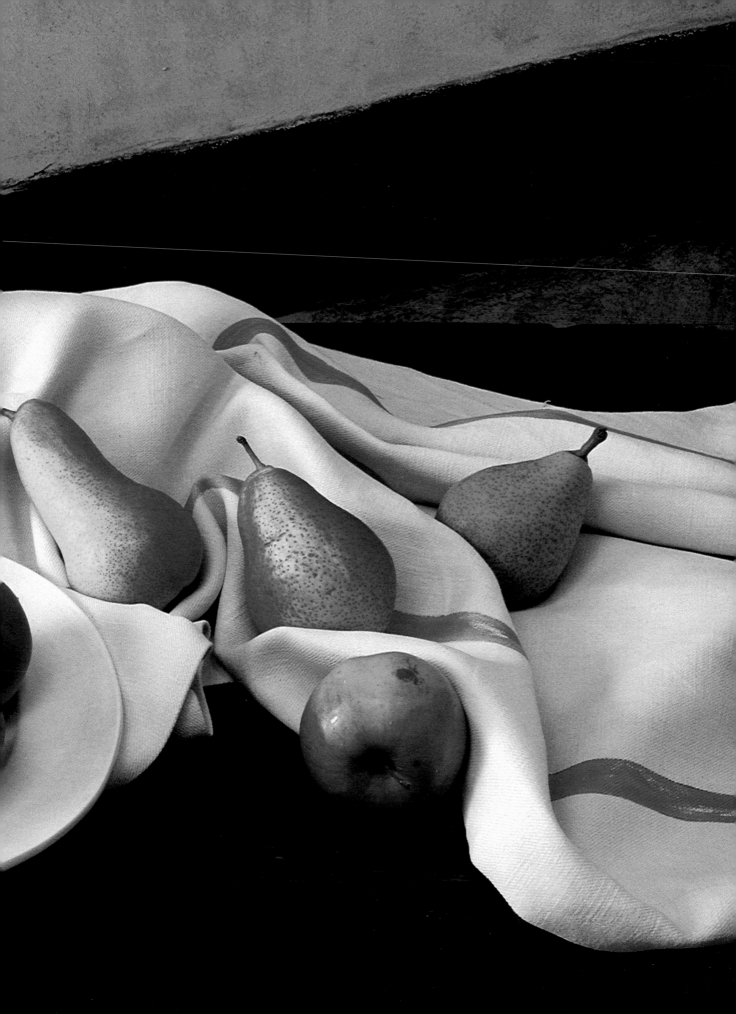

paintings are never confined. They open onto a space which is not limited by the canvas nor concentrated around a patch of paint, they even seem to be in perpetual movement. Cézanne's still life canvases are almost living things, moving in their own light. The objects, put together for the painting which is inappropriately named 'still life', have a life of their own: it is this life which animates Cézanne's paintings. A table is not a solid inanimate object, it is a strange thing made up of geometrical forms, a piece of work made by a carpenter. And it should never be said that Cézanne did not know how to draw, as

some of his contemporaries claimed, rather he drew differently from those around him and from those who had gone before.

Cézanne painted objects and the living world in movement, constantly changing. He went beyond the realism of a moment as seen by the Impressionist and traditional painters and sought to paint the way that objects vibrate in light, the light and movement which to him represented the real essence of life itself. His goal depended as much on his sensitivity as on his powers of observation, and his choice of subjects for his paintings was of great importance. The objects and fruit which he rejoices in through his paintings were part of his everyday life. It was usually the same table in his paintings and what surrounded the table was reduced to an imprecise background, more so since he had left Jas (*Nature morte au vase pique-fleurs*) (Still life with a flower vase). A tablecloth or a brightly coloured piece of material was enough to create an atmosphere and hint at the complexity of space. He would place some local pottery on the table, a jug with a handle, a vase, a cup, a plate, a glass, a bottle, all ordinary everyday objects without value. Only the three skulls or the small plaster figure without arms (falsely attributed to Puget)

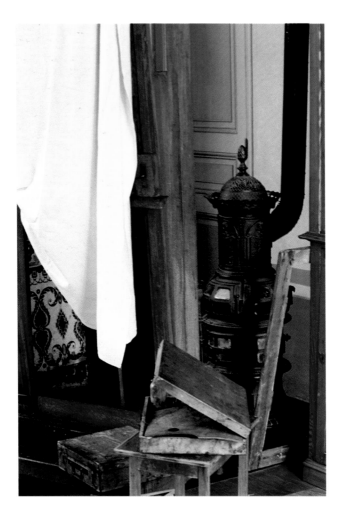

Cézanne, not a strong believer in his youth, finished his days a devout Catholic and attended mass at the cathedral regularly.

were out of the ordinary, there was no crystal nor any precious silverware. He always gave the best position to the fruit he so loved, with its warm colours and shapes which attracted light: apples of course, but also peaches, apricots, oranges, lemons, pears, also sometimes a bread roll, biscuits, eggs, onions. In his studio he would eulogize nature in its simplest form by painting some of the things it provided.

A temple is not just the building, but also the grounds in which it is built; and the garden at Lauves was part of Cézanne's temple, the whole thing part of his subject matter. It was a wild garden, even less formal than the one at Jas. It was quite overgrown, left to itself and occasionally cut back as one would cut back a pathway. There were olive trees, bay trees, lilacs, plum and cherry trees. In front of the house, roses, geraniums and sage bushes provided a splash of colour amidst all the greenery. But Cézanne did not redesign his garden as Monet had done at Giverny, he merely rendered it prettier. Monet had controlled nature, dictating to it so that he could paint it as he wished to, whereas Cézanne had a dialogue with it, added to it, directed it, but never changed it. And he too painted his garden.

The gardener, Vallier, took care of the trees and the flowers and all the little things that needed to be done around the house. He was a quiet peaceful man, a retired sailor. He agreed to pose for Cézanne on the terrace in front of the garden, wearing a straw hat or a cap. As long as he could stand there, lost in his thoughts, he was happy. One of the

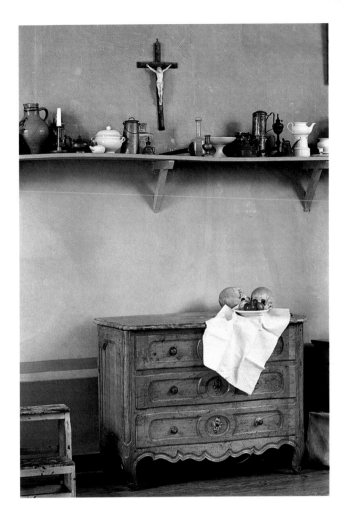

advantages of Lauves was that Cézanne could do portraits outdoors without anyone to bother him. He had not liked to do them at Jas de Bouffan as there were always too many people. One of the family, the workers, or someone visiting would watch what he was doing, or would strike up a conversation. When he was painting Cézanne liked to be surrounded by peace and quiet. More than once he had stopped painting, packed his stuff up and left because he had been interrupted and was no longer able to concentrate. Did people believe that painting just flowed from the fingers, without reflection and thought?

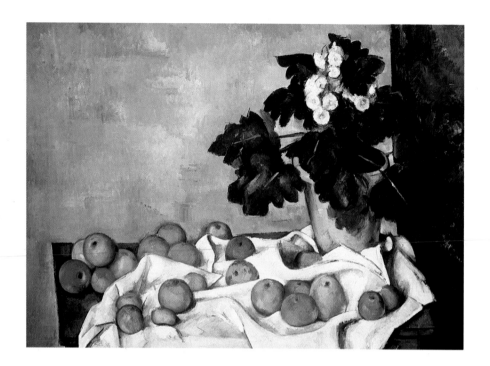

Pot de géraniums et fruits,
Metropolitan Museum, New York

*C*ézanne treasured this
sculpture and always kept it
near by. He believed it to be
a mould of a piece by Puget,
a sculptor he admired
greatly. He often painted
and drew it.

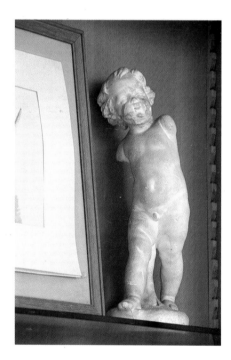

Vallier has earned a place in history as the
man who allowed Cézanne to paint in peace
and quiet. He was a man who was familiar
with the laws of nature, the seasonal changes,
and knew how to let time ripen things
without trying to force them. The same thing
applied to Cézanne's paintings, whose
maturity could not be forced. They needed
time to mature. And it was not by chance that
it was with this man that Cézanne finally
achieved what he had always wanted to
achieve: a painting of a man depicted as part
of the light and colours of nature, as an
integral and essential part of nature. His
silhouette stood well-defined, not melting or
absorbed into the landscape, yet depicted as if
all the light and energy of nature was
concentrated in him.

Here in the garden at Lauves Cézanne
found the 'formula', the one he had tried to
use for the *Grandes baigneuses*. Émile Bernard

took a photograph of Cézanne in front of that canvas, sitting down, seemingly peaceful, his trousers covered in paint, looking at one of the more finished versions of the painting. Cézanne had always been haunted by Manet's *Déjeuner sur l'herbe*, which had pinpointed a new way of painting. He had even tried a version of it without the nudes, with red fruit and himself in the middle, index finger raised in a gesture of explaining something to others. He was still trying to achieve the goal of painting nudes in nature, of representing the female body as naturally as possible without the usual exterior signs of society: Cézanne's nudes were not erotic, they were more Rousseau-like and innocent.

When he was younger he had not been afraid to paint daring scenes (*L'Après-midi à Naples*, *L'Enlèvement*, *Une moderne Olympia*) (Afternoon in Naples, The abduction, A modern Olympia), but now he was older he painted more enigmatic and less commercial scenes which were not at all provocative. They were like ceremonial gatherings in which the characters seemed in perfect harmony with one another and with their surroundings, made up of more trees than water. Their main concern was not bathing, judging by the foreground where baskets of fruit and food are more in evidence than water. In another painting one figure is holding a sort of pan, watched by two others. What are they preparing? As a younger man he had painted *L'Orgie* (The orgy), an amazing painting where an abundant meal was part of a luxurious scene with nudes. Cézanne had come a long

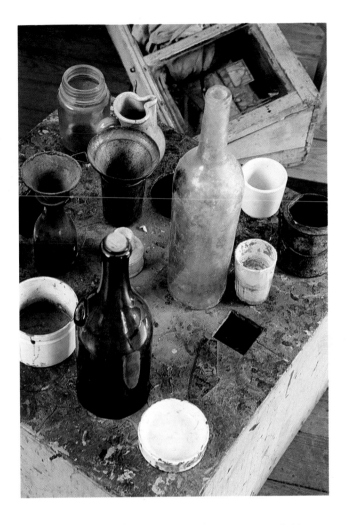

way since then and denuded his painting of all literary intentions, inventing a new representation of the human figure and new harmonies in composition and colour. So the fact that he returned to nude figures and food towards the end of his life shows how important they were to him, and how they were linked in the mind of the romantic man with all his desires and his wish to enjoy life. Thanks to age and his painting, it is obvious that he had found a new balance, a more spiritual concept of life and of man's place in the world. Curiously, nobody noticed that *L'Orgie* was a pastiche of *La Vierge entourée de*

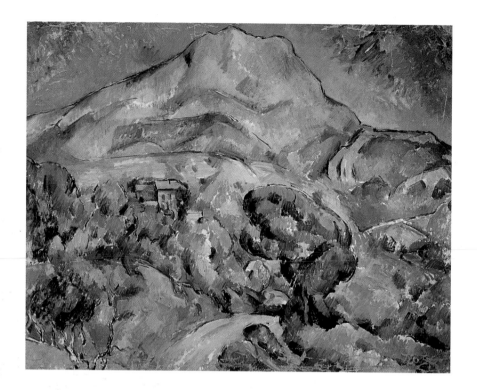

There was an excellent viewing point of the Mont Sainte-Victoire within short walking distance from Lauves. Cézanne was haunted by the mountain, painting his favourite landscape over and over again until the very end of his life.

La Montagne Sainte-Victoire.
The Hermitage, Saint Petersburg.

Saints et de Saintes (The Virgin and the Saints) by Rubens which was exhibited by the Granat museum in Aix in 1860, (Bourguignon de Fabregoules collection). So it was in fact a Christian painting transformed into a pagan one. Thirty-five years later the *Grandes baigneuses*, painted in the studio at Lauves, may have had its origin in this youthful provocation, but now he chose to praise the world rather than lament it.

Cézanne was near his studio at Lauves when he was taken ill. On 15 October 1906, he collapsed in the rain. He was taken home, but got up the next day to work as usual. He wanted to continue his portrait of Vallier, but this last session proved too much for him and eight days later, at rue Boulegon, he died.

He had once referred to himself as the 'man who doesn't exist'. It was as if he had arranged this meeting with death at his favourite location so that in dying there he too would blend into and become a part of the Provence landscape he so loved.

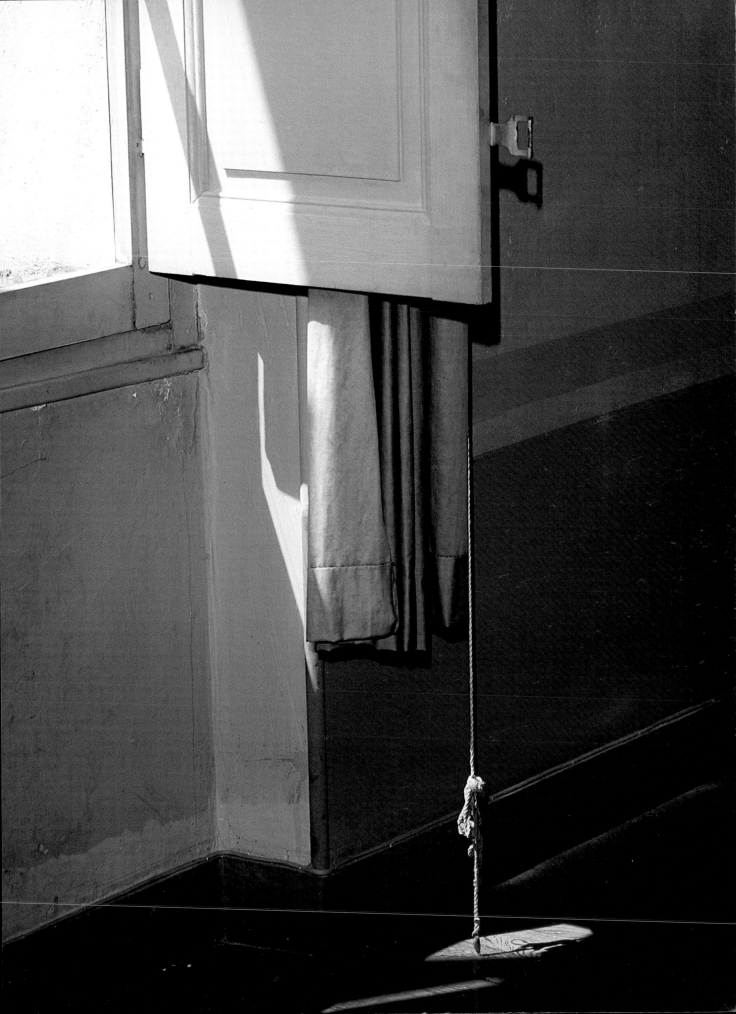

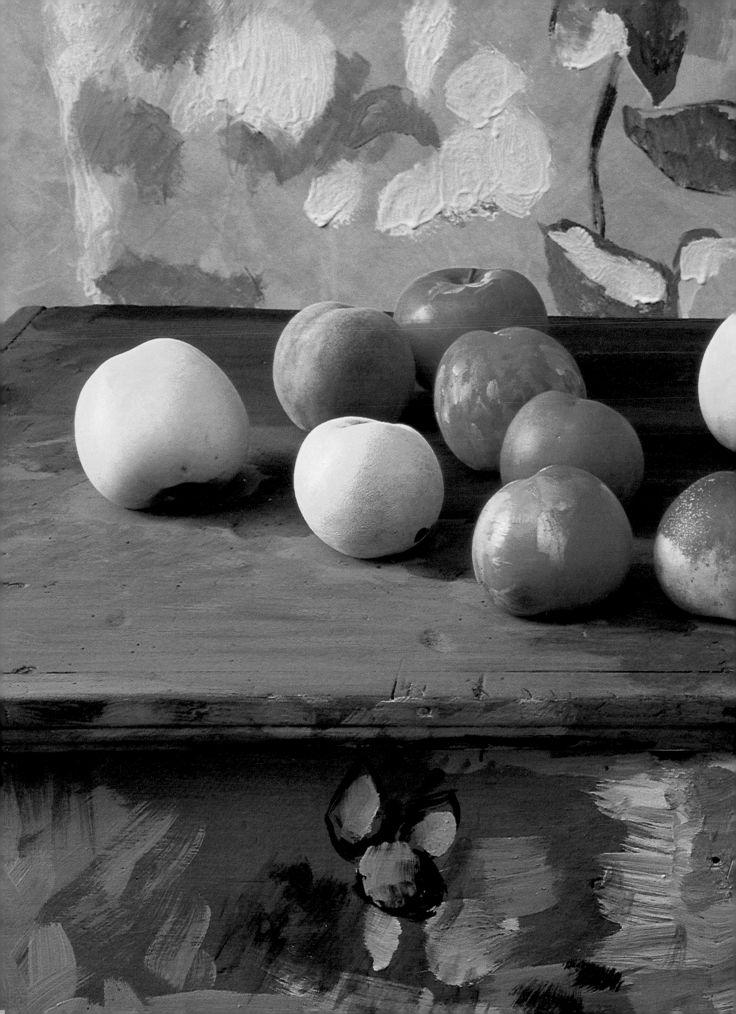

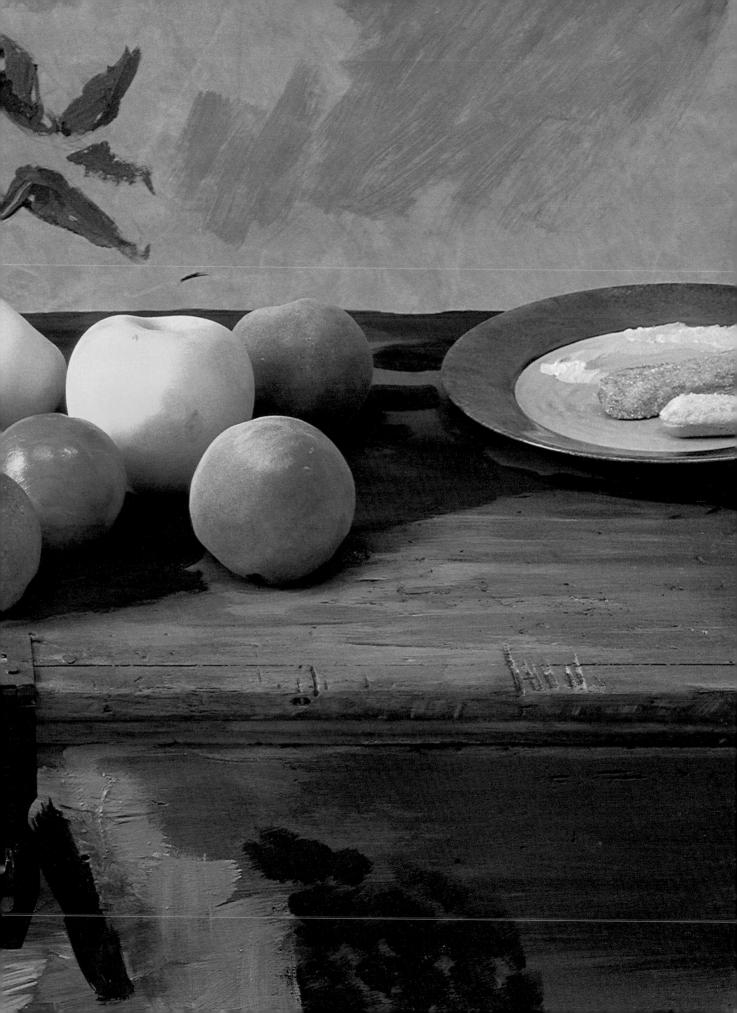

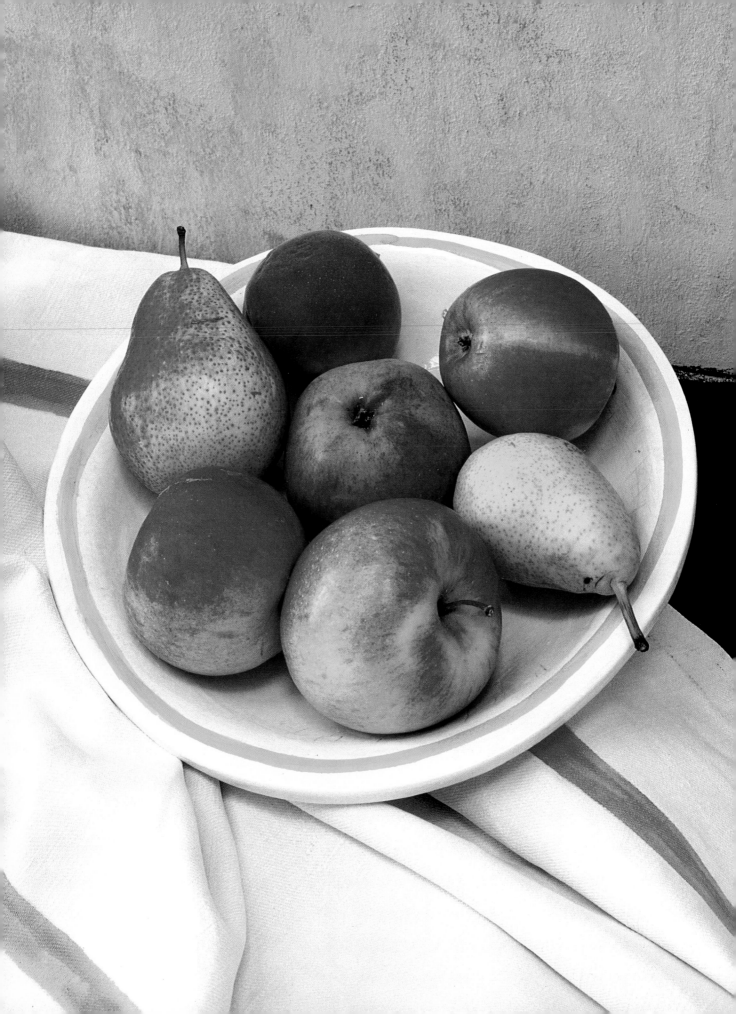

Recipes

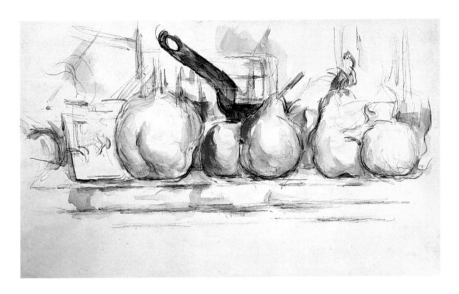

Still life : apples, pears and cooking pot, Musée d'Orsay, Paris.

The heart of Provence offers a more authentic and
basic cuisine than the neighbouring coastal regions.
Garlic, savory, and thyme;
olive oil and olives;
leeks, more delicate in flavour than onions;
an abundance of succulent tomatoes:
these are among the essential ingredients in
Provençal cooking, one of the simplest
yet most flavoursome of French cuisines.

Soups

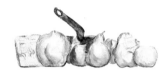

SOUPE AUX PORRIS ET AUX VERMICHELLI
LEEK AND VERMICELLI SOUP

Serves 6

3 medium leeks; bouquet garni (1 sprig thyme or savory, 1 sprig sage, 1/2 bunch parsley stalks); 2 garlic cloves; 1.5 litres / 3 pints chicken or lamb stock (see recipes p.184) well skimmed; 1 tbsp olive oil; 1 generous handful vermicelli; salt and freshly ground black pepper; nutmeg; grated cheese (such as parmesan).

Make a deep cut lenghtwise into the leeks and soak them in warm water to remove all traces of dirt. Keep the dark green top leaves and tie them together in a bouquet garni with the fresh thyme or savory, sage and parsley stalks. Peel the garlic cloves and crush them using a knife handle. Heat the stock gently.

Drain the leeks and slice them finely. Pat them dry with a tea towel. Heat the oil in a stainless steel pan and add the leeks. Reduce to a minimum heat and stir with a wooden spoon for 5 minutes, then add the garlic. Cook for a few minutes more, then pour in the stock and throw in the bouquet garni. Cover and simmer gently for 25 minutes. Then turn the heat up slightly and add the vermicelli. Do not cover and cook until the pasta is done. Add salt if necessary and two or three turns of the pepper mill and a pinch of freshly grated nutmeg. Reduce the heat and partially cover with a lid to allow the vermicelli to swell.

Serve with grated cheese (parmesan or comté) and a few drops of olive oil.

When Cézanne had guests who were not restricted by diet as he was, Madame Brémond would add a generous spoonful of tomato purée (see recipe p.180) to the soup and serve with a side dish of ailloli *(see recipe page 181). To turn this soup into a main meal, she would add chopped potatoes, mashing them into the soup with a fork when cooked, and serve over a boiled egg.*

AïGO BOULIDO
GARLIC SOUP

Serves 6

For the soup:

**6 large garlic cloves; 1 litre / 2 pints water or light
chicken stock (see recipe page 184); 1 sprig thyme;
1/2 a bay leaf; 1 sprig fresh sage; coarse salt.**

For accompaniment:

**6 thick slices fresh, country-style bread; 6 hard-
boiled eggs; 2 tbsp extra-virgin olive oil; grated
cheese (mature comté, gruyère or hardened goat's
milk cheese); salt and freshly ground pepper.**

Peel the garlic cloves, then lightly crush
them in their skins so that they remain whole.
Pour the water or chicken stock into a large pan
and add the garlic, thyme, bay leaf and some salt.
Bring slowly to the boil then lower the heat and
simmer for approximately 5 minutes.   Pick the
sage leaves off the stalks and add to the
simmering stock. Remove from the heat. Cover
and leave to infuse for several minutes.
Meanwhile, toast the bread slices, grate the
cheese and peel the eggs. Warm the soup bowls
and place one slice of toasted bread into each.
Pour a little oil over each slice and top with a
boiled egg.

Remove the thyme and laurel, but not the
sage, from the stock. Using the back of a spoon,
crush the garlic and blend the creamy flesh into
the soup.

Pour the soup over the egg and toast and
serve piping hot sprinkled with freshly ground
pepper and a handful of grated cheese.

*Cézanne was particularly fond of this, the
'queen of Provençal soups' as it was both delicious and
good for his health. Still a classic family favourite*

*today, it is renowned for its medicinal properties.
L'aïgo boulido sauvo la vido is a Provençal French
saying which literally means 'garlic broth saves life'.
This particular soup helps the digestion, though if it is
being served as a starter instead of a main meal, the
boiled egg should be omitted.*

*For variation, thinly sliced carrots with finely
chopped cooked chicken may be added. Although a tasty
alternative, Cézanne himself would probably not have
added anything. He preferred simple and basic cuisine.*

SOUPE D'ÉPEAUTRE
AU PETIT SALÉ
WHEAT AND BACON SOUP

Serves 6

**1 large onion; 350g / 12oz salt pork or bacon;
1tbsp olive oil; 2 medium sized leeks; 2 celery
sticks; 2 carrots; 1 turnip; bouquet garni (1 bunch
fresh parsley and marjoram, 2 cloves); 2 garlic
cloves; 300g / 10oz bulgar wheat , pearl barley or
rice; salt and pepper.**

Peel and chop the onion. Cut the salt pork
or bacon into six pieces without removing the
rind. Heat the oil in a large pan over a medium
heat. Add the onion and bacon pieces and sauté
until golden brown.

Peel and chop the vegetables, keeping
some of the dark green leek leaves to one side for
the bouquet garni. Make the bouquet garni, by
tying the marjoram, parsley and green leek leaves
together, wrapped around the two cloves.

Put the vegetables in the pan and mix
together with the bacon and onion. Add 3 litres /
6 pints water, the garlic cloves, bouquet garni
and a few grains coarsely ground pepper. No salt

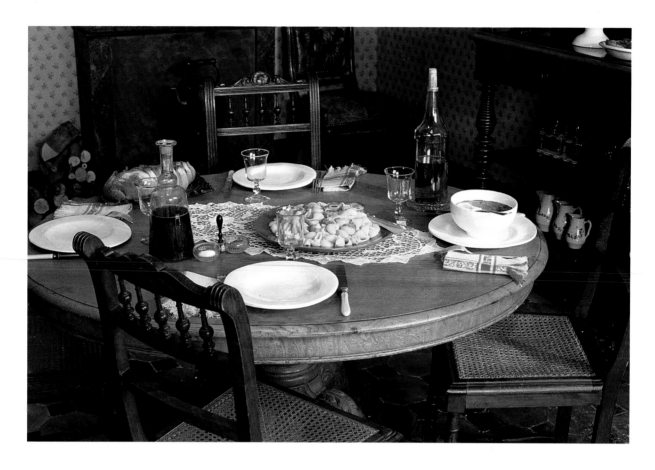

Macaronade and *Aïgo Boulido*, rue Boulegon.

is needed at this point as the bacon is salty. Bring to the boil and leave to bubble for a few minutes, skimming the surface as it boils. Cover and lower the heat and simmer for 45 minutes. Sprinkle in the wheat, barley or rice (which will thicken the soup). Cover and continue simmering for a further 35 to 40 minutes.

Remove from the heat and discard the bouquet garni. Taste and adjust the seasoning. Remove the bacon pieces and pour the rest of the soup into a tureen. The reserved bacon is served separately with *ailloli* (see recipe p.181), or vinaigrette. The soup may also be served with large slices of wholemeal bread, toasted and rubbed with thyme leaves and crushed garlic.

Epeautre *(spelt or chaffy wheat) is a brown seed wheat variety from the mountain regions of Haute-Provence and Basses-Alpes in South-Eastern France. It has a very distinctive taste, but bulgar wheat, rice or pearl barley may be used instead. This winter soup, served with a crisp green salad, is a meal in itself and can be followed with a sheep or goat's milk cheese and a compote of seasonal fruits.*

Petit salé, *also known as* lard salé, *is lightly salted roast pork ready-prepared at a* charcuterie. *Bacon may also be used.*

SOUPE À L'EIGRETO
SOUR SOUP

Serves 6

1 handful spinach; 1 handful sorrel; a few sprigs parsley; heart of 1 cos lettuce; 1 medium sized leek; 1 garlic clove; 2 large potatoes; 1 tbsp olive oil; 2 litres / 4 pints beef stock; 2 eggs; salt and pepper.

The more 'leaves' you use in this soup the better. Chinese cabbage, swiss chard or dandelion leaves, for example, could be added to the above list of ingredients.

Remove the leaves from the spinach, sorrel and parsley. Wash all the leaves carefully, then chop them roughly together with the lettuce heart. Wash and finely slice the whiter part of the leek. Peel and crush the garlic. Peel and chop the potatoes into small chunks.

Heat the oil over a low heat in a stainless steel saucepan. Brown the potatoes and leek for 5 minutes. Then add the spinach, sorrel, lettuce, parsley (and optional extras) and garlic, and cook until soft.

Warm the stock in a large pan and then add all the ingredients from the saucepan. Bring to the boil uncovered, then season to taste. Cover and simmer for approximately 20 minutes. When cooked, pass through a blender.

Pour a ladleful of the soup into a large warmed soup tureen. Beat in two eggs until blended. Add the rest of the soup, a little at a time, beating continuously until it is all incorporated. Serve immediately with grated cheese if preferred.

Celery may be used instead of potato for this recipe, but the soup will need to be thickened. The essential ingredient is the sorrel which gives the soup its tangy flavour and hence it's name: eigreto *which means sharp or sour.*

Starters and Appetizers

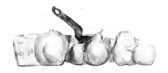

OMELETTE AUX CHAMPIGNONS
MUSHROOM OMELETTE

Serves 6

300g / 10oz mushrooms, preferably wild; 4-5 sprigs flat-leaf parsley; 2 leeks; 4 tbsp olive oil; 2 garlic cloves; salt and freshly ground pepper; 8 eggs.

Clean the mushrooms using a damp cloth. Cut away and discard the earthy base from the stalks. Chop the rest of the stalks finely and thinly slice the caps. Finely chop the parsley and wash and slice the leeks.

Heat 2 tablespoons of oil in a large frying pan and toss in the chopped mushroom stalks and leeks (you could use young onions instead, but Provençal cooks generally prefer leeks for their more delicate flavour). Cook over a low heat, stirring occasionally. Peel and crush the garlic. Pour another tablespoon of oil into the pan and add the garlic and sliced mushroom caps. Season and cook for 3 to 4 minutes.

Meanwhile, beat the eggs with a tablespoon of water and good vinegar, salt and pepper. Add the parsley. Turn up the heat and pour the eggs straight into the pan with the vegetables. Move the pan gently from side to side until the base is covered with a layer of egg. Use a wooden spoon,

while tilting the pan, to draw the cooked egg inwards and allow the uncooked egg to come into contact with the base of the pan. When cooked to your taste, fold the omelette over and slide it onto a plate. Alternatively, when one side is cooked, slide the whole omelette onto a plate, turn the pan upside down over it and flip the omelette back in to cook the other side.

Either way it may be served hot or cold.

Ceps are particularly delicious in an omelette, but any type of mushroom can be used. You could also just use the stalks in the omelette and cook the caps separately in a pan, then fill them with the fried leek, parsley and garlic, sprinkle with breadcrumbs and cook in a hot oven until crispy.

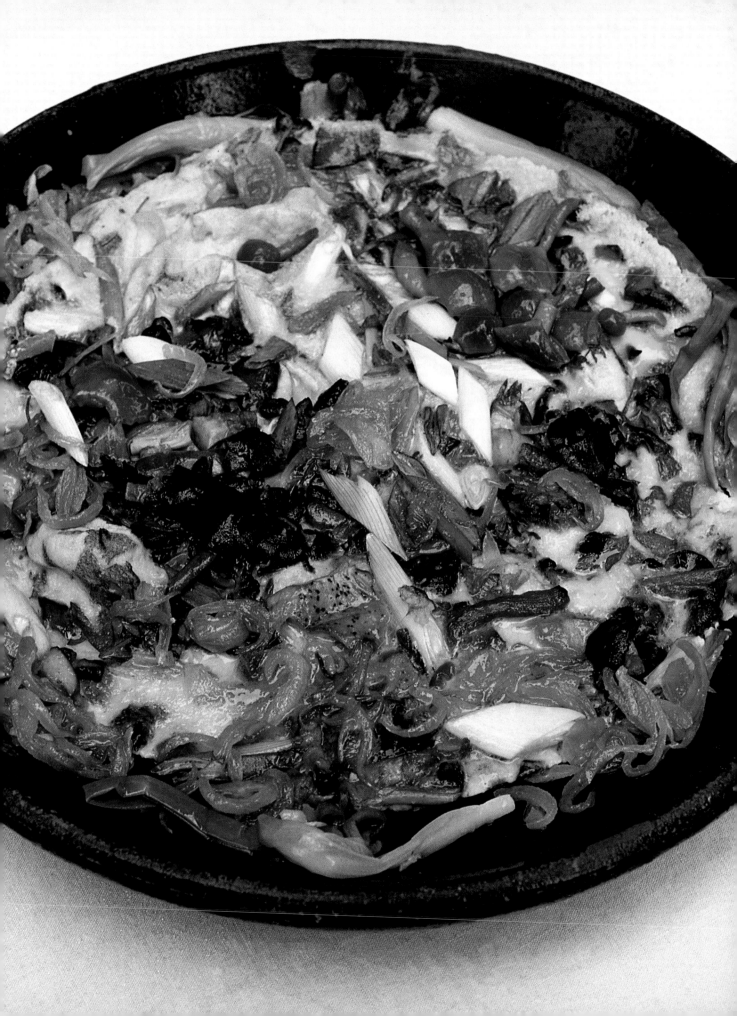

SARDINES À L'AIGRELETTE
FRIED SARDINES IN VINEGAR

Serves 6

2 dozen fresh sardines; 4 garlic cloves; 1 bay leaf;
1 pinch paprika; 1 tbsp coarse salt; freshly ground
pepper; 6-8 tbsp olive oil; 6 tbsp red wine vinegar;
1 sprig flat-leaf parsley; 2 lemons.

Clean the sardines under cold running water, rubbing them between your fingers to remove scales. Place them onto absorbent kitchen paper and gently pat them dry.

Peel and chop the garlic. Break the bay leaf into small pieces and mix with the garlic, paprika, salt and black pepper.

Heat the oil in a large pan. Arrange the sardines side by side (if the pan isn't large enough, cook 8 or 10 at a time dividing the seasoning accordingly) and fry over a medium heat for 3 minutes on one side.

When golden, turn them over using two skimmers or two spatulas and sprinkle with the seasoning. Cook for a further one to two minutes.

Pour the vinegar over the cooked sardines.

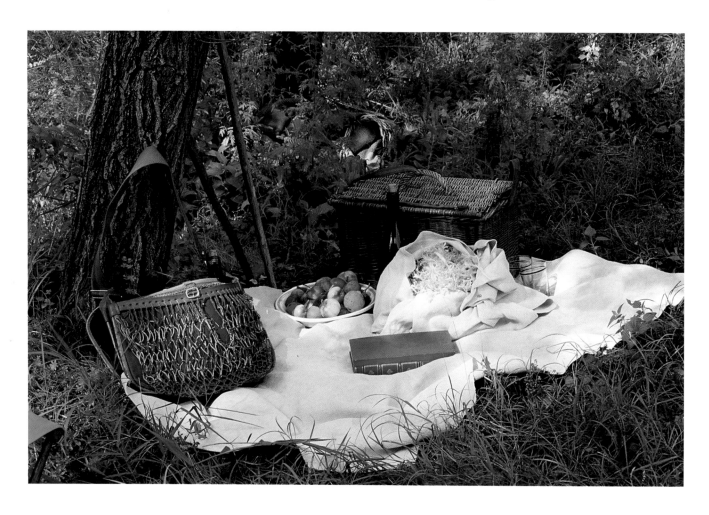

Leave for 30 seconds then transfer the sardines from the pan to a serving dish and keep warm.

Turn up the heat and boil the liquid in the pan until reduced.

Meanwhile, chop the parsley and cut the two lemons into quarters.

Throw a little of the parsley into the evaporating liquid, and sprinkle the rest over the sardines. Then pour the reduced liquid on top of the sardines and serve immediately with the lemon quarters and toasted bread.

If you are particular about the small bones in sardines, they may be cleaned before cooking. Do this by removing head, tail and fins. Slice the underside lengthwise from top to tail and, using your thumb, remove the central bone.

PAN BAGNAT DU VOYAGEUR
PROVENÇAL PICNIC ROLLS

Serves 6

2 ripe, medium tomatoes; 1 celery stick; 1 spring onion; 4 basil leaves; 12 black olives, pitted; 2-3 tbsp vinaigrette; olive oil; freshly ground black pepper; 1 oval or round, freshly baked roll per person; 2 hard-boiled eggs; 2 anchovy fillets; 1 tbsp tuna; 2 garlic cloves.

Peel the tomatoes (though a true Provençal would not!) by first soaking in boiling water to loosen the skins. Then remove the skins and squeeze out the watery seeds. Cut into small slices and put into a mixing bowl. Remove the stringy threads from the celery, then wash and slice thinly. Peel and finely chop the onion. Chop the basil leaves. Mix all together with the olives,

half the vinaigrette and some oil and pepper. Cover with cling film and leave to marinate at room temperature.

Cut each bread roll in two so that the bottom piece is bigger than the top (roughly two-thirds). Remove the soft part of the bread from within and sprinkle the insides of the hollowed out roll with the rest of the vinaigrette and some oil.

Cut the eggs into quarters, then cut each quarter in two. Chop the anchovy fillets.

Fill each roll with some of the mixture from the bowl. Add some of the chopped tuna, eggs and anchovies on top, then cover with the top half of the roll and press together.

These delicious rolls can be served as either a snack or a starter, and are ideal for hikers or for picnics. If you choose to prepare them for a picnic or a journey, wrap them tightly in aluminium foil.

Bread from Marseilles, made with fresh yeast and baked in a wood fire oven was traditionally used, but freshly baked, country-style rolls make a good substitute. Originally, the difference between an ordinary pan-bagnat *and a traveller's pan-bagnat lay in the contents. The latter was normally filled with tuna, anchovies, bitter olives and several different vegetables - if you could afford it. Otherwise, the plain version is simply bread dipped in vinaigrette. Bagnat in Provençal French means soaked or moistened.*

CRESPEOU AUX HERBES
HERB, CHEESE AND ONION OMELETTE

Serves 6

1 medium onion or leek; 1 garlic clove; 1 handful young sorrel leaves; 4 swiss chard leaves (the green part only); 2 tbsp olive oil; salt and pepper; 8 eggs; 1 pinch cayenne pepper; 100g / 4oz grated cheese.

Peel and roughly chop the onion or washed leek. Peel and crush the garlic. Wash and dry the greens, roll them up and cut into thin strips.

Place a large frying pan over a medium heat and add a tablespoon of oil. When the oil is hot, add the onion or leek and stir with a wooden spoon until slightly brown. Add the garlic and greens. Reduce the heat and leave for a few minutes to soften, then remove the pan from the heat. Add a little salt and pepper.

Beat the eggs together with 2 tablespoons water and the cayenne pepper (a spoonful of flour may be added at this point. This will result in a more pancake-like consistency). Turn the vegetables onto a warmed plate, pour the second tablespoon of oil into the pan and place over a high heat. Light the oven at 180°C (gas mark 4 , 350°F) and warm a plate a little wider in diameter than the pan you are using.

Pour the eggs into the pan and shake until the base of the pan is covered with an even layer of egg. Sprinkle the vegetables and cheese on top, then lower the heat and stir them into the omelette with a wooden spoon.

Cook for a few minutes, then, holding the warmed plate tightly over the pan, turn the pan upside-down so that the omelette drops onto the plate. Return the pan to the heat, adding a little more oil if necessary. Then slide the omelette back into the pan to cook the other side. Cook for a further 5 minutes, then cover the pan and place in the oven for a short spell which makes the omelette puff up nicely. Serve warm with a sprinkling of red wine vinegar or cold in slices.

The crespeou *was popular for picnics and was often served with* pan bagnat. *The above ingredients can be varied. Other vegetables may be used, though they should not be mixed, or small fish may be added. In Provence, it is customary to serve a number of different omelettes of varying flavours and colours. Not only are they delicious, but they make an attractive presentation when sliced.*

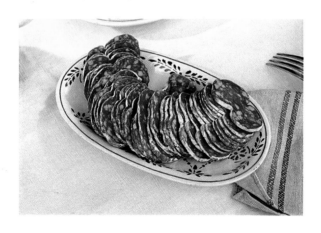

GAIETO DE FOIE DE PORC
PORK LIVER PARCELS

Serves 6

1 large pig's membrane (caul); 8 garlic cloves; 5 juniper berries; peppercorns; 1 sliver dried orange peel; 1 sprig flat-leaf parsley; 3 sage leaves; handful freshly chopped aromatic herbs (chervil, tarragon, chives, basil, rosemary etc.); pinch of grated nutmeg; coarse salt; 1kg / 2lb thickly cut streaky bacon; 1kg / 2lb of pork liver; wine or cider vinegar; 1 liqueur glass eau-de-vie de marc or fruit brandy.

Caul is the delicate net of membranes and fat from the stomach of a pig and is used here to wrap the stuffing. If you can't find any at your butcher you could use bacon sewn with string to wrap the parcels but you would miss the visual delight. *Eau-de-vie* is a spirit distilled from grape residue after wine-pressing and often flavoured with fruit such as pear or plum. Brandy could be substituted.

Soak the caul overnight in cold water, to which salt and vinegar have been added, making sure it remains intact.

Peel and crush the garlic. Crush the juniper berries with the peppercorns and orange peel. Chop the parsley, sage and other herbs of your choice. Mix all these together and add the nutmeg. Divide the mixture equally into two bowls and add salt.

Dice the bacon and cut the liver into thin strips. Put the bacon in one of the bowls of herb mixture and the liver in the other. Mix well with the ingredients in each bowl and cover with cling film. Refrigerate for 24 hours.

The following day, drain and dry the caul, then leave to marinate for a further hour in the marc or brandy.

Prepare a baking dish and some trussing string. Remove the two bowls from the fridge. Drain the caul, dividing the marc/brandy between the two bowls. Spread the caul out onto your work surface, making sure it has not been torn. If you discover any tears, cut strips from the outer edges and place them onto the holes. Cut the caul into twelve squares. On each square place some of the bacon mixture followed by the liver mixture, another portion of the bacon mixture and so on, finishing with the bacon mixture, until the contents from each bowl have been evenly distributed between the twelve squares. Wrap the caul around the meat and tie each square up with trussing string to make a parcel. Each parcel should be roughly the size of an orange. Preheat the oven at 210°C (gas mark 7, 425°F) Transfer the parcels to a baking dish and cook for approximately 35 minutes. Serve cold as a starter or snack.

Cézanne used to pack these little parcels in his lunchbag when he went on an excursion to his country cabin. But in Aix and most Provençal bourgeois households, gaieto *- known as* gaillette *or* caillette *in other regions - would be prepared differently. Trussed like a roast, it was cooked in a pressure cooker for at least an hour, with a generous splash of regional dry white wine. It was generally served cold and cut into slices like a pâté.*

AUBERGINES GRILLÉES
GRILLED AUBERGINES

Serves 6

6 aubergines; 2 tbsp olive oil; 2 garlic cloves; 6 anchovy fillets; 1/2 tsp chopped parsley; 1 unwaxed lemon; freshly ground pepper.

Wash the aubergines and remove the tops, but do not peel or slice them. Place them low under the grill, or in a very hot oven set at 240°C (gas mark 9, 475°F), or they may be charcoal grilled. Whichever method you choose, cook them well, turning regularly, until very soft to the touch. Leave them to cool a little, then slice each aubergine in two lengthwise and lay each half face down in the oil and steep for at least one hour.

Meanwhile, peel and crush the garlic, remove small bones from the anchovies and chop them up. Mix them together with the parsley, pepper (do not add salt as the anchovies are salty enough) and the juice from the lemon.

Spread this mixture over each aubergine half and then join the two halves back together. Wrap each aubergine tightly in aluminium foil and keep cool until ready to serve.

This snack is ideal for picnics and Cézanne liked to eat it with pan bagnat *(see recipe p.135). It can also be served at home with boiled eggs and chopped tomatoes sprinkled with basil.*

BERLINGUETO
STUFFED EGGS

Serves 6

A solid, palm-sized ball of dry bread (taken from the soft part of a loaf); 2 tbsp light fish stock, milk, white wine or water; 5 anchovy fillets; 3 garlic cloves; 6 basil leaves; pinch ground pepper; 4 sprigs flat-leaf parsley; 2 tbsp olive oil; 6 hard-boiled eggs; 2 tbsp white breadcrumbs; salt.

Soak the bread in either fish stock, white wine, milk or water. Then squeeze out any excess liquid. Rinse the anchovy fillets if they are salted and pat them dry with absorbent kitchen paper.

Peel and chop the garlic. Put it into a mortar or large bowl with the basil leaves and bread and some coarsely ground black pepper, and pound into an aromatic paste. Cut the anchovies into pieces, making sure there are not too many bones. Continue to pound the paste, gradually adding the anchovies followed by the chopped parsley and a spoonful of oil (if the anchovies were preserved in oil, you could use this).

Peel the eggs and cut them in half lengthwise. Remove the yolks and blend them into the anchovy paste. Season to taste.

Arrange the twelve egg halves in a gratin dish. Before placing the eggs in the dish, cut 2mm/1/8in off the base of each half so that they stand firm in the dish.

Preheat the oven at 210°C (gas mark 7/ 425°F).

Fill the hollows of each egg half with the mixture to form a small dome. Sprinkle with breadcrumbs, pour a little oil over each one and cook 'au gratin' until crisp and golden.

Serve piping hot with a tomato sauce or purée (see recipe page 180).

To vary the recipe the egg halves may be placed on a bed of spinach or topped with a thin layer of béchamel sauce, turning this appetizer into a light main meal.

This dish was very popular in the Carpentras region. It is possible that its name originated from a type of dome-shaped boiled sweet called a berlingot, *made in the region.*

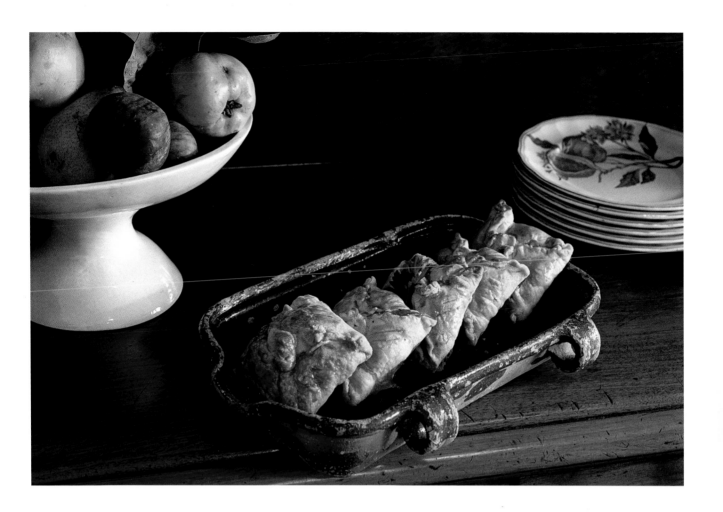

PETITS PATÉS CHAUDS
HOT SAVOURY PASTIES

Serves 6

600g/1 1/4lb shortcrust pastry; 200g / 7oz smoked ham; 200g / 7oz cooked chicken breast; 3 swiss chard leaves (the green part only) or an equivalent amount of spinach; 2 eggs; rum, eau-de-vie de marc (see p 137) or cognac; 1 pinch saffron powder; 2 pinches savory; salt and pepper; 100g / 4oz breadcrumbs; 1/2 lemon; 1 garlic clove; 150g / 5oz sausage meat; 1 tablespoon olive oil; 1 egg yolk.

Roll out the pastry into a square or rectangle. Cut out twelve 10cm/4in squares.

Dice the ham and chicken (turkey or pheasant may be used instead, but they have a stronger flavour). Chop the swiss chard or spinach. If you opt for the latter, young spinach should be used and the stalks removed before chopping. Beat the two eggs in a bowl together with the rum, marc or cognac then mix in the salt and pepper, savory, saffron powder and breadcrumbs. Grate the rind from the lemon into the mixture.

Peel and crush the garlic and mix together with the sausage meat and chopped ham and chicken. Add salt and pepper. Using your hands coated with a little oil, combine the meat with the egg mixture until smooth. Then mix in the greens, but with a lighter touch, followed by the lemon juice.

If you have time it would be worth carrying out a quick cooking test: take a small ball of the mixture, about the size of a hazelnut, flatten it and fry for a few minutes on either side. By doing this you can taste and adjust the seasoning accordingly.

Beat the egg yolk with a little water or milk. Lightly grease a baking sheet and preheat the oven to 210°C (gas mark 6-7, 400-425°C).

Divide the filling into twelve equal balls and place each ball in the centre of the pastry squares. Flatten a little and moisten the edges of the pastry. Then bring the four corners of the pastry square into the middle and seal the sides by pinching them together to form a little pasty. Leave a small opening at the point where the corners meet to allow steam to escape. Brush the top of each pasty with the egg yolk and place them onto the baking sheet.

Bake for 20 minutes then reduce the temperature to 150-180°C (gas mark 2-4, 300-350°F) and cook for a further 10 minutes. Turn off the oven and, with the door ajar, leave the pasties to stand for 5 minutes. Serve hot.

Puff pastry may be used instead of shortcrust. It is richer and perhaps more appropriate for Sundays or special occasions. Madame Brémond often dispensed with the pastry, wrapping the stuffing in cabbage leaves or in a crépine *(pig's caul) and cooking them au gratin . If Cézanne didn't take the little meat pasties with him on a painting excursion, she would serve them at table with a bowl of tomato sauce.*

BOUGNETTES DE BRANDADE
COD AND POTATO CROQUETTES

Left-over brandade or creamed salt-cod (see recipe p.143); potatoes (2 parts left-over brandade to 1 part potato purée); 1 egg per 200g / 7oz of mixed brandade and potato mixture; salt and pepper; flour; oil for frying.

Weigh the left-over *brandade* and decide how many eggs you will need for this amount plus half again of added potato purée. Weigh out the required amount of potatoes, peel and cook them well, then mash them. Beat the egg(s) and mix into the potatoes with salt and pepper, to make a creamy purée. Then blend together with the left-over *brandade*.

Sprinkle work surface and hands with flour. Take a portion of the mixture, roughly the size of an egg, and roll it into a ball between the palms of your hands. Place the ball onto the floured surface and flatten it to form a fish cake. Repeat until all the mixture has been used, adding flour to work surface and hands when necessary.

Heat the oil in a deep pan and fry over a moderate heat, turning occasionally, until crisp and golden.

Serve with tomato purée (see recipe p. 180), a fennel sauce (white roux sauce with added butter, lemon juice and blanched chopped fennel) or green herb mayonnaise. Alternatively, serve with *raïto* (see recipe p.181) and a *mesclun* salad: a salad traditionally made from young shoots which grow wild in the South of France. Most commonly used leaves are rocket, chicory, curly endives, lambs' lettuce, but groundsel, dandelion leaves and chervil may also be added. Serve with vinaigrette.

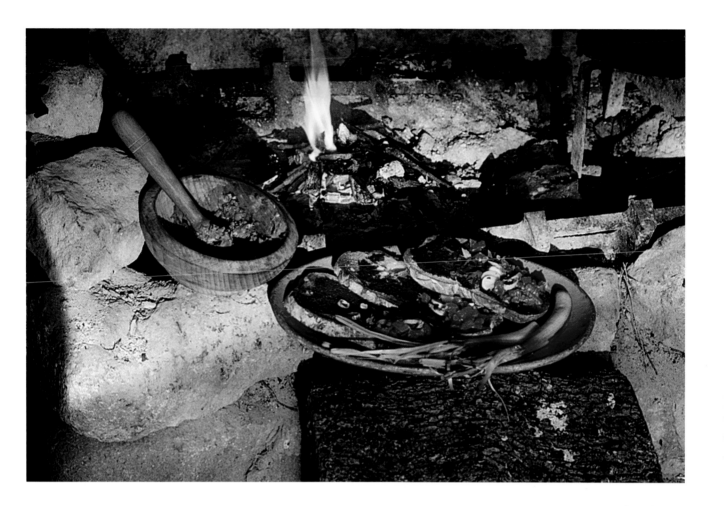

TARTINES FRITES AU ANCHOIS
FRIED ANCHOVY BREAD

Serves 6

1 baguette or French loaf; milk; olive oil for frying;

2 tbsp tomato purée (see recipe p.180); 200g / 7oz

anchovy spread (see recipe p.182).

Cut the French loaf into twelve slices approximately 1.5cm / 3/4in thick. Soak the slices in milk for a few minutes on either side. Place them over a grillpan or wire cooling tray to drain off the excess liquid. Then use absorbent kitchen paper to pat them dry.

Heat the oil in a skillet or sauté pan and fry the bread on each side until golden brown.

Remove them with a slotted spoon, placing them on absorbent paper to soak up excess oil.

While they are still hot, use a spatula to spread each slice with a thin layer of tomato purée followed by a layer of anchovy spread. Serve immediately.

This snack can of course be varied, by using other ingredients to spread over the fried bread slices, such as grilled peppers in olive oil, garlic mayonnaise or chopped garlic with a sprinkling of basil or parsley, or leftover boumiano *(see recipe p.162), etc.*
The above photo features a mortar containing the ingredients of an anchoïade *(see recipe p.182) and the slices of toast are spread with a tapenade of crushed tomatoes, chopped basil and garlic.*

Fish

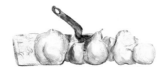

AÏGO-SAÙ
PROVENÇAL FISH SOUP

Serves 6

**1.5kg / 3lb white fish; 1 large leek; 6 large
potatoes (choose a floury but firm variety); 2 garlic
cloves; 1 large onion; 2 tbsp olive oil; 1 celery stick;
1 fennel bulb; 2 tomatoes or 1 tbsp tomato purée
(see recipe p.180); bouquet garni (1 bay leaf; 1
sprig parsley, 1 sprig thyme, 1 sliver dried orange
peel (optional)); coarse salt and black pepper; 1
bowl rouille (see recipe p.183); grated cheese.**

Any type of white fish may be used for this
dish, as long as it is fresh - whiting, gurnard,
conger eel, scorpion fish, wrasse are all suitable and
rainbow wrasse is particularly good. Gut and rinse
the fish, cutting each into three pieces, without
removing the heads which are full of flavour.

Peel the leek, putting the dark green top
leaves to one side for the bouquet garni. Slice and
wash to remove all traces of dirt and grit. Remove
from the water and pat dry. Peel, wash and dry the
potatoes, then cut into chunks. Peel and crush the
garlic. Peel and finely chop the onion.

Heat the oil in a large pan. Toss in the
onions and cook until translucent. Add the leek
and potatoes and stir fry for 10 minutes, reducing
the heat if they are browning too quickly.

Meanwhile, wash and slice the celery into
rounds and cut the fennel bulb into six. Wash and
quarter the tomatoes, squeezing each piece gently
to remove the watery seeds. Make a bouquet garni
by tying together the parsley, thyme, bay leaf, the
dark green leek leaves you have put to one side and
the orange peel if desired.

Push the vegetables to the edge of the pan
and place the fish pieces in the centre. Brown for
3 minutes on each side. Add the celery on top of
the fish followed by the fennel and the garlic.
Using a spatula, move the fish pieces gently
around the pan so that the vegatables slip in
between them. Then add the tomatoes and the
tomato purée, and turn the heat up high. Add 1
1/2 litres (3 pints) water, salt and pepper and the
bouquet garni. Cover the pan three quarters over
with a lid and bring to the boil.

Reduce the heat and cover almost
completely again. Simmer for 10 minutes. (This
may be extended to 15 minutes if you don't
object to the fish fragmenting).

Remove the fish pieces and place into
individual heated bowls. Pour the soup into a
heated tureen, discarding the bouquet garni, and
ladle over the fish. Place a dish of grated cheese
and a dish of *rouille* between each place setting,
to garnish the soup if desired.

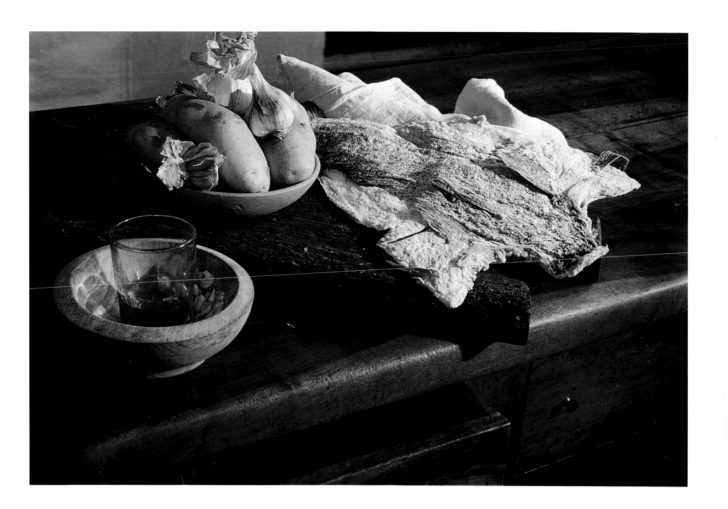

BRANDADE DE MORUE
CREAMED SALT COD

Serves 6

**600g/1 1/4lb salt cod fillets; 1/2 litre/1 pint boiled
milk; 1/2 litre/1 pint olive oil; pinch grated nutmeg;
freshly ground white pepper; 1 unwaxed lemon.**
For the stock:
**1 bouquet garni (1 bay leaf, 1 sprig parsley and
thyme); 1 sprig fennel; 2 garlic cloves; ground
pepper.**

Soak the fish overnight in cold water to remove the salt. The water should be changed a few times, making sure to lift the fish when replacing fresh water, otherwise the salt which collects at the bottom of the dish will remain trapped under the fish. Twelve hours should be sufficient time, but taste the fish before straining to make sure it is properly desalinated.

Prepare an aromatic stock by boiling the bouquet garni, fennel sprig, peeled garlic and pepper together in unsalted water. Leave to cool.

Put the fish into the saucepan containing the cold stock. Place uncovered over a low heat and simmer gently. The stock should not be brought to a boil as this will make the fish tough.

Remove from the heat and cover. Leave to poach for 10 minutes.

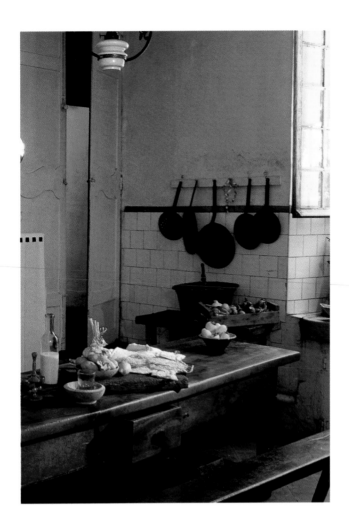

the fish vigorously with a wooden spoon, adding alternately one tablespoon of oil and one of milk until both liquids have been well incorporated into the fish. The alternation of the warmed milk and oil and energetic beating or 'gangassage' are essential in the making of a perfect brandade which should be rich, smooth and creamy in texture. Season with salt and pepper, add a little grated nutmeg and the lemon juice and peel.

Serve the *brandade* piping hot with boiled potatoes cooked in their skins, and croutons which have been rubbed with garlic and thyme or 'farigoulette'.

The locals have another name for this dish: gangasso *which literally means 'to stir'. But if you prefer to adopt more modern methods of preparation a mixer may be used instead of hand beating with a wooden spoon. For a richer* brandade, *the milk can be substituted with single cream.*

If you have any leftovers, they can be used for croquettes *(see recipe p.140), added to a savoury flan or fried in a pan with some eggs.*

Meanwhile, wash and dry the lemon. Grate the rind and squeeze the juice of one half into a cup.

Once poached, remove the fish from the stock and place it on absorbent kitchen paper to soak up excess liquid. Remove the skin and bones. Take the two garlic cloves from the stock and squeeze out the flesh, which has become creamy during cooking. Pound the garlic and fish together in a mortar until blended. Smear a little oil onto the bottom of a large stainless steel pan and add the pounded fish. Pour the milk and oil into two separate, small pans.

Place all three pans over a low heat. Beat

"AURADE "À LA PROVENÇALE
SEA BREAM PROVENÇAL

Serves 6

**1 sea bream (approximately 1.7kg / 3 1/2 lb);
1/2 bunch flat-leaf parsley; 4 fresh fennel stalks; 2
lemons; 1 fennel bulb; 3 courgettes; 3 tomatoes; 2
sweet onions; 3 garlic cloves; 1/2 wine glass olive
oil; 1 wine glass dry white wine; 1 spray basil
(large leaves); 100g / 4oz black olives, pitted; salt
and freshly ground pepper.**

Clean and scale the fish or ask your
fishmonger to prepare it for you. Make sure the
insides are nice and dry, then season and fill with
the parsley stalks (keeping the leaves for the
sauce), chopped fennel stalks and one half of a
lemon thinly sliced.

Lightly grease a large baking dish (choose
one which is also flameproof). Thinly slice the
rest of the lemons, the fennel bulb, the washed
unpeeled courgette, washed tomatoes and peeled
onions. Arrange them in the baking dish in
alternate rows.

Peel and crush the garlic and finely chop
the parsley leaves. Sprinkle a little of each over
the vegetables in the baking dish and partially
cook over a low heat. You could begin to cook the
fish at the same time, but it may cook more
quickly than the vegetables. It is safer to pre-cook
the vegetables for approximately 10 minutes.
This will soften them and will give juices the fish
can cook in.

Preheat the oven to 210°C (gas mark 6-7,
410°F)

Place the fish on the bed of vegetables and
sprinkle with the remaining garlic and parsley.
Pour the oil and white wine over the top. Add
salt and pepper and bake in the oven. Baste at

regular intervals and 15 minutes into the cooking
time, reduce the oven temperature to 180°C (gas
mark 4, 350°F). After a further 10 minutes,
sprinkle the fish with the basil leaves and olives,
baste again and reduce the temperature to 150°C
(gas mark 2, 300°F). Cook for 10 more minutes
then serve immediately, straight from the baking
dish.

Daurade *or sea bream was considered a
speciality and was often prepared in this way for
special occasions, accompanied with toasted bread spread
with* ailloli *(see recipe p.181) - or* 'oursinade' -
ailloli *mixed with a little fish stock and dressed up
with* 'laugnes' *which are Mediterranean sea urchins.*

Meat, Poultry and Game

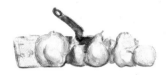

CARBOUNADO
BRAISED MUTTON

Serves 6

2 garlic cloves; 2 1 1/2cm/ 2/3in slices of mutton (350g/12oz), taken from the leg; 1 small sprig rosemary; 150g / 5oz salted bacon; 1 bunch spring onions; 4 new turnips; 3 baby carrots; 3 or 4 swiss chard leaves; 3 celery sticks; 4 large tomatoes or 2 tbsp tomato purée (see recipe p.180); olive oil; 1 pinch grated nutmeg; salt and pepper; 2 wine glasses dry white wine.

For the accompaniment:

2 young globe artichokes; 1 lemon; 1 kg / 2lb fresh, shelled white haricot beans (dried or canned can be used); 1 bouquet garni (1 bay leaf, 1 sprig parsley, 1 sprig thyme); 1 garlic clove.

Peel and thinly slice the garlic and distribute over the upper side of one of the mutton slices. Sprinkle over with rosemary leaves, then put the other slice of mutton on top. Leave to stand in an oiled platter.

Dice the bacon. Peel, wash and dry all the vegetables. Leave the spring onions whole, quarter the turnips and cut the carrots into four. Remove the stringy threads from the celery sticks and swiss chard leaves, then chop them up. If you are not using purée, quarter the tomatoes, squeeze out the watery seeds and place them face down so that the excess juice drips away.

Grease the base of a large, heavy-bottomed pan with olive oil. Place over a high heat and when the oil is hot enough, throw in the bacon and stir until it begins to brown. Using a slotted spoon, transfer the bacon onto a plate. Then add the two mutton slices, unseasoned sides down. Cook for three minutes, then turn them over, reducing the heat immediately so that the rosemary does not burn. Put the bacon back into the pan and wait a further 3 to 4 minutes before adding all the vegetables, except for the onions and tomatoes. Turn the mutton slices once again, using a spatula or two wooden spoons, taking care not to pierce the meat. Some of the bacon and vegetables will work their way under the meat slices and brown. Cook for 7 to 8 minutes then add the onions and tomatoes (or the tomato purée) and a dash more oil. Stir all the contents together for a few more minutes then pour in the wine. Season with the nutmeg, pepper and a little salt (not much is needed as the bacon is already salty). Cover tightly. If the lid of your pan or casserole contains a reservoir for water, make sure it is always full. If you have an ordinary lid, soak a thick cloth in water and place it on top. Reduce the heat and simmer for 1 3/4 to 2 hours.

While the stew is simmering, you have plenty of time to prepare the vegetable side dishes.

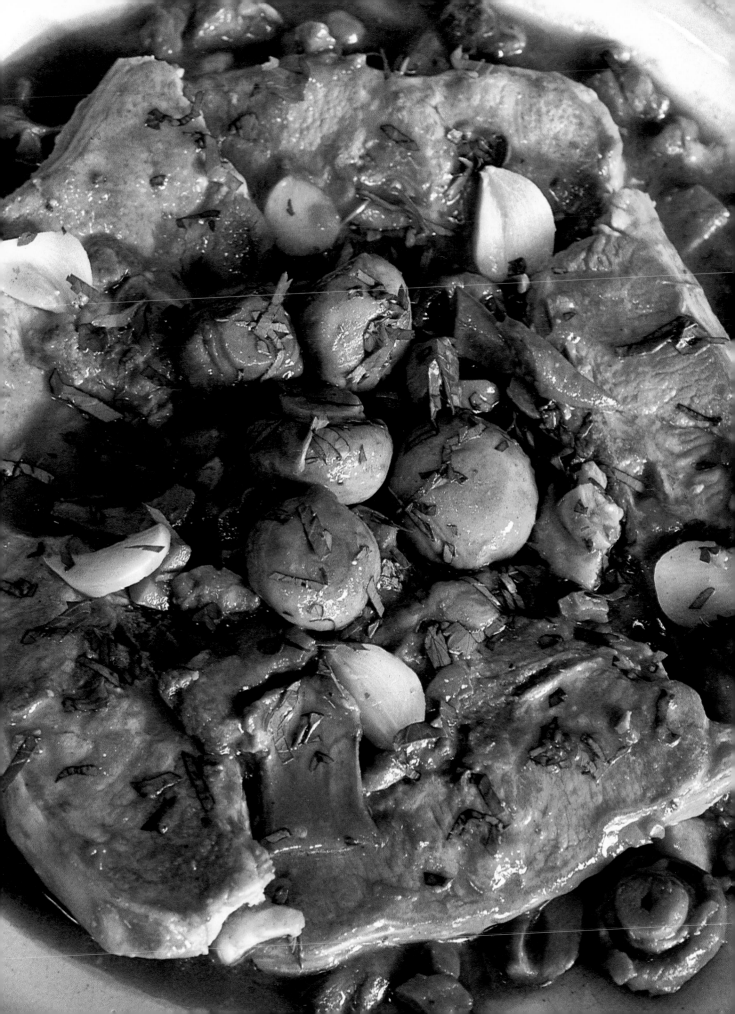

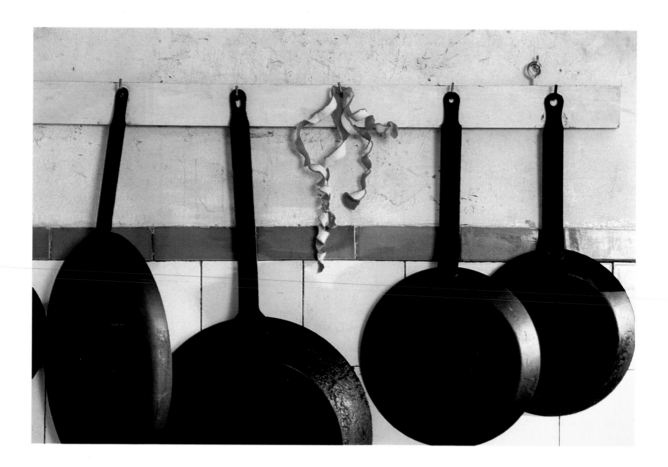

Remove the outer leaves from the artichokes, cut off the hard leaf tips and the stalk. Cook the artichokes in a water for about 20-25 minutes with a little oil, lemon juice and salt and pepper. The fresh haricot beans should be boiled in water with garlic and a bouquet garni.

Serve the *carbounado* straight from the pan. There should only be a little liquid left, which should be dark in colour and full of flavour. Serve with the drained artichokes and haricot beans.

Carbounado *is a traditional dish, venerated by the great French poet Mistral who often served it at his table. Its name is derived from the word 'carbonise', because the juices often stick to the pan, becoming a lovely dark brown meaty concentrate, which gives this dish its particular flavour.*

PINTADEAU FARCI AUX CHAMPIGNONS STUFFED GUINEA FOWL WITH MUSHROOMS

Serves 6

150g / 5oz wild mushrooms (ceps); juice of 1/2 lemon; bouquet garni (4 parsley sprigs, sliver of lemon peel); 1 leek; a handful of the soft inside of a loaf of bread; 2 tbsp milk; salt and freshly ground pepper; 3 juniper berries; 150g / 5oz sausage meat; 1 garlic clove; 2 young guinea-fowl or 1 large guinea-fowl, with livers; 2 tbsp olive oil.

Clean the mushrooms with a damp tea towel. Separate the heads and slice into thin strips.

Cut away the earthy part of the stalk and chop the rest. Douse the mushrooms with the lemon juice.

Separate the parsley stalks from the leaves and tie them up with the leek's top leaves and a piece of lemon peel to make a bouquet garni.

Crumble the bread into a mixing bowl and pour in the milk. Add the salt and pepper, crushed juniper berries, sausage meat and then garlic, finely chopped. Mix all the ingredients together carefully and leave to one side.

Cut the leek into slices about 2cm/1in thick. Pour one tablespoon of oil into a casserole, large enough to hold the bird(s). Place over a medium heat and add the leek. Cook until lightly golden then transfer to a plate with a slotted spoon. Next brown the liver(s) for about 4 minutes, adding salt and pepper towards the end. Remove them onto a chopping board and when cooled, chop them up and add them with the leeks, to the bread and sausage meat mixture. Stuff the inside of the bird with the mixture and sew up the opening. Once stuffed, the guinea-fowl can be kept in a cool place overnight.

Preheat the oven to 210-240°C (gas mark 7-9, 425-475°F). About an hour before the meal, pour the rest of the oil into the casserole and place over a reasonably high heat. Brown the guinea-fowl on all sides. Season with salt and pepper. When nicely browned, add the bouquet garni and place the casserole in the oven for 40 minutes if you are cooking the young guinea-fowl and 50 minutes for a larger bird. Baste with the cooking juices at regular intervals.

15 minutes before the cooking time is up, add the mushrooms. If desired, they can be replaced by young onions, fennel bulbs, celery hearts or sour apples. Lower the temperature to 180°C (gas mark 4, 350°F) until cooked. Serve immediately.

BLANQUETTE DE VEAU À L'AIXOISE
BRAISED VEAL (AIX STYLE)

Serves 6

1kg / 2lb knuckle of veal; 1 onion; 1 leek; 2 garlic cloves; 2 tomatoes or 4 tbsp tomato purée (see recipe p.180); 3 tbsp olive oil; 1 tsp flour; 1 bouquet garni (1 bay leaf, 1 sprig parsley and thyme); 1 sprig savory; 1/2 sprig rosemary; 1 fennel stalk; 1 sprig basil; salt and pepper; 2 wine glasses dry white wine; 2 wine glasses water; 2 tbsp bitter olives; 500g / 1lb celery hearts.

Cut the meat into 3cm / 1in cubes. Peel and finely chop the onion. Wash and slice the leek. Peel and crush the garlic. Wash and cut the tomatoes into quarters, squeezing each piece gently to remove watery seeds.

Pour the oil into a large pan and place over a medium heat. Toss the cubes of meat into the oil and brown on all sides. Add the onion and leek and stir. Leave to cook for 5 minutes then sprinkle with the flour (preferably using a flour dredger). Stir and leave to cook for a few minutes more. Then add the garlic, tomatoes, bouquet garni, herbs and salt and pepper. Pour in the white wine and the same amount of water. Cover and simmer over a gentle heat for a maximum time of 45 minutes.

Add the olives and replace the lid. Peel, wash and dry the celery hearts and add them to the stew. Cook for a further 20 minutes. Remove the bouquet garni and serve.

This dish may be served directly from the pan or casserole dish.

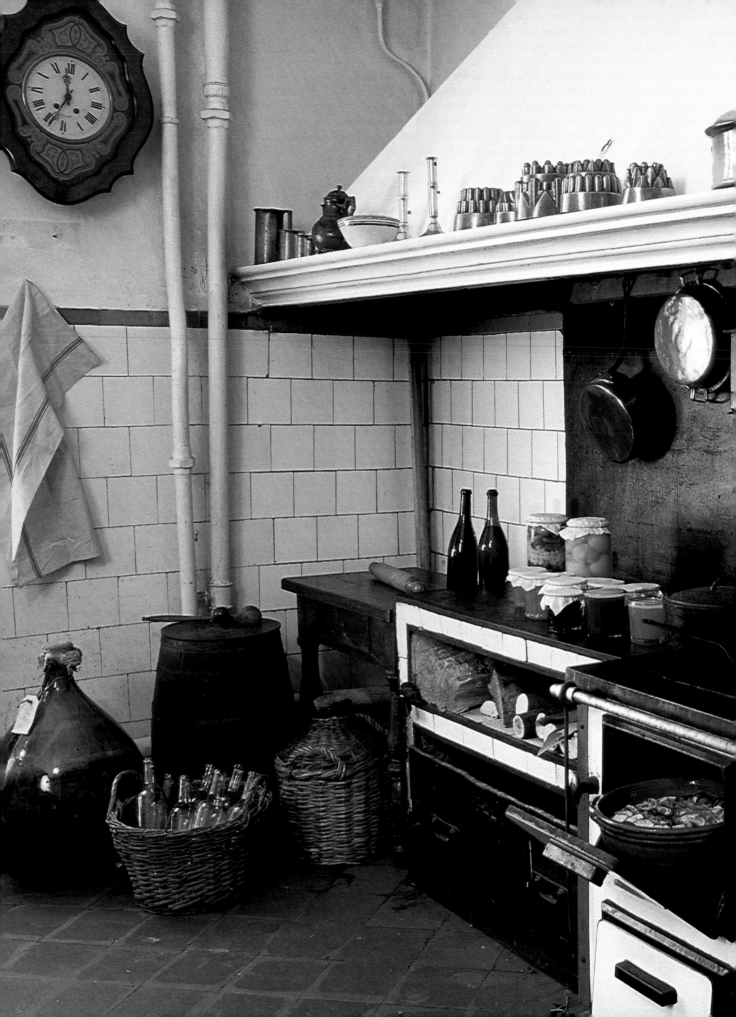

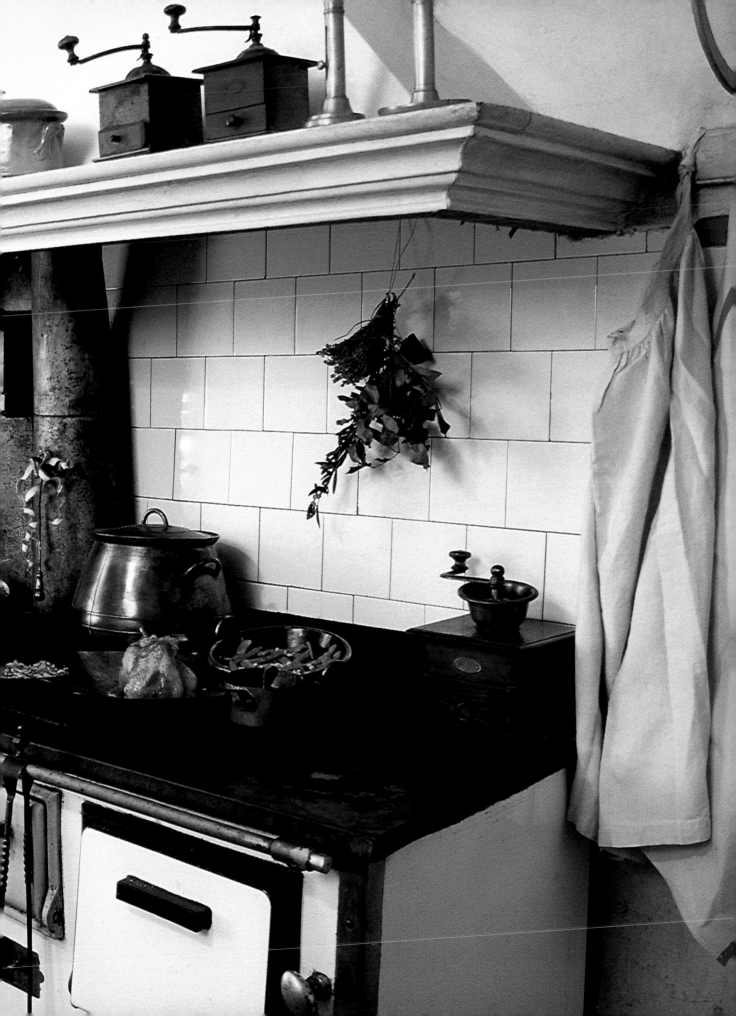

FASSUM
STUFFED CABBAGE

Serves 6

1 green cabbage; 1 bunch parsley; 75g / 2 1/2oz raisins; 1 large garlic clove; 1 red onion; salt and freshly ground pepper; 200g / 7oz bacon; 150g / 5oz pork liver; 1 ball, the size of an orange, stale bread (taken from the soft middle of a loaf); 1 tsp olive oil.

For the cooking stock:

1 carrot; 1 leek; 1 celery stick; 1 garlic clove; bouquet garni (1 bay leaf, 1 sprig thyme, 1 sprig rosemary, 3 or 4 juniper berries); rock salt; black peppercorns.

Remove the hard and damaged outer leaves of the cabbage. Wash the cabbage by dipping it in cold water with vinegar. Blanch for 10 minutes in salted water, then strain. Rinse once more under cold running water and strain again. Leave the cabbage, head down in the colander to make sure all excess water drips out.

Meanwhile, prepare the stuffing. Remove the stalks from the parsley, reserving them for the bouquet garni, and finely chop the leaves. Rinse and dry the raisins. Peel and chop the garlic and onion very finely. Place all these ingredients in a bowl with a little salt (not too much as the bacon is already salty) and freshly ground black pepper.

Remove the rind from the bacon (but do not discard), cut into small pieces and put through a meat-mincer with the pork liver and lastly the bread, which will help extract any meat left in the mincer. Mix together with the ingredients in the bowl and leave to stand.

Take the cabbage and pull back the outer leaves to remove the heart, which should be about the size of a grapefruit. Chop the heart quite

finely and, with the oil, add to the rest of the ingredients in the bowl. Mix all together carefully, then fry a small ball of the stuffing to test whether the seasoning needs adjusting.

Place the cabbage onto a piece of muslin spread over a dry tea towel (in Provence, a piece of old net curtain was often used). Pull back each leaf, without detaching from the stalk, and insert a generous spoonful of stuffing between the leaves, filling the centre of the cabbage where the heart was with the rest. Close the leaves over the stuffing and wrap the cabbage in the muslin, tying it together at the top.

Wash and peel the stock vegetables and place them in a pan, just deep and large enough (but not too large) to fit the cabbage. Add the bacon rind, garlic, bouquet garni (made from a bay leaf, a sprig of thyme, the parsley stalks, the dark green leaves from the leek and the rosemary sprig all tied together around the juniper berries). Add salt and pepper.

Lastly, put the stuffed cabbage on top and pour over with enough boiling water or light chicken stock (see receipe p.184) so that it is completely submerged. Cover with a lid and bring to the boil over a medium heat. Reduce the heat to a minimum and skim the surface until the liquid is clear. Simmer gently for two hours.

Remove the cabbage from the stock and strain well. Cut away the muslin bag and slice. Serve with vinaigrette or green herb mayonnaise. *Fassum* may also be served cold as a starter, accompanied with *ailloli* (see recipe p.181).

The stock can be kept and makes a very good soup if you blend in the vegetables and discard the bouquet garni and bacon rind. You could even add 'pastina' or small pasta, as Madame Brémond did, such as vermicelli or cappellini.

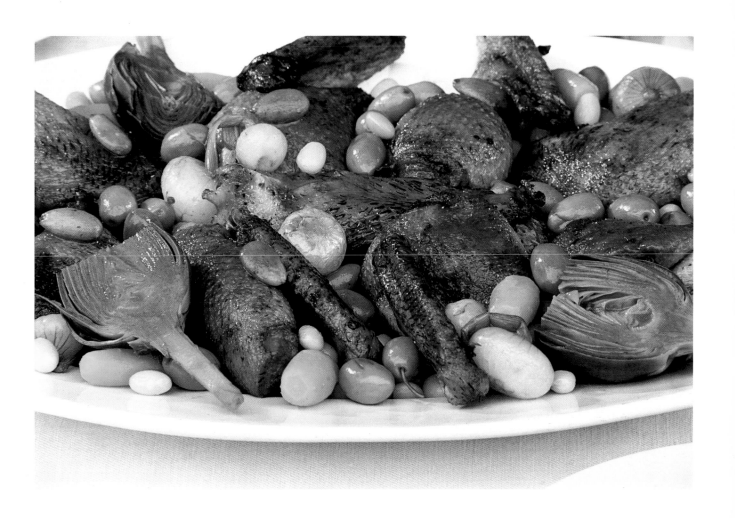

CANARD AUX OLIVES ET AUX CAROTTES
DUCK WITH OLIVES AND CARROTS

Serves 6

1 duck (2kg / 4 1/2lb); 100g / 4oz smoked or Parma ham; 1 bunch small onions; 6 carrots; 1 tbsp olive oil; 2 garlic cloves; 10cl / 3 1/2 fl oz Banyuls (strong sweet red wine) or dessert wine; 250ml / 8 fl oz chicken stock; 1 liqueur glass brandy; 150g / 5oz green olives, pitted; salt and freshly ground pepper.

Cut the duck into pieces and, if it is fatty, cut off the excess fat to use for cooking instead of the oil. Cut the ham into strips. Peel the onions, leaving them whole with a little of the stalk. Peel and slice the carrots.

Melt the duck fat or heat the olive oil in a casserole over a low heat, and brown the duck pieces on all sides. Remove from the casserole and replace with the carrots. Cook for 5 minutes, then add the onions. When golden, remove with a slotted spoon. (If you have used fat from the duck, you can empty it into a bowl and conserve it in the fridge to use at a later date for frying). Put the pan back over a low heat and replace the onions and carrots. Add the ham and garlic, peeled but left whole, and then add the duck. Cook for a few minutes before adding the wine and stock. Leave on the heat until it begins to bubble gently.

Preheat the oven at 180°C (gas mark 4, 350°F). Heat the brandy and arrange the duck pieces on top of the vegetables in the casserole. Keep a box of matches ready. Pour the hot brandy over the duck pieces, and then light to flambé the meat. When the flames die down, season to taste, not forgetting that the olives and bacon are already salty.

Cover the casserole tightly with a lid (to seal the casserole properly you can soak a cloth in flour and water and wrap it around the lid), and cook in the oven for one and a half hours. Half

way through the cooking time, check the level of the liquid and add a little hot stock if necessary. About ten minutes before the duck is cooked remove the lid and add the olives. Reduce the temperature to 150°C (gas mark 2, 300°F), replace the lid and cook until done. Switch off the oven, but do not remove the casserole. Leave it to stand for 10 minutes then transfer to a heated dish.

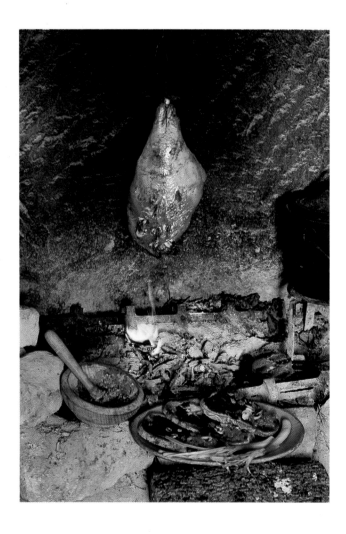

Gigot d'Agneau à l'ail et aux petits oignons
Lamb Cooked in Garlic and Onions

Serves 6

1 fresh bay leaf; 3 garlic cloves; 2kg / 4lb leg of lamb; 2 tbsp olive oil; 1 1/2kg / 3lb small onions; 2 large tomatoes; 1 pinch sugar; 2 wine glasses white wine (preferably from the Provence region); 1/2 litre / 1 pint chicken stock (see recipe p184); salt and freshly ground pepper.

Break the bay leaf into small pieces. Peel the garlic, leaving two of the cloves whole and crushing the third, in a mortar, with some rock salt. Remove the outer fat from the lamb as this improves the cooking. Rub the creamed garlic into the lamb.

Preheat the oven at 240°C (gas mark 9, 475°F). Place the lamb onto a large, flat, ovenproof dish and baste with a tablespoon of oil. Sprinkle the bayleaf pieces on top and cook in the oven for 20 minutes.

Peel and chop the onions. Wash and quarter the tomatoes. Squeeze each quarter gently to remove watery seeds.

Remove the lamb from the oven and place it onto a large dish. Spread the onions onto the baking tray, pouring half the remaining oil over them. Sprinkle with sugar and put the baking tray back into the oven for 5 minutes until the onions are golden brown. Remove the tray from the oven once more. Push the onions to the sides and place the lamb joint back in the centre of the tray. Reduce the oven temperature to 230°C (gas mark 8, 450°F) and cook for a further 15 minutes, basting with the cooking juices two or three times, until the onions are nice and soft. Then remove from the oven.

Heat the white wine in a saucepan without bringing to the boil. Add the tomato pieces and the two uncrushed garlic cloves to the onions on the baking tray and pour the white wine over the meat and vegetables. Then turn the leg of lamb over and return to the oven. Cook the lamb for a further 10 minutes.

Meanwhile heat the chicken stock. Pour some of the heated stock evenly around the leg and pour the rest over the lamb itself. Return to the oven to braise for a further 40 minutes (adding freshly ground pepper after 15 minutes) turning the lamb and basting it regularly, to obtain a glaze. If you notice the upper side of the lamb becoming too dark, cover with aluminium foil and add a little more stock to obtain a nice, thick gravy.

Turn the oven off, but do not remove the meat. It should be left to stand for at least 10 minutes before carving. Slice the lamb and arrange the pieces on a warmed dish, surrounding the meat with the onion and tomato sauce.

Madame Brémond was always careful in selecting a good leg of lamb, making sure it had an abundant layer of white fat and checking that the flesh was light pink in colour. She would of course remove all excess fat from the lamb given Cézanne's dietary restrictions. Though she would then use the melted fat from the roasting pan, which had absorbed flavour from the vegetables, to sprinkle over gratinated potatoes, macaroni or salsify.

NOUGAT DE BŒUF
BEEF STEW

Serves 6

1 calf's foot; 1 oxtail; 1kg / 2lb topside of beef; 1kg / 2lb chuck steak; 600g / 1 1/4lb flank or brisket; 200g / 7oz diced streaky bacon; bacon rind (enough to cover the bottom of your casserole dish); 4 onions, each studded with 2 cloves; 2 carrots; 3 leeks; 5 garlic cloves; 1 piece dried orange peel; 1 tbsp tomato purée (see recipe p180) or two large ripe tomatoes; 2 tbsp capers; 1 tbsp peppercorns; 1 bouquet garni (1 bay leaf, sprig thyme and parsley); 1 bottle red wine (preferably Corsican); 1/2 liqueur glass brandy; 1 wine glass red wine vinegar; 1/2 wine glass olive oil; 3 anchovy fillets; salt.

It is essential to use a variety of meat cuts for this recipe. Your butcher should be able to provide you with a good selection of lean and fatty, tender and muscly cuts. It is this variety which gives the casserole it's rich flavour and special consistency.

Split the calf's foot in two and cut the oxtail into six or eight pieces. Cut the meat into 80g-100g/3-4oz chunks and slice the bacon. Take a large pan and cover the bottom with the bacon rind, the fat facing down. The rind will prevent the meat from sticking to the bottom of the casserole and gives the sauce a creamy texture.

Peel and chop the onions and other vegetables. Peel the garlic, leaving the cloves whole and crush them using the flat of a knife blade. Cut the orange peel into small pieces. Mix the garlic and orange peel with the tomato purée, 1 tbsp capers and the peppercorns. Mix the spice mixture and vegetables together.

Spread a layer of this vegetable and spice mixture over the bacon rind and top with a layer of meat and the bouquet garni, followed by another layer of the vegetable and spice mixture and so on until all ingredients are in the pan. Pour the wine, brandy, vinegar and oil over the top. Cover and leave in the fridge to marinate overnight.

The next day, place the covered pan over a medium heat. Bring to the boil, then reduce to a simmer. Place a heat diffuser under the pan, making sure it is tightly covered, and simmer for four hours without removing the lid.

Crush the anchovies in a mortar with some of the cooking juices and stir them into the stew 20 minutes before it has finished cooking. Once the cooking time has elapsed, check the level of the liquid. Not much is needed but there should be enough left for the *macaronade* (see recipe p.168) which is the ideal accompaniment to this dish. If more liquid is needed, then add some hot, lightly salted stock (not wine). Sprinkle the stew with the remaining capers just before serving with the *macaronade* which can be prepared while the stew is simmering.

ÉPAULE D'AGNEAU FARCIE
STUFFED SHOULDER OF LAMB

1 shoulder of lamb; 1 bouquet garni (1 sprig savory, 1 sprig thyme and 1 sprig rosemary); 1 glass white wine; salt and coarsely ground black pepper.
For the stuffing:
1 sweet onion; 1 garlic clove; 3 swiss chard leaves; 3 tbsp olive oil; 4 sprigs flat-leaf parsley; 1 egg; salt; 1 thick slice raw ham; 1 slice stale bread, crusts removed; 1/2 wine glass dry white wine; 150g / 5oz lean minced pork; 8 black peppercorns; 5 juniper berries; 1 unwaxed lemon; 100g / 4oz green olives.

Ask your butcher to bone the shoulder and trim the fat from the meat so it can be easily rolled. Keep the bones.

To make the stuffing, peel and chop the onions finely and peel and crush the garlic. Wash and cut the swiss chard leaves into strips. Heat a spoonful of oil in a pan, then add the onions and cook them over a low heat until soft. When the onions are translucent, add the garlic. Cook for one minute, then cover with the swiss chard strips. Mix together with the onion and garlic, then cover the pan, remove from the heat and leave to cool at room temperature.

Finely chop the parsley and beat together with the egg and a little salt (not too much as the bacon and olives are already quite salty). Dice the ham into small cubes. Soak the bread in the white wine and add to the beaten egg and parsley with the diced ham, minced pork, pepper and juniper berries. Mix all these ingredients together well.

Once the mixture in the pan has cooled, stir and incorporate with the rest of the mixed ingredients. Wash the lemon and grate a little of the rind into the mixture. Stone the olives.

Preheat the oven at 210°C (gas mark 7, 425°F). Lay the shoulder of lamb out on your work surface, with the opening facing you. Spread the stuffing over the meat and sprinkle the olives on top. Roll up the meat and sew together with trussing string to form a neat shape which resembles the shoulder before it was boned.

Smear oil onto a baking dish roughly the size of the lamb shoulder and place the meat on it. Baste with oil and sprinkle with salt, pepper and herbs. Squeeze some lemon juice over the top. Add the bones to the dish (this will give flavour to the sauce). Cook for 10 minutes then turn the meat over and splash with white wine. Cook for 1 1/2 hours - or 1 3/4 hours if you prefer the lamb well done - turning the meat over twice and basting at regular intervals.

Turn the oven off and leave the meat to stand, with the oven door slightly open, for a further 15 minutes. This will make carving easier.

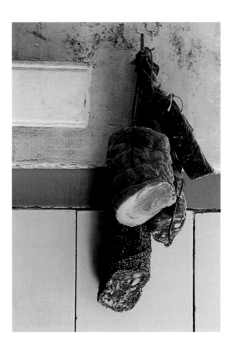

If you have any left over lamb, it can be served cold in slices with a *mesclun* salad (see recipe p.140).

ADOBO DE JARRET DE PORC
ROAST PORK

Serves 6

1 leg of pork; 1 large carrot; 1 onion studded with a clove; 1 garlic clove; 2 tbsp tomato purée (see recipe p.180); 1 large piece bacon rind; 1 tbsp olive oil; salt and pepper; 1 kg / 2lb shelled broad beans; 2 leeks, white part.

For the marinade :

1 garlic clove; 1 carrot; dark green top leaves of 2 leeks; bouquet garni (1 bay leaf, 1 sprig sage, 1 sprig parsley, 1 sprig thyme); peppercorns; 1 bottle white wine (preferably from Provence); 1 tsp olive oil; 1 wine glass chicken stock (see recipe p.184).

To make the marinade, peel and crush the garlic, grate the carrot, tie the dark green leek leaves together with the sage, bay leaf, thyme and parsley to make the bouquet garni and place all together in a large terrine with the peppercorns (but no salt), the wine and olive oil. Put the leg of pork into the terrine and if there is not enough liquid to cover it completely, top up with chicken stock. Cover with kitchen film and marinate overnight in a cool place.

Transfer the meat to a colander to strain. Peel the carrot and onion, leaving them whole for the time being. Peel and chop the garlic. Pat the meat dry with a clean cloth. Make small cuts into the meat and insert garlic pieces. Preheat the oven to 210°C (gas mark 6-7, 400-425°F).

Pour the oil into a large, heavy-bottomed pan, which has a tightly fitting lid. Place over a medium high heat and brown the pork evenly on all sides. When the pork begins to brown add the whole onion. This should caramelize and its flavour will penetrate the meat. Pour the marinade into the pan and as soon as it reaches boiling point, reduce the heat and add the tomato purée, carrot and bacon rind. Cover and cook in the oven for 2 hours. Lower the oven temperature to 180°C (gas mark 4, 350°F) , turn the meat over, replace the lid and cook for a further 30 minutes.

Wash, soak and slice the white of the leeks and add to the casserole. Add the broad beans 10 minutes later. Cover and cook for a further 8 to 10 minutes.

Serve the vegetables in a large heated dish with some of the sauce (the bouquet garni, bacon rind and the clove, if you can find it, should be discarded). Remove the bones, cut up the meat and serve with the rest of the gravy.

You could ask your butcher to bone and roll the leg of pork if you prefer a roast served in even slices. In this case, keep the bone and add it to the casserole during cooking for flavour.

LAPIN EN PAQUETS
RABBIT PARCELS

1 large rabbit, preferably wild; 1 small bunch fresh thyme; 1 sprig rosemary; 1 sprig savory; 2 pig membranes or cauls (see page 137); 2 garlic cloves; 1/2 tsp grated nutmeg; 2 wine glasses olive oil; 5 medium tomatoes; salt and freshly ground pepper.

Joint the rabbit into six pieces: two thighs, two front legs including the ribs, the saddle cut in two along either side of the back bone. You can ask your butcher to do this for you. Keep the rest of the carcass and back bone to make a stock later on.

Pick the leaves off the herb stalks, keeping the latter to one side for the stock.

Rinse the cauls. (If they were conserved in brine, soak them for 20 minutes in warm water.) Dry them carefully and divide each one into three squares. Each square should be large enough to wrap around one of the rabbit pieces.

Peel and crush the garlic cloves with salt

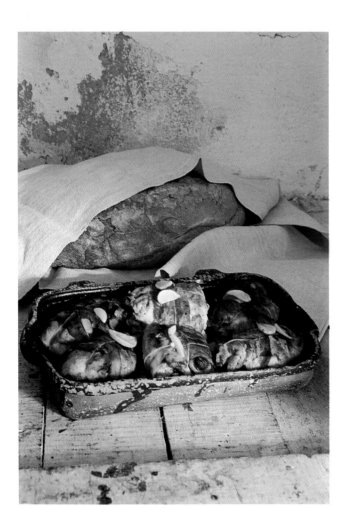

and mix with some freshly ground pepper and the nutmeg. Place the garlic mixture into a bowl and blend with the lightly chopped herbs. Pour the olive oil into another bowl.

Spread the six membrane squares over your work surface. Dip each rabbit piece into the oil and then coat with the spiced garlic and herb mixture. Wrap each piece of rabbit in it's membrane square and leave to cool. The rabbit parcels are now ready for cooking.

Wash and slice the tomatoes and remove the seeds. Heat the remaining oil in a frying pan and gently brown the tomatoes for 2 minutes on either side. Add salt and pepper as you turn them, using a spatula so that they do not break. Transfer them to a baking dish using a slotted spoon, arranging them carefully side by side.

Preheat the oven at 210°C (gas mark 7, 425°F). Place the rabbit parcels on top of the tomatoes and sprinkle over with oil or some stock. If you prefer the latter, then it should be prepared in advance by boiling the bones in water with a bouquet garni until reduced to a creamy liquid.

Cook the rabbit parcels for 20 minutes, basting frequently with the cooking juices. Turn each parcel over and reduce the oven temperature to 180°C (gas mark 4, 350°F). Cover with aluminium foil to prevent the meat from becoming too dry and cook for a further 15 minutes. Remove the foil and cook for 5 more minutes until the tops of the parcels are lightly caramelized. Serve warm.

Vegetables

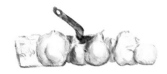

BOUILLE D'ÉPINARDS ET DE LIMAÇONS
SNAILS WITH SPINACH

Serves 6

6 dozen snails; beef or chicken stock (see recipe p.184); 2 medium onions; 2 garlic cloves; 100g / 4oz bacon; 3 tbsp tomato purée (see recipe p.180); 1 large bunch fresh, young spinach; 1 bouquet garni (fennel stalk, parsley stalks, sprig savory); 1 strip dried orange peel; salt and freshly ground black pepper; 2 wine glasses dry white wine; 1 wine glass olive oil.

In France, snails are often purchased live and left unfed for two to three days. Then for a further three to four days, they would be fattened, in this case with a flour, savory and thyme based feed. Live snails are hard to come by, though they are sometimes sold fresh and are widely available frozen or canned. Soak the snails in warm water, then blanch them for 10 minutes in stock or boiled salt water (or else prepare them according to instructions on package).

Meanwhile, peel and chop the onions and garlic. Cut the bacon into strips. Pour half the oil into a large pan and place over a medium heat. Toss in the bacon and cook until brown. Then add the onion and when it is translucent, add the garlic and tomato purée. Stir for a few minutes, then add the spinach leaves which have been washed and dried. Strain the snails and transfer them to the pan.

It is important to time this preparation accurately as the fresh snails will only remain tender if transferred to the pan while still hot.

Add the bouquet garni, orange peel, salt and pepper, white wine and the rest of the oil, then cover. Reduce the heat to a minimum and simmer gently for 35 to 40 minutes. If the liquid evaporates too rapidly, some of the stock used to blanch the snails may be added.

Serve with thick slices of toasted country-style bread, not forgetting to supply each person with a long needle or nail to remove the snails from their shells.

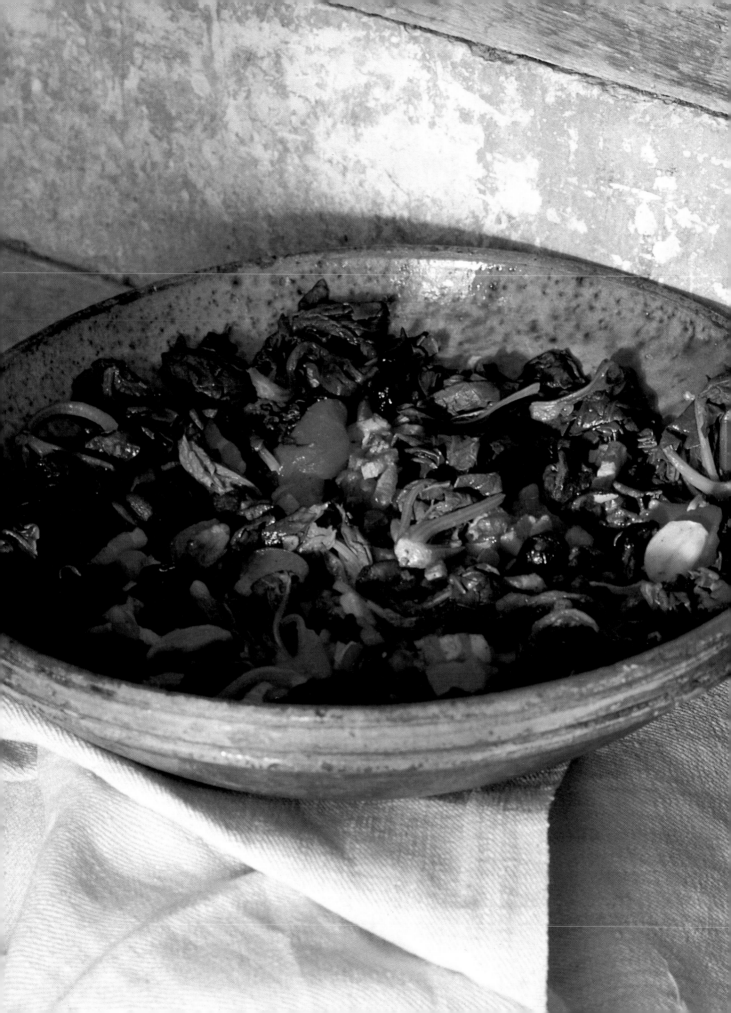

ARTICHAUTS EN BARIGOULE
BRAISED STUFFED ARTICHOKES

Serves 6

**12 small artichokes; lemon juice or vinegar; 150g /
5oz bacon, lightly smoked; 2 garlic cloves; 3 large
onions; 1 large carrot; a few sprigs of flat-leaf
parsley; 1/2 tsp savory; 1 egg-sized ball stale
bread (without crusts); salt and freshly ground
pepper; 2 wine glasses dry white wine; 1 wine
glass olive oil.**

Remove the outer leaves from the
artichokes, cut off the hard, sharp leaf tips and
trim down the stems. Fill a large container with
water and plenty of lemon juice or vinegar and
throw in the artichokes.

While they are soaking, cut the bacon into
strips. Peel and chop the garlic and two of the
onions. Then chop the carrot and third onion
keeping them separate. Remove the parsley leaves
from their stalks and chop them finely. Tie the
parsley stalks together. Put the chopped parsley,
savory, crumbled bread, chopped onions and
garlic, into a bowl. Mix well, add salt and pepper
and bind together with a splash of white wine
and some olive oil. Put to one side.

Take a large, cast-iron pan and place over a
fairly high heat. Add a little oil and toss in the
bacon. As soon as the bacon begins to brown add
the remaining chopped onion and carrot. Stir and
cook until they begin to brown, then remove
from the heat. Mix with the bread and herb
mixture.

Strain the artichokes and wipe them with a
clean dry cloth. Put a generous spoonful of the
stuffing into the heart of each one and arrange
them upright in the pan. Sprinkle oil and plenty
of pepper over the top, then pour in the

remaining wine and an equal amount of water or
chicken stock (see recipe p.184). Cover three
quarters over with a lid and bring to the boil.
Reduce the heat and simmer very gently for 1
hour and 10 minutes. The artichoke stems should
always be immersed in liquid, so keep a little
white wine and stock by the pot and add when
necessary to maintain the level of the liquid.
Serve directly from the pan.

*In some parts of Aix-en-Provence, larger
artichokes are used. The choke is removed and sausage
meat and mushrooms are added to the stuffing.*

BOUMIANO (BOHÉMIENNE)
AUBERGINES BOHEMIENNE

Serves 6

**1kg / 2lb aubergines; 1 onion; 3 garlic cloves;
1kg / 2lb tomatoes; 3-4 tbsp olive oil; 2 salted
anchovies; 1 tbsp milk; 1 tsp flour; freshly ground
black pepper; 1 heaped tbsp breadcrumbs; salt.**

Cut the washed, unpeeled aubergines into
thick rounds, then cut each round into quarters.
Sprinkle the pieces with salt and leave in a
colander to 'sweat' and draw out the liquid.
Meanwhile, peel and chop the onion and garlic.
Peel (see p.135), deseed and crush the tomatoes.

Pour a tablespoon of oil into a large, high-
sided frying pan and place over a medium heat.
Add the onions and stir with a wooden spoon
until lightly golden. Add the garlic and stir for
another minute, then reduce the heat to a
minimum.

Pat the aubergine pieces dry with a clean
cloth and toss them into the frying pan. Turn up

the heat and cook the aubergines for 7 to 8 minutes, stirring occasionally, to soften them. Pour in the rest of the oil and, when it is hot, add the tomatoes. Use a slotted spoon to put the tomatoes in so that the juice can be strained off before they go into the pan. Mix together with the aubergines and add pepper. Leave to simmer uncovered over a low heat for a further 15 minutes, stirring occasionally.

Meanwhile, run the anchovies under cold water rubbing them between your fingers to remove salt and bones. Place the fillets in a bowl containing the milk and leave to soak.

Place a small stainless steel pan over a low heat and add a little oil, then sprinkle in the flour. Beat with a wooden spoon until smooth, then gradually add the milk from the bowl of anchovies, stirring continuously, and two tablespoons of water to obtain a type of oil-based béchamel, commonly used in Provençal cooking. Cook for five minutes to eliminate the floury taste. Crush the anchovies and mix into the sauce. Pour over the vegetables and serve immediately.

This dish can also be served au gratin, or 'en tian' in Provençal French. To do this, simply rub the bottom of a baking dish with garlic and brush with oil. Transfer the *boumiano* into the dish and sprinkle with breadcrumbs (mixed with a little grated cheese, such as comté, if preferred). Splash with a few drops of olive oil and bake in a hot oven for 5 to 7 minutes until brown and crispy.

Serve directly from the dish.

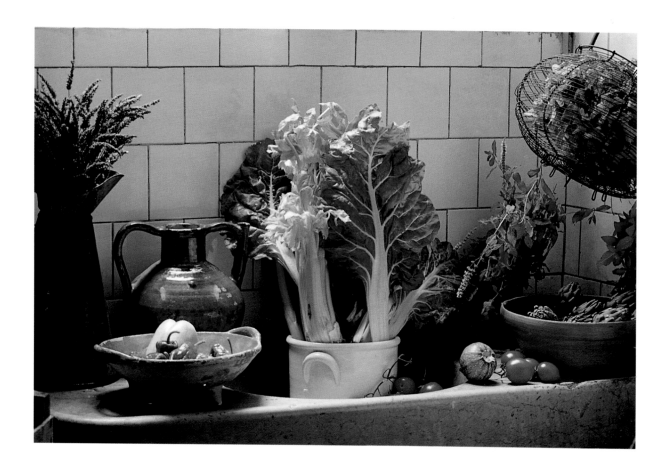

DAUBE D'HARICOTS ROUGES
RED KIDNEY BEAN CASSEROLE

Serves 6

600g / 1 1/4lb dried red kidney beans; 150g / 5oz thick bacon slices; 1 thick bacon rind; 1 medium leek; 2 garlic cloves; 1 tomato or 2 tbsp tomato purée (see recipe p 180); 1 large, preferably pink onion; 4 cloves; 1 bouquet garni (1 bay leaf, sprig parsley and thyme); 1 celery stick; 1 sprig sage; 1 bottle red wine (preferably from the Provence region).

Rinse the kidney beans and leave them to soak in warm water for at least 3 hours.

Rinse the bacon under running water and cut into short strips. Peel the leek, putting the dark green top leaves to one side to add to the bouquet garni. Wash and dry carefully to remove all traces of grit, then slice. Peel the garlic cloves, leaving them whole. Wash and quarter the tomato and squeeze each piece to remove watery seeds. Peel and quarter the onion. Stud each quarter with a clove. Wash and chop the celery stick. Prepare the bouquet garni and include the leek leaves.

Select a large, heavy-bottomed casserole pan for cooking. Place over a medium heat and throw in the bacon strips. Cook until browned on all sides and transfer to a bowl using a slotted spoon. Now add the onion and leek to the fat and lightly brown for approximately 5 minutes. Remove the onion and leek and put to one side with the bacon strips.

Arrange the rind on the bottom of the pan, fat-side down. Drain and add the kidney beans, bacon, onion, leek and other remaining ingredients. Lastly, pour in the wine. If it does not cover all the ingredients, top up with water

or a light stock. Cover with a lid. Soak a cloth in water, wring it out, then place it on top of the lid. The cloth should be dampened periodically during cooking, making sure it does not dry out.

Reduce the heat to a minimum and leave to simmer gently for approximately two hours. If towards the end of the cooking time, you think there is too much liquid, uncover the pan slightly to reduce. Season to taste.

This was one of Cézanne's favourite dishes - a meal unto itself. His cook sometimes added a ham bone, to enrich the flavour.

SALADE DE POMMES DE TERRE DU JAS
JAS DE BOUFFAN POTATO SALAD

Serves 6

500g/1lb small, new potatoes; 450-500ml/16 fl oz vegetable stock; 1 sprig thyme; a few sprigs flat-leaf parsley; 1 small pepper; 1 tsp coriander seeds; 1 unwaxed lemon; olive oil; salt.
For the sauce:
200g / 7oz black olives and 200g / 7oz green olives, all pitted; 1 garlic clove; 1 pinch cayenne pepper; 1 sprig fresh thyme; 5 tbsp olive oil; 1/2 wine glass wine vinegar; 3 hard-boiled eggs to decorate.

Blanch the green olives for a few seconds in boiling water, then rinse. Put them into a bowl with the black olives. Peel and crush the garlic and add to the bowl with the cayenne pepper, thyme, olive oil and vinegar (which you can replace with lemon juice if you prefer). Mix all the ingredients together and leave the olives to soak for an hour.

Peel the potatoes and shape them into ovals.

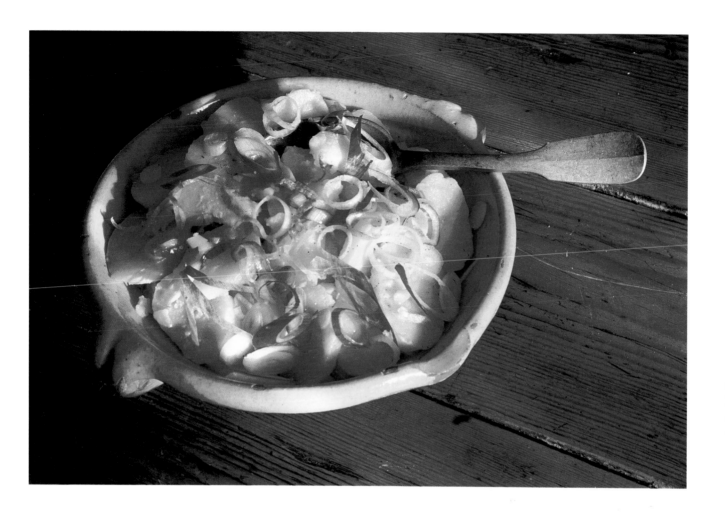

There should be about 60 potatoes. Plunge them into cold water.

Pour the vegetable stock into a large pan. Separate the thyme leaves from their stalks. Chop the parsley and crush the coriander seeds. Tie the thyme stalks with the parsley, pepper, coriander and peel from the lemon, in a piece of muslin. Add the muslin bouquet garni to the pan with a splash of olive oil, cover with a lid and bring to a boil over a medium heat. Then using a slotted spoon, transfer the potatoes to the stock. Add salt if necessary and a little pepper. Bring it back to the boil, cover and reduce the heat to a minimum. Simmer gently for 15 to 20 minutes. Check with the point of a knife that the potatoes are cooked, then remove from the heat.

Turn the potatoes and stock into a large, heatproof salad bowl and allow to cool a little before removing the muslin bag. Add the juice from the lemon and a spoonful of olive oil. Taste and adjust the seasoning. Leave to cool at room temperature.

When the potatoes are cold, strain them and pour the olive marinade over them. Beat the vinegar into the remaining olive oil and add. Sprinkle with chopped parsley and decorate with the eggs sliced into rounds or cut into quarters.

Serve with a bottle of chilled white wine and a bowl of anchovies.

TIAN DE LÉGUMES
VEGETABLE GRATIN

Serves 6

2 bunches swiss chard; 2 garlic cloves; flour; 2 tbsp olive oil; 150g / 5oz grated cheese (preferably comté); whole nutmeg; a few sprigs flat-leaf parsley; 2 egg yolks; 1 wine glass single cream; 2 tbsp white breadcrumbs; salt and pepper.

Separate the green from the white part of the swiss chard, keeping the white but only the green from three of the leaves for this recipe (the rest can be used at a later date in an omelette, quiche or stuffing). Clean the white part and remove the filaments, then cut into 3-4cm/1-2 in pieces. Cook for 15 minutes with the garlic cloves, in boiling water to which you have added salt, a little flour and a dash of oil.

Meanwhile, grate the cheese and nutmeg and finely chop the parsley and the greens. Preheat the oven to 210°C (gas mark 6-7, 400-425°F). Grease the bottom of a terrine or baking dish. Beat the egg yolks together with the cream and season lightly.

Strain the cooked swiss chard and garlic. Mash the garlic and spread over the base of the baking dish. Cover with a layer of swiss chard, a little parsley and greens mixed together, some grated cheese with nutmeg, then another layer of swiss chard and so on, finishing with a layer of cheese. Pour the egg and cream mixture over the top and sprinkle with breadcrumbs and a little olive oil. Bake in the oven until brown and crispy. Serve warm.

Le Tian is a very popular dish in Provence, generally made from leftovers. There are endless different variations. Here are a few alternative suggestions:

- Aubergine tian or gratin, made with aubergines, tomatoes and basil and topped with grated cheese; or fry the aubergine slices and make a béchamel sauce with egg yolk.

- Cardoon tian. Cook the cardoon in the same way as the swiss chard and add béchamel instead of the egg and cream.

- Other vegetables suitable for a tian include marrow, spinach, courgettes, onions and leeks.

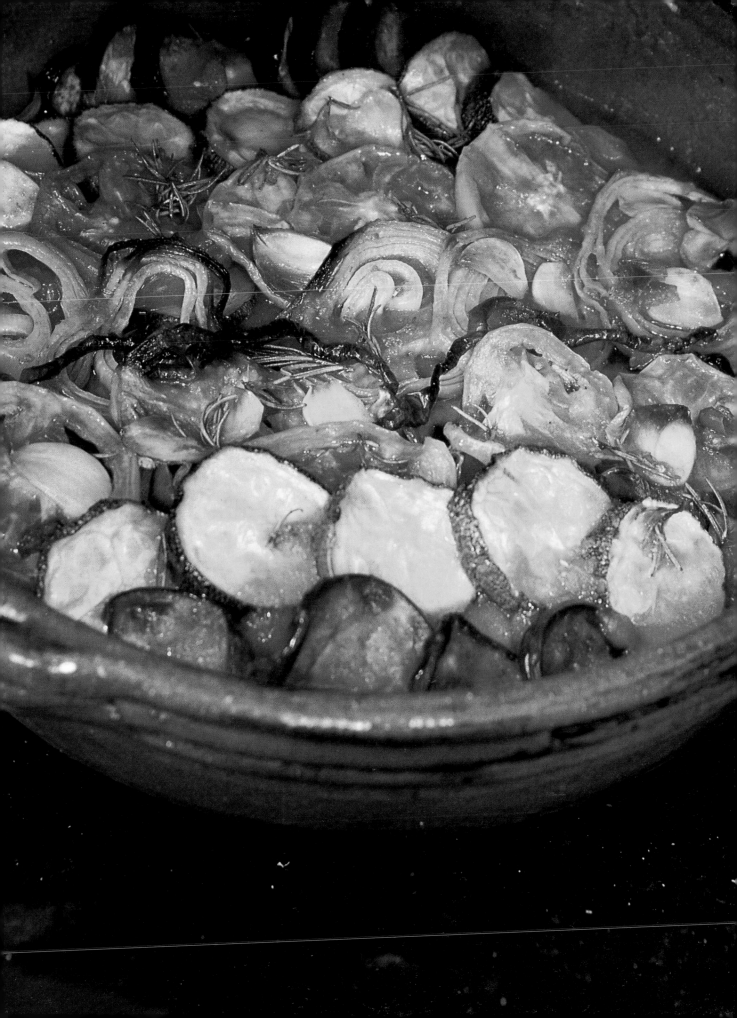

MACARONADE AU JUS D'AGNEAU
MACARONI WITH LAMB SAUCE

Serves 6

500g / 1lb thick macaroni; 100g / 4oz grated cheese; 1 tbsp olive oil.

For the sauce:

2 onions; 4 garlic cloves; 1 sprig rosemary; 1kg / 2lb braising lamb; flour; 2 tbsp olive oil; 1 bouquet garni (1 bay leaf, sprig parsley and thyme); 1 tsp ground cinnamon; salt and pepper; 350ml / 12fl oz dry white wine; 150g / 5oz green olives*.

First make the sauce. Peel and chop the onions. Peel and crush the garlic. Remove rosemary leaves from the stalks and chop finely. Dice the lamb into small cubes (2-3cm / 1in). Dust them lightly with flour.

Pour the oil into a large pan and when it is hot, add all the lamb at once to brown, stirring continuously, over a medium-high heat so the meat browns without cooking. Using a slotted spoon, transfer the browned lamb to a bowl.

Now toss the onions into the casserole and fry gently for 4 to 5 minutes stirring continuously. As soon as they begin to brown, add the garlic and stir. Add the lamb and mix together with the bouquet garni, chopped rosemary, cinnamon and salt and pepper. Then pour in the white wine.

Cover, reduce the heat to a minimum and simmer gently for 35 minutes, stirring occasionally.

Remove the lid to check the wine has reduced. Add enough water or a light vegetable stock (or half water and half chicken stock) so that the meat is barely covered. Cook for a further hour, still over a very low heat or, better still, in a preheated oven 180°C (gas mark 4, 350°F) which should be reduced to 150°C (gas mark 2, 300°F) after 30 minutes. Stir from time to time making sure the casserole is tightly covered. Add the olives 15 minutes before cooking is completed.

Cook the macaroni al dente. Pour some oil into the bottom of a baking dish and arrange a layer of macaroni on top. Sprinkle with grated cheese, then use a large spoon to add generous amounts of sauce taken from the lamb casserole, leaving the meat and vegetable pieces (to be served separately, either with the *macaronade* or for a different meal). Repeat at least once more, finishing with a layer of grated cheese. Put in the oven at 240°C (gas mark 9, 475°F) until heated through and the topping crisp and golden.

Serve with the lamb and vegetable pieces if desired or just with a simple salad.

The lamb stew made in this recipe can also be used for a different meal. Simply reheat and skim off the fat. Accompany with rice or bulgar wheat served with the sauce.

The *macaronade* can also made in the same way using a beef sauce. The juices from the *nougat de boeuf* (see page 156) can replace the liquid from the lamb and the *nougat* and *macaronade* can be served together or separately.

*Olives cassées *are recommended for this recipe. These are olives whose skins have split, but whose stones are untouched. Once the bitter flavour disappears, they are then preserved in aromatic brine in a tub of cool water for ten days. They may be difficult to come by, but are a real delicacy.*

PATANO
POTATOES WITH OLIVES AND BACON

Serves 6

3 garlic cloves; 1 large onion; 200g/ 7oz thickly sliced bacon; 2 tbsp olive oil; 12 medium-sized potatoes; 200g / 7oz black olives; a few bitter olives; 1 bayleaf; 1 tomato or 2 tbsp tomato purée (see recipe p180); 1 wine glass veal or pork stock (see recipe p.184); 3 sage leaves; freshly ground pepper.

Peel and chop the garlic. Peel and slice the onion thinly.

Cut the bacon into strips without removing the rind which gives a creamy texture to the dish.

Pour a tablespoon of oil into a heavy, preferably cast iron, casserole and place over a medium heat. When the oil is hot, toss in the bacon. Stir for about 5 minutes until brown on all sides.

Peel, wash, dry and cut the potatoes into large chunks.

Transfer the bacon from the casserole into a bowl, using a slotted spoon so that the fat remains in the casserole. Add the onions to the fat and stir until golden. Transfer into the bowl containing the bacon. Then, turn the heat up a little, add the potatoes and stir with a wooden spoon until they too are uniformly brown. Put the bacon and onions back into the casserole and, without stirring, add the garlic and olives, sprinkle the chopped bay leaf on top, and add the tomato purée or the tomato (quartered and each piece squeezed to remove watery seeds). Leave for five minutes, then mix all ingredients together. Add a generous amount of pepper, but no salt.

Pour in the stock and reduce the heat. Cover with a lid and leave to cook for 35 to 40 minutes. The sage leaves should be added just 10 minutes before the end of cooking.

Serve in a large, warmed bowl.

This rustic recipe can be varied by adding pistou *(a sauce made from basil, garlic, olive oil and cheese, pounded into a paste) or by using a whole head of garlic, peeling the cloves but leaving them whole. In both cases, the sage should be omitted. Add with the stock and cook in the oven at a low temperature for 45 to 50 minutes. This takes longer, but the dish will be smoother and richer as a result.*

Desserts

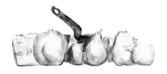

FRISOUNS
BATTER BISCUIT CURLS

Serves 6

**150g / 5oz flour; 150g / 5oz caster sugar; 3 large
eggs; 1 1/2 tbsp orange flower water; 25g / 1oz
butter or 1 1/2 tbsp peanut oil; icing sugar.**

Preheat the oven to150°C (gas mark 2,
300°F). Grease a baking-sheet with oil or butter
and put in the fridge to cool.

Mix the flour and caster sugar and set
aside. Break the eggs into a bowl and beat with
the orange flower water until smooth. Then,
using a wooden spoon, gradually beat in the flour
and sugar until the mixture is smooth and
creamy.

Take a teaspoonful of the mixture and form
a 10cm/ 4in strip (roughly the length of your
index finger) onto the greased baking-sheet. For
more evenly shaped *frisouns*, an icing-bag may be
used. Make sure that there are generous spaces
between each strip as they will spread out when
cooking.

Bake in the oven for 5 minutes. When the
frisouns are golden brown, remove the baking-
sheet and place as near to the open oven door as
possible, so that it remains warm. Quickly detach
each one from the tray and roll up into a curl over
the handle of a wooden spoon. Slide off onto a
plate. If you can enlist help for this operation it
would speed up the process and prevent the last
pieces from becoming too dry and cracking as
they are rolled. If not, it is advisable to bake
them in several small batches.

When cool, sprinkle with icing sugar and
serve with cream flavoured with rum, lemon or
vanilla.

Another regional speciality - called bugnes,
oreillettes *or* ganses *depending on whether you come
from Arles, Marseilles or Aix - can be made using the
same ingredients, but with triple the amount of flour
(i.e. 450g / 15oz) Prepare the mixture in exactly the
same way, then cover with a damp cloth and leave to
stand for an hour. Roll out the dough as thinly as you
can, cut into rounds and fry in oil until golden
brown. When cool, serve as above.*

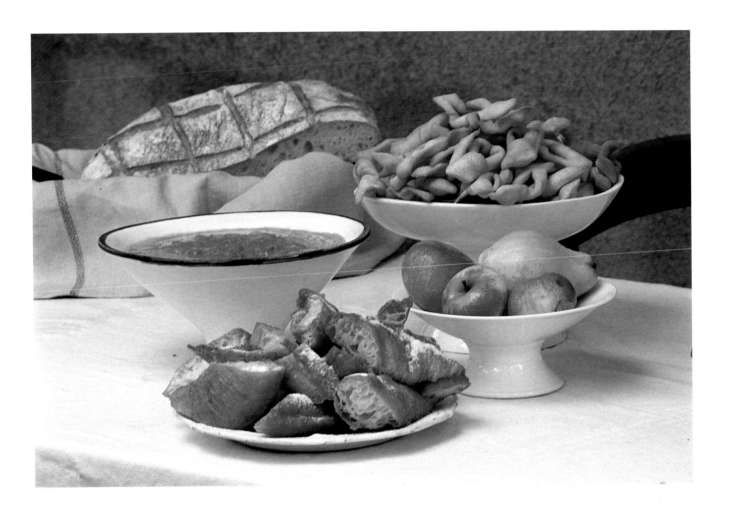

CHICHI FREGI
SWEET FRITTERS

Serves 6

500g / 1lb flour; salt; 6 eggs; 250ml / 8fl oz chilled boiled milk; 1 tbsp orange flower water or grated rind of one unwaxed orange or lemon; oil for frying (vegetable or olive).

Mix the flour and salt in a large bowl and make a well in the centre of the flour. Separate the eggs, putting the whites into another large mixing bowl with a tiny pinch of salt. Beat the yolks together with the orange flower water and half of the milk and pour into the well. Gradually incorporate the flour to obtain a creamy mixture.

Mix in the remaining milk a little at a time. The resulting mixture should be smooth but not runny.

Whisk the egg whites until stiff and fold them carefully into the mixture. Heat the oil in a deep frying pan.

Put the mixture into an icing bag with a wide nozzle. When the oil is hot, hold the icing bag over the centre of the pan and squeeze the mixture into the oil in a circular movement to form a wide spiral. Cook for a few minutes on each side until golden.

Transfer on to absorbent kitchen paper to soak up any excess oil.

Repeat until all the mixture has been used. Sprinkle with icing sugar and cut into pieces. Serve immediately.

These delicious fritters are usually served with mulled wine or home-made bitter orange wine (see recipe p.175)

In Cézanne's day, provençal housewives made chichi *with chick pea flour (which can still be found in oriental grocer shops) or even from puréed peas.*

POIRES ET COINGS AU MIEL
HONEY GLAZED PEARS AND QUINCES

Serves 6

12 cooking pears or 12 quinces; 1 clove; 1 vanilla pod; 1 star anise pod; 250g / 8 1/2oz liquid honey or caster sugar; 1 unwaxed lemon.

Pour 1.5 litres of water, preferably mineral water, into a stainless steel pan with a base large enough to hold all twelve fruits. Add the spices and honey (or sugar). Peel the fruit without removing the stem, and stand them upright in the pan. If the water does not cover the fruit then top up until the liquid just covers them. Wash and cut the lemon into quarters and add to the fruit. Place the pan over a medium heat and bring to the boil. Reduce the heat to a minimum and simmer gently for 20 minutes. Use a skewer or long needle to check whether the fruit is cooked. The flesh should be soft enough for the skewer to pass straight through to the core with ease, but firm enough to remain whole without breaking. Remove the pan from the heat and leave the fruit to cool in the syrup.

Transfer the fruit to a large fruit bowl and refrigerate. Replace the syrup over the heat and reduce to a third of its volume. Remove the spices and lemon, then dip the fruit into the warm syrup. Put them back in the fridge to cool. Repeat this process, until all the syrup has been used and you should finish up with 12 beautifully glazed pears or quinces. They can be served cold or placed under a grill briefly to caramelize just before serving.

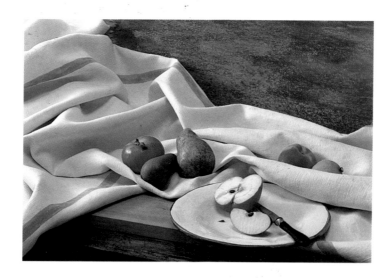

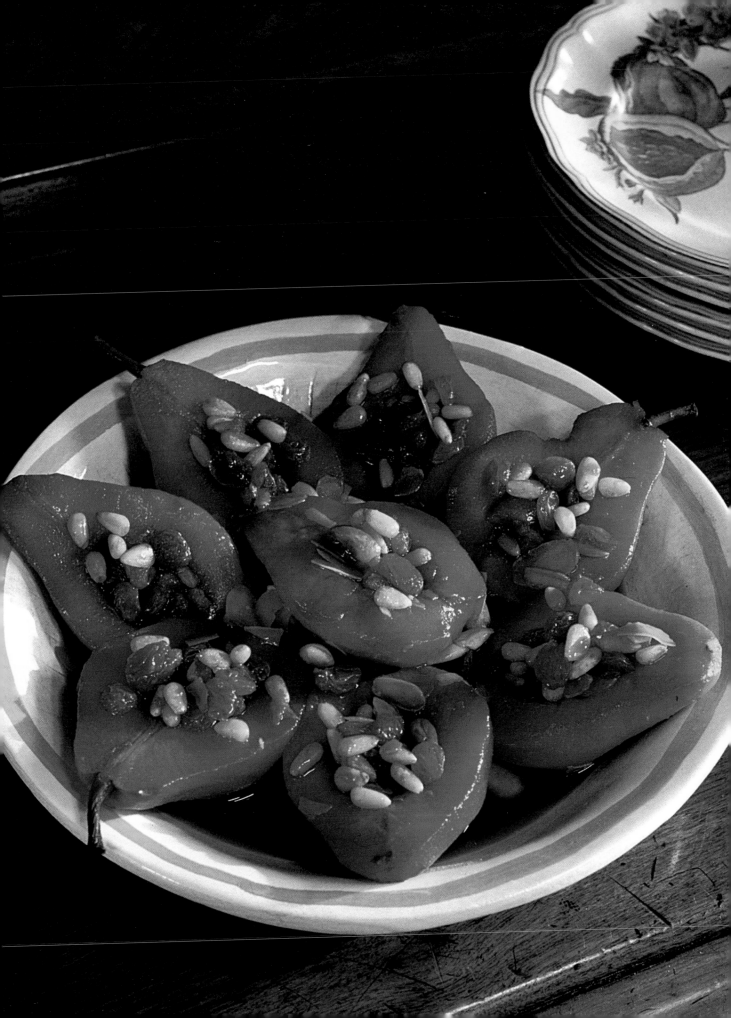

BROUSSE AU MIEL ET AUX AMANDES
FROMAGE FRAIS WITH HONEY, ALMONDS AND MARMALADE

Serves 6

600g / 1 1/4lb fromage frais (or fresh goat's cheese); 4 drops bitter almond essence; 3 tbsp honey (preferably thyme honey); 50g / 2oz split almonds.

For a 500g / 1lb pot of marmalade:

3 oranges; 1 unwaxed lemon; 1 small piece cinnamon stick; 1 small pinch grated nutmeg; 1 clove; 175g / 6oz granulated sugar.

Prepare the marmalade the night before. Scrub the fruits under running water then douse in boiling water to remove all traces of dirt. Dry. Remove 1/2cm / 1/8in off both ends of the oranges and lemon and cut the rest into thin slices over a stainless steel pan, so that none of the juice escapes. Leave the fruit slices to marinate overnight in the cinnamon, nutmeg, clove, half the amount of sugar and 30cl / 1/2 pint bottled water. (Do not use tap water as this contains too much calcium).

Place the saucepan of fruit slices and marinade over a low heat, add 20cl / 7fl oz water and bring to the boil uncovered. Reduce the heat to a minimum and simmer gently for 20 minutes. Remove from the heat, add the rest of the sugar and leave to cool without covering.

When cool, remove the clove and cinnamon stick and return to a low heat, still uncovered. Bring the marmalade back to the boil. As soon as boiling point is reached, remove from the heat and cool. The marmalade will keep for several days in the fridge.

Heat the honey in a bain-marie or double boiler. Put the fromage frais into a bowl and beat vigorously with the warm honey and almond essence. (Take care not to add more than 3 to 4 drops as almond essence is toxic in large doses). Pour the mixture into a dessert dish and refrigerate for 30 minutes. Decorate with almond halves and serve with the marmalade.

For a more elaborate presentation you can make a decorated dome shape. Take 2 gelatine leaves, soften in cold water, strain and add to the honey as it is being heated in the bain-marie. Put the mixture into a dome-shaped mould and refrigerate for at least 2 hours. Turn out, decorate and serve as above.

TARTE AUX PASSERILLES
CHEESE AND SULTANA FLAN

Serves 6

For the pastry:
200g / 7oz flour; 1 pinch salt; 75g / 3oz caster sugar; 1 sachet vanilla sugar; 150ml / 5fl oz oil; 1 large egg.

For the filling:
1 bunch swiss chard leaves (green part only); 250g / 8 1/2oz sultanas; 100g / 4oz brown sugar; 1 pinch salt; 100g / 4oz grated cheese; 2 eggs; 1 sachet vanilla sugar .

First make the pastry. Sift the flour and salt into a large bowl and mix in the caster and vanilla sugar. Make a well in the centre and pour in the oil (leave a teaspoonful to grease the flan ring with) and add the beaten egg. Beat the oil and egg together in the well, then gradually draw the flour in from the edges and blend with your fingertips until a dough is formed. Turn the dough out onto a floured surface and knead lightly. Sprinkle the dough and mixing bowl with flour. Put the dough back into the bowl, cover with a damp cloth and keep in a cool (but not too cold) place while preparing the filling.

Remove the green leaves from the white stalks (do not discard these stalks as they can be used elsewhere - cooked au gratin, for example, as described in the recipe on p.166). Wash and dry the greens, roll them up and slice them into fine strips which should then be dried in a very cool oven. (Traditionally they would have been left to dry under the Provençal sun.)

Rinse the sultanas, then place them in a bowl and pour hot water over them. Leave to soak until swollen and then strain. In another bowl, place the sugar, salt (a very small pinch), grated cheese, sultanas and dried greens. Mix together well with the eggs, which should be beaten beforehand.

Preheat the oven to 180°C (gas mark 4, 350°F). Grease a flan ring.

Roll the pastry out onto a floured surface and line the flan ring. Prick the base with a fork and put a few dried beans on top, to stop the pastry from changing its shape while cooking. Bake blind for 10 minutes.

Gather the leftover pastry, roll out and cut into narrow strips equal in length to the diameter of the flan ring. Take the flan ring out of the oven, remove the dried beans and fill the pastry case with the mixture. Use the strips to make a lattice finish and bake for 15 minutes. As soon as the flan is cooked sprinkle with vanilla sugar.

Serve hot or cold with a dessert wine.

The grated cheese gives this flan a very distinctive taste, but if you prefer a smoother taste, fromage frais may be used instead.

VIN D'ORANGES AMÈRES
ORANGE WINE

3 bitter oranges; 1 unwaxed lemon; 2 cloves; 1 vanilla pod; 1 liqueur glass eau-de-vie de marc (see page 137); 1 bottle dry white wine; 175g / 6oz granulated sugar.

Wash and dry the fruit. Cut into quarters and place in the bottom of a large preserving jar together with the sugar, cloves and vanilla pod, split in half lengthwise, (but only three-quarters of the way down). Pour the marc over the fruit followed by the wine and stir.

Seal the jar hermetically and leave in a cool, dark and dry place for 45 days.

Following pages: Cheese and Sultana Flan.

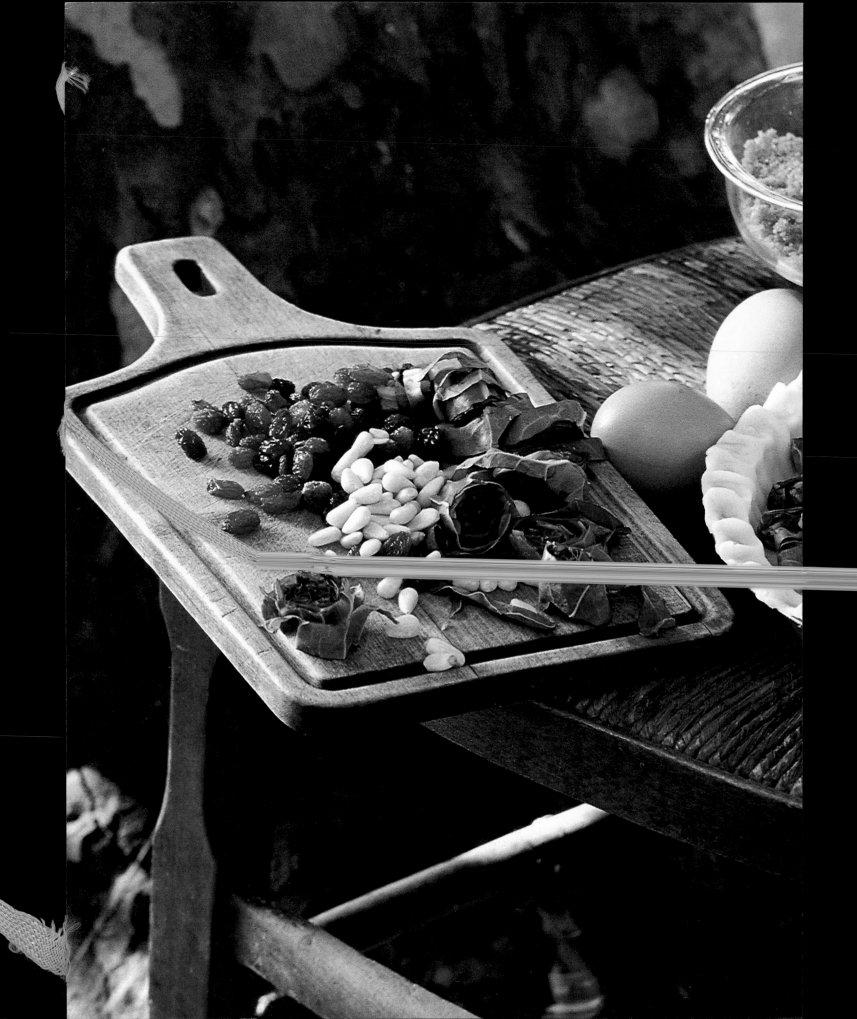

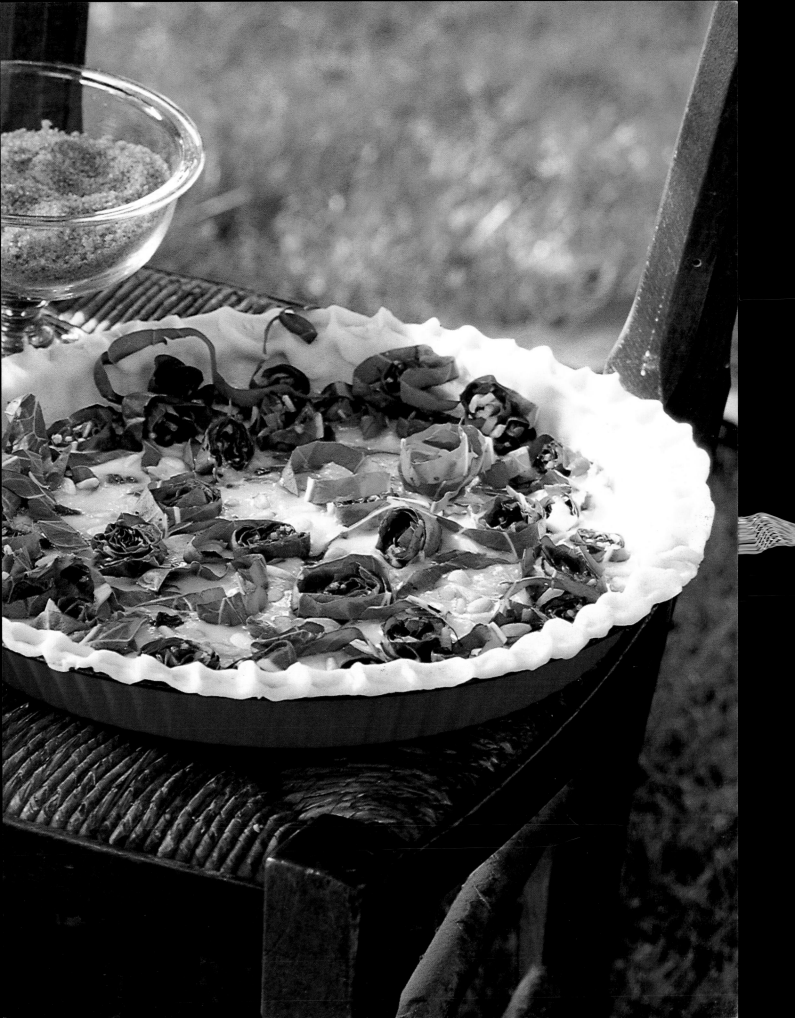

BLANC MANGER PROVENÇAL
BLANCMANGE PROVENÇAL

Serves 6

100g / 4oz candied fruits; 50g / 2oz sultanas;
100ml / 31/2 fl oz lavender honey; 250ml / 9fl oz
milk; 1/2 litre / 1 pint crème fraîche; 3 egg yolks;
4 gelatine leaves.

Chop the candied fruits. Soak the sultanas in boiling water until swollen then strain well.

Heat the honey to liquefy it, but do not boil. Remove from the heat and put aside.

Heat the milk in a medium pan with the crème fraîche. Put aside.

Whisk the egg yolks vigorously in a bowl until they begin to lighten, then gradually add the honey, whisking continuously but less energetically. Then whisk in the warm milk and cream. Pour all the ingredients into a clean, medium-sized pan.

Soften the gelatine in a bowl of cold water. Place the pan of blancmange mixture over a medium heat and cook for about 10 minutes, taking care the liquid does not bubble at all. Stir continuously with a wooden spoon in the shape of a figure eight, so that the cream does not stick to the bottom.

Strain the gelatine and stir into the until dissolved. Pour a little of the blancmange into a mould, then sprinkle over some candied fruits and sultanas. Repeat the process until the ingredients are finished. Allow to cool at room temperature then refrigerate overnight. Turn out of the mould into a fruit bowl or dessert dish. Decorate with pieces of candied fruit.

GATEAU D'AIX AUX AMANDES
AIX ALMOND CAKE

Serves 6

25g / 1oz butter or 1 tsp vegetable or peanut oil to
grease the cake tin; 6 eggs;   salt; 1/2 unwaxed
lemon; 250g / 8 1/2oz ground almonds; 250g / 8
1/2oz caster sugar; 3 drops vanilla essence; 100g /
4oz cornflour; 50g / 2oz granulated sugar; 75g /
3oz flaked almonds.

Grease a 25cm / 10in round cake tin and put in the fridge to cool. Separate four of the eggs and whisk the remaining two eggs in a separate bowl with a pinch of salt.

Grate the rind of the lemon half and mix together in a large bowl with the ground almonds and caster sugar. Gradually incorporate the whisked eggs and four egg yolks into the dry ingredients, beating vigorously with a wooden spoon until smooth and creamy. Add the vanilla essence and cornflour and blend in.

Preheat the oven to 210°C (gas mark 6-7, 400-425°F). Whisk the egg whites until firm. Beat one spoonful of the egg white into the cake mixture, then fold in the rest of the egg white, one spoonful at a time. This should be done gently, without beating or whisking the mixture, to obtain a light and airy cake.

Turn the mixture into the cake tin and sprinkle the granulated sugar and flaked almonds over the top. Bake in the oven for 30 minutes. Check that the top of the cake is not browning too quickly. If this is the case, reduce the heat to 150-180°C (gas mark 2-4, 300-350°F) after 20 minutes and cover with a piece of buttered greaseproof paper.

Turn off the oven, but leave the cake to stand inside with the oven door ajar for 6-8 minutes. Then remove the cake from the tin and leave to cool on a wire cooling tray.

This cake can be eaten for breakfast or tea. It can also be served as a dessert with custard, which has been flavoured with orange flower water, or with a fruit compote.

CROISSANTS ET CORNES
ALMOND CROISSANTS

For 20 small croissants or cornes:

1 tbsp apricot jam; 200g/7oz ground almonds; 150g /5oz caster sugar; salt; 3 egg whites; 75g/3oz almond flakes; 1 tsp soft brown sugar; 1 tbsp milk.

Heat the jam in a bain-marie or double boiler and strain it to remove small pieces of fruit. Place the ground almonds, caster sugar and a very small pinch of salt in a mixing bowl. Add the strained jam and beat with a wooden spoon until smooth.

Beat the egg whites lightly until frothy but not stiff. Using a wooden spoon, gradually blend enough egg white into the mixture to form a dough which should be smooth and thick enough to be rolled in the hand.

Divide the dough into pieces the size of a walnut and over a dry, floured surface, roll them into fingers which taper off at the ends. Brush with lightly beaten egg white, then roll them in the flaked almonds.

Lightly grease a baking sheet and arrange in scattered rows. Form into half-moon shapes by pushing the ends inwards. Bake in a preheated oven for 10 to 15 minutes at 180°C (gas mark 4 / 350°F). Dissolve the brown sugar in the milk

and brush over the croissants 5 minutes before they are cooked.

Turn off the oven and with the door slightly open, leave the cooked croissants to sit for a while.

The croissants or *cornes* are usually served with coffee or at tea time. They will keep for several days if stored in an airtight tin.

In some Provençal villages they are shaped into little balls and rolled in finely chopped pine nuts. Hence the alternative name of Pignolats (pignons *is French for pine nuts). If you opt for the* pignolats, *they will need to be baked for a little longer.*

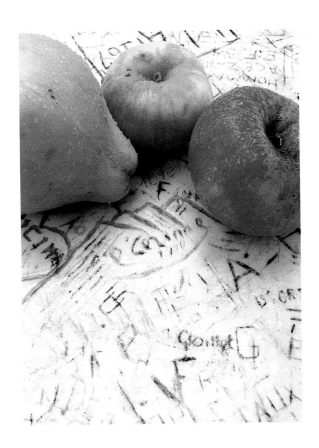

Stocks and Sauces

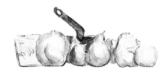

LE COULIS
TOMATO PURÉE

Serves 6

**2 kg/ 4lb ripe, fat tomatoes; coarse salt; olive oil;
bouquet garni (parsley stalks, sprigs of thyme,
laurel, fennel, savory); freshly ground pepper.**

Wash and dry the tomatoes. Cut them in half vertically and score a cross into the skin of each half.

Using the point of a knife, remove as many of the inner seeds as you can. Sprinkle salt over the cut side and leave 'to sweat' for 30 minutes. Squeeze each half between your fingers and place onto a wire tray or grill pan, cut side down, for a further 30 minutes, to allow the maximum amount of liquid to drip out.

Cut the tomato halves into smaller pieces. Pour some oil into a large, high-sided frying pan and place over a medium heat. Toss the tomatoes into the oil, stir for one or two minutes, then crush them with a wooden spoon. Reduce the heat to a minimum and cook for 20 minutes.

Put the bouquet garni into a large preserving jar or earthenware pot together with some coarsely ground pepper and a little olive oil. Pass the tomatoes through a fine sieve, lined with a piece of muslin, or blend in a vegetable mill or food processor on a fine setting. When the purée has been well strained, pour it back into the pan, add salt and pepper and reduce for 20 minutes over a low heat, stirring occasionally. Remove from the heat and allow to cool without covering. Pour into the preserving jar or pot, packing it down well, to make sure there are no air bubbles. One way of doing this is to fold a dish cloth in four and bang the jar down on it several times. Cover the tomato paste with a thin film of olive oil to preserve it.

Whenever you use purée from the jar, be sure to smooth the surface back over and pour over a fresh layer of oil.

Madame Brémond would take handfuls of the tomato paste and roll them into balls between her oiled palms. They were left to dry under the Provençal sun and stored in preserving jars with a bouquet garni and oil. So whenever she needed tomato purée for a recipe, she would simply dip into the jar and pull out a purée ball - a perfect measure.

AILLOLI
GARLIC MAYONNAISE

Serves 6

8 garlic cloves; 800ml/ 1 1/3 pints olive oil; 2 egg
yolks; juice from 1 lemon; salt and pepper.

Peel and chop the garlic. Put the pieces
into a wooden or marble mortar and pound to a
smooth paste. A pinch of salt may be added to
ease the process. Dilute with a few drops of olive
oil, then add the egg yolks one at a time,
working them in with the pestle. Add the salt
and slowly work in the olive oil, a trickle at a
time, turning the pestle in a circular motion and
always in the same direction. The *ailloli* will
gradually thicken. Add some pepper then
incorporate the lemon juice in the same way.

If the *ailloli* appears too thick, add one or
two teaspoons of water a few drops at a time. If,
on the contrary, it is too thin i.e. if the pestle does
not stand upright in the mayonnaise, then put one
spoonful of *ailloli* into a bowl and with a wooden
spoon, beat in just under half a glass of boiling
vinegar. Gradually work this mixture back into
the rest of the mayonnaise with the pestle,
removing the excess oil which comes to the
surface (which can be kept to dress a salad).

*Ailloli is very versatile and can be served with
fish, snails, stews, cold meats and steamed vegetables.
Cézanne liked to spread it on toast which he usually
ate with a tomato and a hard-boiled egg.*

LA RAÏTO
RED WINE FISH SAUCE

Serves 6

1 large red onion; 3 tbsp olive oil; 1 level tbsp
flour; 300ml / 10fl oz light stock; 1/2 litre / 1 pint
red wine (preferably from Provence); 2 garlic
cloves; 1 tbsp tomato purée (see recipe p.180); 1
bouquet garni (1 bay leaf, 1 sprig thyme, 1 sprig
parsley); salt; black pepper; 1 tbsp capers; 1
handful black olives.

Chop the onion. Heat some oil in a frying
pan, then toss in the onions and fry until golden.
Sprinkle with a little flour and continue stirring.
As soon as the flour and onion begin to brown,
pour in the heated stock. When it begins to
bubble, add the red wine. Reduce the heat and
bring back to the boil, then add the garlic cloves,
which have been peeled and lightly crushed
inside their skins, the tomato purée and the
bouquet garni. Season to taste.

Simmer without covering until the liquid
has been reduced to a third of its original volume.

Blend in a vegetable mill or food processor.
Add the capers and olives.

*Raïto is traditionally served with cod and most
other poached fish and enhances the flavour of boiled
potatoes. This is the only Provençal sauce made with
red wine and onion and is believed to have been brought
to Marseilles by the Phoenicians.*

ANCHOÏADE FAMILIALE
ANCHOVY SPREAD

Serves 6

12 salted anchovies; 12 anchovy fillets in oil; 1 small glass milk; 12 whole almonds; 4 hazelnuts; 1 small, fresh onion; 3 garlic cloves; 1 red pepper; 2 basil sprigs; 3 parsley sprigs; 3 walnuts; 1 pinch fennel seeds; 1 tbsp orange flower water; olive oil.

A few hours before preparation of the anchoïade remove the salt from the whole anchovies by running them under cold water while rubbing them between your fingers. Separate them and remove as many of the bones as you can, then rinse in a bowl containing cold water. Pour the milk into another bowl and transfer the anchovies into the milk. If the milk does not cover them completely, top up with water until they are submerged. Leave to desalinate for at least 2 hours.

Blanch the almonds and hazelnuts to remove their 'skins'. Peel the onion and garlic and chop roughly with the red pepper. Pick the basil and parsley leaves off their stalks and chop them finely.

Remove the anchovy fillets from their oil and wipe them with absorbent kitchen paper. Remove all visible bones and chop the fillets into small pieces. Drain, dry and chop up the desalinated anchovies.

Place the onion, red pepper and garlic in a mortar and pound. When they begin to blend into each other, add the chopped anchovies. Resume pounding and continue while gradually adding the almonds, hazelnuts, walnuts and fennel seeds, until all ingredients have blended into a smooth pâté.

Still pounding, trickle in the orange flower water and the oil.

Transfer the *anchoïade* to a preserving jar and refrigerate until use.

This is the deluxe version for special occasions, but if you want to prepare a simpler anchoïade *for daily use, then just pound the anchovies with garlic, a few parsley or basil leaves, some olive oil and a few drops of red wine vinegar.*

Right :
Table de cuisine : pots et bouteilles.
The Louvre, Paris.

ROUÏA
ROUILLE

Serves 6

2 red peppers; 2 garlic cloves; coarse salt; 250ml /

9fl oz olive oil; 1 slice stale bread; stock.

Cut open the red peppers, remove the seeds and rinse and chop the flesh. Peel the garlic. Crush the red peppers and garlic in a mortar, adding a pinch of salt and a tablespoon of olive oil.

Remove the crust from the bread and moisten the soft part with stock. Add the moistened bread to the mix of peppers and garlic. Continue pounding, while slowly pouring the rest of the oil into the mortar, until the paste has the consistency of mayonnaise. If it separates, add a teaspoon of very hot stock. Just before serving, beat in some stock (four or five parts stock to one part *rouille*). Instead of the bread, you can use a slice of well-cooked potato if you prefer.

Rouille is traditionally served with *bouillabaisse* or Provençal fish stew but can also be served with a chicken dish, diluted with chicken stock.

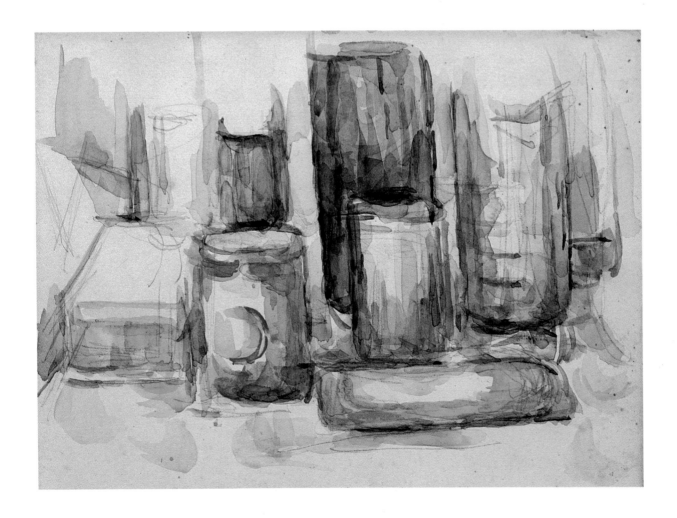

BOUILLON DE VOLAILLE
POULTRY STOCK

For 3 litres/5 1/4 pints of stock

2kg/4 1/2lb poultry giblets (neck, wings, feet, carcass); 2 white onions; 2 carrots; 2 leeks; 2 celery sticks; 4 garlic cloves; 1 bouquet garni; 1 small piece fresh root ginger; 1 wine glass (about 200ml/7fl oz) dry white wine or cider; coarse salt; white pepper.

Clean the giblets, cut off the claws from the feet and the beak if the head is to be used. Rinse thoroughly and take out the cartilage from the neck. Blanch the feet and remove the skin, which should come off easily.

Hold one onion directly over a flame to brown it and then stud it with cloves. It will flavour and colour the stock. Fill a cooking pot with 4 litres/7 pints of water and drop in the vegetables together with the giblets. Cover and bring rapidly to the boil. Skim as often as necessary. When the liquid is clear add the bouquet garni, ginger and white wine. Season with salt and, only at the end, pepper. Simmer over a very low heat for 3 hours at least. Strain the stock and keep at low temperature until it is used.

The vegetables and the cooked meat (which was scraped off the bones and skin) can be prepared as a salad served with a simple oil and vinegar or *rémoulade* (mustard) dressing.

BOUILLON DE VEAU
VEAL STOCK

The basic ingredients are the same as for the poultry stock: vegetables, herbs and spices, and wine.

Purchase 2kg/4lb of veal knuckle or neck bones, broken into small pieces. Toss the bones in cold water and heat up. Regularly skim off the foam and add the vegetables, seasoning and wine.

Leave to simmer over a low heat for 3 hours. Strain the stock and it is ready for use.

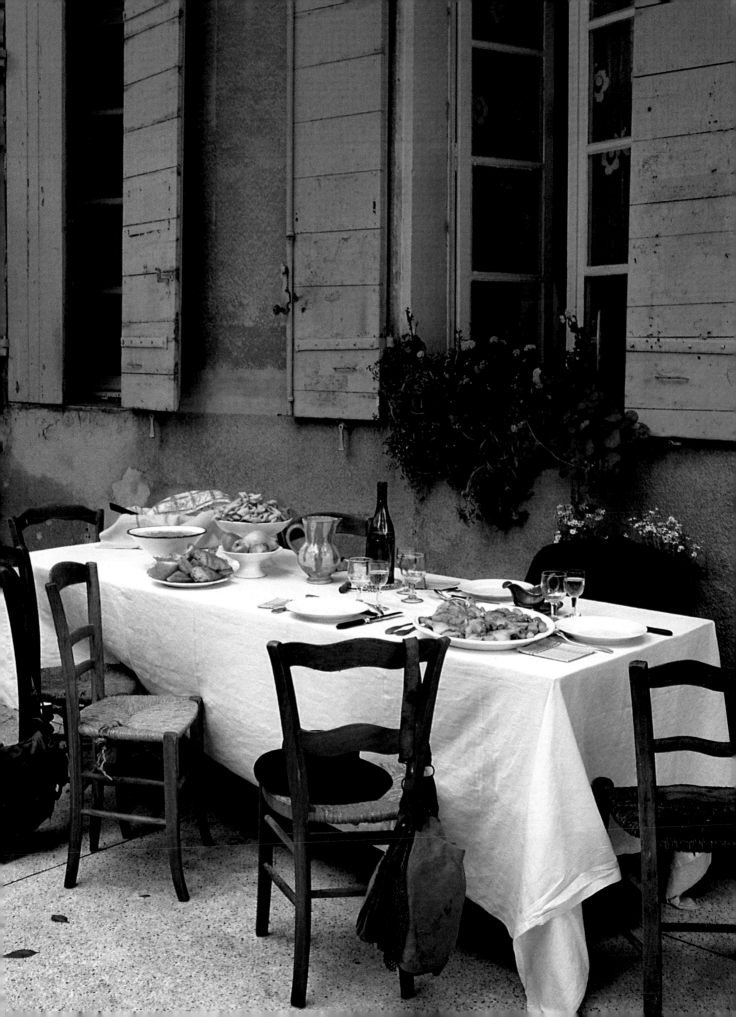

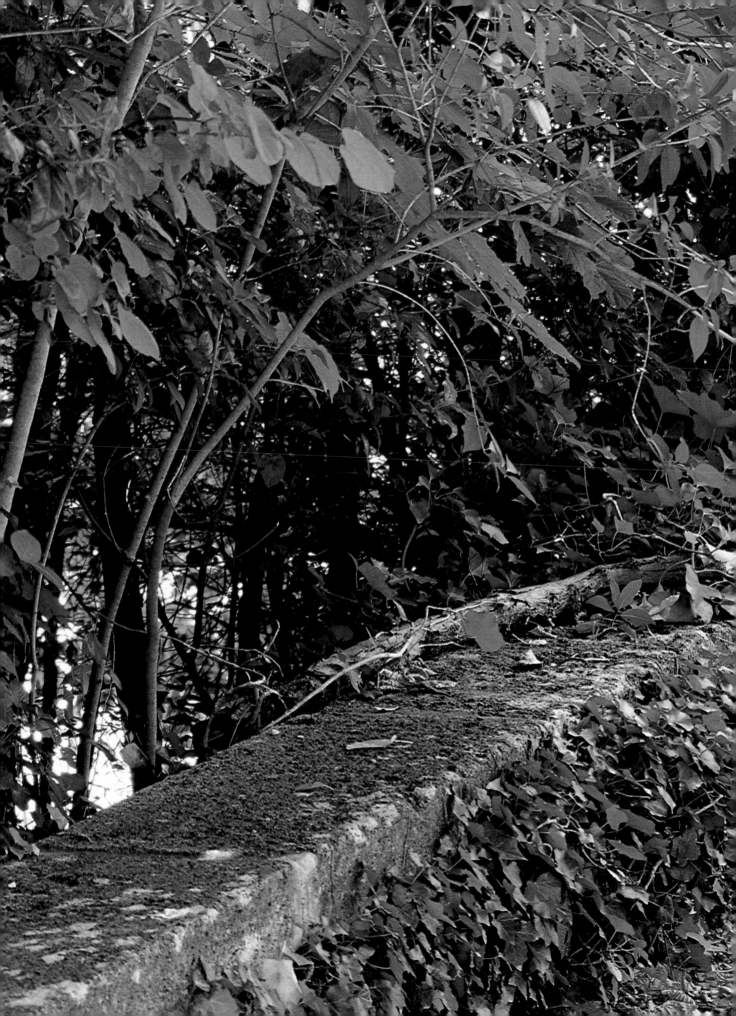

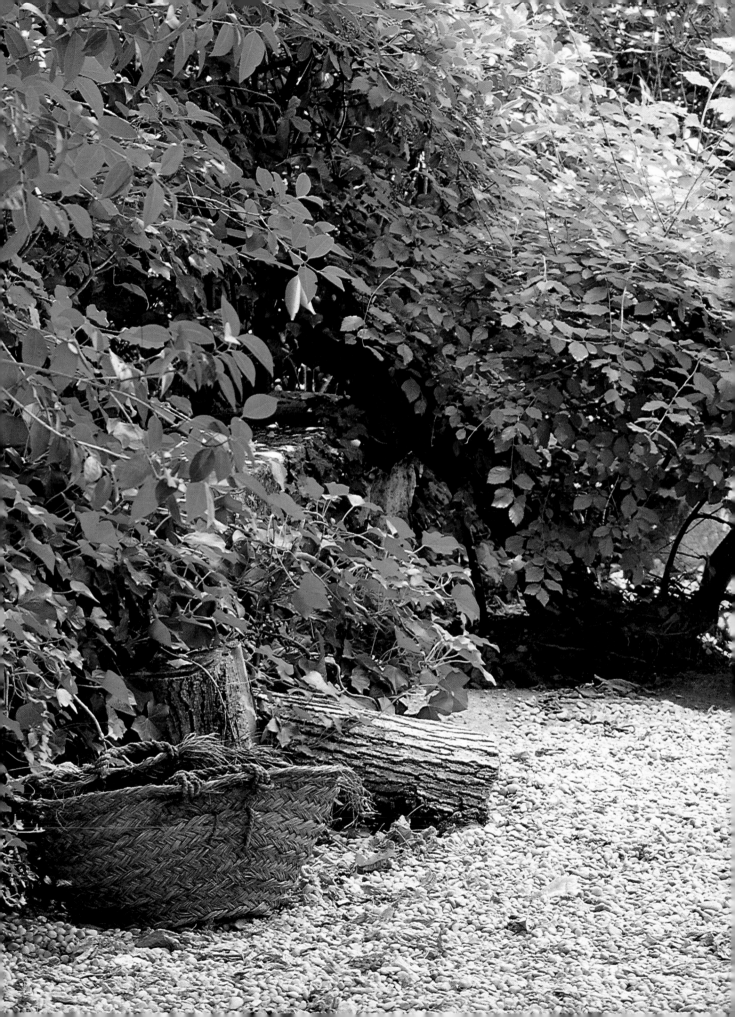

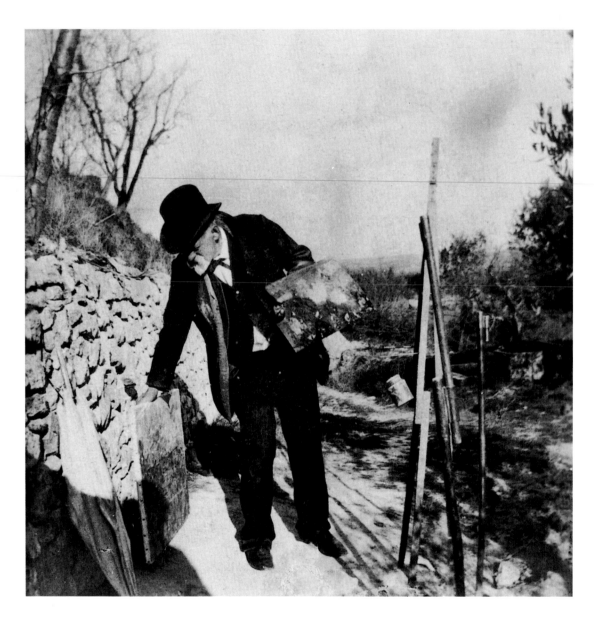

Portrait of Cézanne painting at Aix-en-Provence.
Photograph taken in January 1904 by Maurice Denis.

Acknowledgements

To illustrate the lifestyle of Paul Cézanne was quite a challenge.

I wanted to find the authentic historical sites in Provence which the great artist frequented and painted and

have tried to reflect the atmosphere of the place where he was born

and chose to spend his whole life.

None of this would have been possible without the help of many who I would like to take this opportunity to

thank:

M. Philippe Cézanne who gave his support to this project;

M. Picheral, the mayor of Aix en Provence

and all the staff at the town hall, especially

M. Guarrigue, M. Corsy and his daughter Anna Haworth Corsy

who so kindly gave us access to Jas de Bouffan;

M. Coutagne chief curator of the Musée Granet;

Mme Bourges curator of the Atelier Cézanne;

M. de Pinguern who opened the doors of

Bibémus for us; the Infirmeries du Roy René for their hospitality;

M. and Mme Calonder; Le Relais Cézanne in Tholonet;

M. and Mme Walter at the river Arc;

Mme Tsaut and M. and Mme Bonzon.

Jean-Bernard Naudin

Recipes

*We would like to thank Barbara Guarneri for her collaboration
throughout production.*

*Our thanks to all the galleries, antique dealers and boutiques
who kindly lent us the objects needed in the making of this book.
Many thanks to:*

*Au Puceron Chineur, Éric Dubois, Fuchsia linge et dentelles anciens,
Fanette, Art domestique ancien, la Maison ivre, Mère-Grand, L'Or du Temps,
Éric Aubry, Garance, Brocante du Panarbo, Devine qui vient dîner, galerie Didier Ludot,
Jeanine Normand, Odette Delain, Olivier Blanchard, Denise Corbier, M. Girard,
Alexandre Biaggi, Anne Vincent, Catherine Verneuil, Roger Normand, Aliette Texier,
Hélène and Raymond Humbert, Michel Bihen, Mokuba, l'Ourartien,
le Village des Antiquaires de Lignanes, Le Forum des arts at Lignanes Puyricard,
La Tuile à Loup, Michel Léger, Terre de Provence, Marlène Chabert, Jacqueline Blanchard,
Chichi chez Freddy, Antiquités et Brocantes au Pays d'Aix, Elsa Halfen, La Licorne,
le Cochelin, La Table en fête, Paul Ollivary, Aux Armes de Furstenberg,
Jardins Imaginaires, Maison de Famille, Mis en demeure,
P.-M. Castellani, Kitchen Bazaar Autrement.*

*Our special thanks to the Laboratoire Gorne
for their collaboration in the processing of the films.*

Bibliography

Cézanne, les années de jeunesse (1859-1872).
Musée d'Orsay exhibition catalogue,
RMN, Paris, 1988.

Cézanne, les dernières années (1895-1906).
Grand-Palais exhibition catalogue,
RMN, Paris, 1978.

Conversations avec Cézanne. Texts by Émile Bernard,
Jules Borély, Maurice Denis, Joachim Gasquet,
Gustave Geffroy, Francis Jourdain, Léo Larguier,
Karl Ernst Osthaus, R. P. Rivière et J. F. Schnerb,
Ambroise Vollard. Collection edited by
P. M. Doran, Macula, Paris, 1978.

M. R. Bourges, *Itinéraires de Cézanne.*
Ville d'Aix-en-Provence, 1982.

Paul Cézanne, *Correspondance*
(collected, annotated and prefaced by John Rewald).
Grasset, Paris, 1985.

Gustave Cocquiot, *Cézanne.* Paris, 1919.

Michel Hoog, *Cézanne « puissant et solitaire ».*
Découvertes Gallimard, Paris, 1989.

Henri Perruchot, *La Vie de Cézanne.* Librairie Hachette,
Paris, 1856, Livre de Poche edition.

Gilles Plazy, *Cézanne ou la peinture absolue.*
Liana Levi, Paris, 1988.

Gilles Plazy, *Cézanne.* Éditions du Chêne, Paris, 1991.

John Rewald, *Cézanne.* Paris, 1986.

Lionello Venturi, *Cézanne.* Skira, Lausanne, 1978.

Émile Zola, *L'Œuvre.* Chronology, introduction
and archive research by Antoinette Ehrard.
Garnier-Flammarion, Paris, 1974.

Photography Credits